# Unity of Heart

## Culture and Change in a Polynesian Atoll Society

## Keith Chambers
## Anne Chambers

Southern Oregon University

WAVELAND
PRESS, INC.
Long Grove, Illinois

For information about this book, contact:
Waveland Press, Inc.
4180 IL Route 83, Suite 101
Long Grove, IL  60047-9580
(847) 634-0081
info@waveland.com
www.waveland.com

**Cover:** Celebration at Kaumaile Primary School, Nanumea, July 1996

Printed in the United States of America

10   9   8   7   6   5

For
The children of Nanumea
and
Our children, Nonu, Kilea, and Tavita

The people of Nanumea are the implicit co-authors of this book. Elders and young people alike have guided us, patiently accepted our questions and mistakes, and have warmly welcomed us back when we have returned after long absences. Both on Nanumea and in Funafuti the Nanumean community cared for us and facilitated our work, to an extent that has delighted us. We hope that all Nanumeans will find something of interest here, perhaps something of value. Of course, any errors and infelicities which remain are ours alone.

*Gātama a Nanumea—a te tuhi tenei he meaalofa foliki mai ia māua. Fakafetai lahi. Fakamolemole fakamagalo mai manafai e hē tonu a mā mafaufauga mo muna i konei.*

# Contents

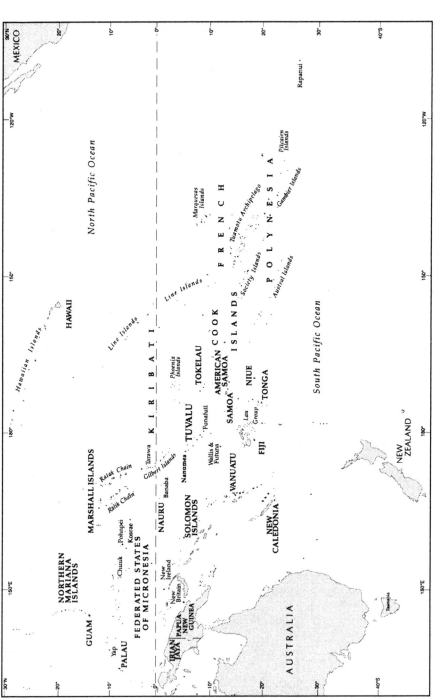

**Figure 1  Pacific Islands.** Used with permission from The Center for Pacific Island Studies, University of Hawaii at Mānoa, by Mānoa Mapworks, Inc.

# Geographic Note

Nanumea, northernmost of the atolls and reef islands that make up the nation of Tuvalu, is located in the middle of the Pacific Ocean near the International Date Line, a few degrees south of the equator (see fig. 1). From its sandy, palm-fringed shores, no other islands are visible. The dark blue Pacific, three of four miles deep here, serves as a bridge to other places—but also as a barrier, linking Nanumea to its Tuvaluan neighbors while ensuring the atoll's separation and uniqueness. The courageous Polynesian voyagers who discovered the islands in this archipelago perhaps two thousand years ago developed a unique version of human society. The nine coral islands they claimed and populated stretch over some four hundred miles of ocean. Using the grid lines of latitude and longitude, Tuvalu can be enclosed in an imaginary rectangle ranging from 5 degrees to 11 degrees south, and 176 degrees to 180 degrees east. Within this area the islands comprise just ten square miles of land, none of it reaching higher than twelve to eighteen feet above sea level. The area within the rectangle contains, besides these bits of land, 90,000 square miles of ocean. Tuvalu's exclusive economic zone under international law is 900,000 square kilometers, about 350,000 square miles. The tiny islands that now form the nation of Tuvalu are minute landfalls in the vast Pacific Ocean.

U.S. National Archives, no. 80-G-418560

*Part of Nanumea atoll from the air, Motu Foliki in foreground, village penninsula to right (1943)*

# Preface

When we arrived in June 1973, the Ellice Islands (as Tuvalu was then known) was administered together with a neighboring Micronesian society as one of Great Britain's last remnants of empire, the Gilbert and Ellice Islands Colony. We were graduate students in anthropology, eager for the experience of fieldwork and glad to be able to visit the central Pacific region on which our studies had long focused. That first trip spanned twenty-one months, seventeen of which were spent in Nanumea itself, with the remainder including research in government archives in Suva, Fiji, and stays in the District Centers of the Gilbert Islands (Tarawa) and the Ellice Islands (Funafuti).

A decade later, in 1984, we returned to Tuvalu and Nanumea for six months of further research. By this time we had become a family and our two young daughters, ages three and six, came with us. It felt like a home-coming after a longer-than-expected absence, and we were pleased to introduce our children to our Nanumean friends and to a new way of life. Twelve years passed before we were again able to spend time in Tuvalu, from May to July 1996. Much of this was in Nanumea and again the whole family was involved—our daughters, now nineteen and nearly sixteen, were joined by their eight-year-old brother. Most recently, Keith visited Funafuti for two weeks in 1998 to meet with Nanumean and Tuvaluan leaders regarding this book. Though work and family commitments have limited the length of our recent visits, we remain committed to a long-term relationship with our adopted Polynesian home. We hope, God willing, to continue our involvement for a long time to come.

ꝫ

## OUR APPROACH

We write here about Nanumean life and culture as we have come to know it through interacting with this vibrant and largely self-reliant community over the course of several decades. Our book is an ethnographic account, grounded in the anthropological tradition of documenting diverse lifestyles. It offers two types of learning opportunities to an interested reader. One of these is understanding something of the cultural logic of a way of life whose fundamental assumptions differ to a striking degree from those that have dominated social life in the West for the last century. Curiosity and imagination, as well as an ability to set aside temporarily one's own cultural assumptions, are essential to this endeavor. Readers may also use their understanding of Nanumean society as a vantage point to reflect on their own lifestyle and culture. The social realms familiar to most Western readers are truly as "cultured" and "exotic" as those of any South Seas island—though it can be difficult to grasp this fully without the perspective offered by a contrasting cultural example.

While our experience of living in Tuvalu and "doing anthropology" there frame our ethnographic description, our understanding of this community is a still-developing process, not an accomplished fact. Our perspectives have evolved and changed since our first visit long ago, redefined by our own life experiences, by emerging ideas in anthropology, and by the unfolding events of life in Tuvalu and Nanumea. By writing in a personal style and by including some of the events that shaped our understanding, we hope that readers can learn from the experience of cultural anthropology: the effort to step beyond one's own cultural values and assumptions and to develop an empathetic understanding of another way of life. With that respect for a social world quite different from one's own may come a heightened appreciation for the fundamental commonalties underlying all human societies. We hope that Nanumean and Tuvaluan readers, as well as to those from other Pacific societies, will also value this ethnography. We would like to think that it will encourage their thought and discussion on the values and goals of their own communities.

Social "reality," of course, can only be rendered provisionally. Any ethnographic description is an interpretation, a product inevitably influenced by the fieldworker's own experiences, assumptions, understandings, and biases. Just as the "insider's point of view" must be as numerous and varied as the number of "insiders," so, too, ethnographic constructions and the knowledge of participants always differ to some extent. We acknowledge the contingent nature of our ethnographic narrative, knowing that it reflects our own cultural backgrounds and the personal experiences we have brought to the research. We urge readers to recognize that our portrayal is not only our own creation, but one that is still evolving. It may present, as many accounts of other societies have done before it, too neat a picture, not taking enough account of cultural contradictions and individual idiosyncrasies or perhaps reflecting too unthinkingly our own biases. We look forward to collaborating with the Nanumean community in continuing to make ethnographic revisions in the future.

Our decision to adopt a shared author's voice in this book, writing as "we" rather than as two individual authors, stems from the close collaboration that has always characterized our fieldwork. Each of us has written separate research notes and kept journals reflecting on our experiences, and we have published separately, too, but we wanted to approach this book as a collaborative project because the data we have shared and discussed over the years have come truly to be joint information. Although we recognize that our genders and idiosyncratic experiences contribute to somewhat different orientations for each of us, we do not attempt to separate our ethnographic understandings here or to document differences between what each of us "knew." As fieldwork progressed, we read each other's notes, compared experiences, discussed the drama of community life, and debated our analyses. A conscious intertwining of our research experience and our shared knowledge resulted. This is the reality that shapes this book.

ह৯

## NANUMEA AND TUVALU

Nanumea is one of the eight distinctive communities that together compose the country of Tuvalu. (The ninth island, southernmost Niulakita, was not permanently inhabited until this century.) Each of these communities has particular traditions, a separate home island or atoll on which members' shared identities and histories focus, and a strong pride in its own uniqueness. Though the national government has sought to cultivate a national identity, particularly since independence in 1978, home-island loyalty remains basic to daily life and politics even in the urban capital. Nonetheless, it would be misleading to write about Nanumea or any other Tuvalu community as if it were a fully self-sufficient or separate entity. Not only are people's lives intertwined with those of their relatives from other islands, but national government policies and globalization pressures also reach to all the islands. Furthermore, an increasingly significant percentage (some 40 percent and growing) of members of each outer island live in the capital today. Increasingly, orientation toward a traditional outer island community is diminishing.

Pressures toward national uniformity and unity, on one hand, and an impetus toward community loyalty and unique cultural identities, on the other, counterbalance in Tuvalu life today. For the purposes of the general reader seeking to understand daily life in a small Pacific island community, the distinctions between Nanumea and the other seven Tuvalu communities may be superfluous. On the other hand, those familiar with Tuvalu or any other Pacific island society will be keenly interested in the details of Nanumean social organization and the cultural attitudes that make this community unique.

This creates a dilemma. Regional differences are as salient in contemporary Tuvalu as is the growing sense of a national identity. Our own research experiences parallel, in a sense, those of all Tuvaluans— grounded initially in a single community, but increasingly drawn toward the center and a more national perspective. Our response in this book has been to maintain a primary focus on Nanumea but also to connect this focus with Tuvalu-wide patterns and concerns. We discuss some of the national and international aspects that impinge on Nanumean life, as well as the relationship between the outer island Nanumean community and the group of Nanumeans living in the capital. Urban/outer island relationships are currently being redefined in Tuvalu and these provide a major focus for contemporary social change. Thus, our work moves freely between specific descriptions of Nanumea itself and a more generalized view of Tuvalu, of which Nanumea is a part. We believe that this approach best reflects the cultural complexity of this small island nation. Readers are reminded that an ethnography focusing on another Tuvalu community would share many similarities with this work. Though a general cultural pattern would be recognizable, innumerable social, economic, political, and cultural differences between each community make it difficult to generalize from this ethnography to Tuvalu society as a whole.

Finally, this book focuses primarily on the last quarter century of Nanumean experience. Elders' memories, traditional accounts of important events, and historical material have been used to extend the time frame backward. We have tried to make time references definitive where these are important and to point out major changes that we have noticed or been told about. It is, of course, illusory to present any society as timelessly traditional. Cultural change is as natural for Nanumeans and other Tuvaluans as it is for members of all human societies. Upheavals and cultural watersheds in the community's past may have been as transformative as the forces of Westernization and globalization that Tuvaluans face today. Nonetheless, Nanumeans see some facets of their culture and society as emblematic and enduring and we have focused much of our discussion on these aspects.

# Acknowledgments

We are humbled, as we look back over the quarter century during which this work has taken shape, to realize how many people have been essential to its creation. Without them, our efforts would never have come to fruition or would have been much the poorer. It is a joy to remember these individuals and their assistance. Yet many of these memories are tinged with sadness, too, since many of those we would like to thank have now passed on.

We are indebted to the entire Nanumean community but some individuals especially facilitated our work at different times and in different places. The following list is probably not complete, although we have tried to make it so. Forgive any omissions, please, since they reflect only our faulty memories.

*Initial work, Wellington, Tarawa, Nanumea, Suva, Funafuti (1973–75)*: This included preparatory work at Bishop Museum (Honolulu), Victoria University (Wellington) and in Tarawa, then colonial capital of the Gilbert and Ellice Islands Colony, archival and records research (in Suva, Funafuti, and Wellington), and our first visit to Nanumea.

*Honolulu*: Edwin H. Bryan, Jr. and Harold St. John, Bernice Pauahi Bishop Museum.

*Wellington, Auckland, Suva*: Ray Watters, Nancy Pollock, Co-Directors of the Victoria University of Wellington Rural Socio-Economic Survey of the GEIC; also David Winchester and Robin Mita at Victoria University. Fellow research team members Betsy Sewell, Bill (and Nola) Geddes, Roger Lawrence; also, linguist Peter Ranby. The helpful staffs of the Western Pacific Archives (Suva) and Alexander Turnbull Library (Wellington); also anthropological colleagues Derek Freeman from Canberra, Ivan Brady, and Jay (and Toki) Noricks in the United States.

*Tarawa*: Bob Bryden and agriculture department staff including Dave Harrison, Tony Arnott, David Brechtefeldt, Neil and Nafiata McNaughton, Dave Wimblett; Eric Bailey (census commissioner and philosopher), Richard Turpin of the colonial service, magistrate Jeremy Fordham and family, Graham Worthington and family, and surveyor extraordinaire Roger Moffitt.

*Funafuti*: District officer Colin Redston; Tito Isala (on the referendum voyage).

*Nanumea*: Our grateful thanks to the following household heads and their family members (in the arbitrary order of our initial census visit): Masiasi, Uti, Inosia, Uni, Talape, Hipa, Matauaina, Alesana, Tulimanu, Kanipule, Usia, Tauila, Malau, Tiao, Taeamo, Utu, Vaha, Fakaoko, Sioo, Poutaiki, Sepola, Teiapa, Famasani, Telea, Otaota, Tautahi, Misa, Levi, Haleti, Kaino, Tekapu, Sasa, Manuao, Tepou, Palota, Falelima, Elika, Vailahi, Sone, Maluuluu, Malesa, Tauno, Mono, Samuelu, Kilo, Tufa, Filemoni, Tepaa, Tefono, Samu, Malie, Pulusi, Sue, Amelina, Valenga, Tuia, Mosikepu, Peia, Heiloa, Talu, Tapeva, Isaako, Maito, Venu, Paseka, Tulo, Timi, Make, Takitua, Ke, Lufo, Pinoka, Hailama, Rongorongo, Tongia, Kaifou, Tekiu, Maka, Talisua, Talitiinga, Taulialia, Olikene, Tinilau, Filipi, Monise, Teaitala, Petaia, Tie, Tefaiva, Tipu, Tefolaha, Hetoifaiva, Ioane, Iosefatu, Taulu, Taulau, Taniela, Kahifa, Iakopo, Niko, Sauni, Kalo, Poke, Petio, Saulo, Alapati, Fualia, Simoe, Talikai, Seselo, Peo, Naomi, Tiligaa, Setalia, Viliamu, Seve, Tenganui, Katea, Teuea, Kauani, Polevia (and Siaumau), Fiataumata, Telangai, Talila, Lepa, Tanielu, Laiti, Tuilimu, Vaelei, Puti, Puanini, Pou, Toia, Temai, Pulepule, Tutu, Temumuni, Malota, Kauapa, Teakaka, Malona, Sela, Lototele, Lipine, Alaelua, and Telavi. Our special thanks (for nurturing, support, and instruction) to Salailoto, Emalia, Haukata, Faatu, Laumua, Tepula, Toko, Pensula, Milo, Kanakope, Failelei, Nasese, Peleise, Misalaima, Milo, Laupulaka, Mamele, Langatili, Temio, Tovine, Amasone, Tiligaa, Telalo, Laina, Mengaa, and most especially to Sunema Rongorongo.

*Middle period, Trondheim, Auckland, Funafuti, Nanumea (1977–87)*: Preparation and writing while we lived in Trondheim and Auckland, as well as Funafuti and some five months in Nanumea:

*Trondheim*: Jan Brogger and his staff at the Socialantropologisk Institute, University of Trondheim, and Unni Dahl and her family.

*Auckland*: Paul and Kris McLaren and family, Julie Park and family, Judith Huntsman, Marie and Peter Cameron and family, Liu and Kailelei Tepou and family, Andre Brett, Peter Ranby, and Doug Munro.

*Funafuti*: Peter and Fuafua McQuarrie and family, Alaelua and her household. Also Pasoni Taafaki, Dr. Alesana Seluka, and Seluka Alesana.

*Nanumea*: Special thanks to Salailoto Make, Sosemea and Tinamoe Samuelu, Laina and Line Teuea, Tie and Emalia Maheu, Neemia and family, Pilikosi and Eseta and family, Lisa Pilikosi, Faanumi and Haulagi and family, and Tulaga Manuela.

*Contemporary scene, Suva, Funafuti, Nanumea (1996–present)*: Stays in Suva, Funafuti, Nanumea in 1996, and Funafuti in 1998.

*Suva*: Peter and Fuafua McQuarrie, Tito Isala, Jeff Liew.

*Funafuti*: Fili and Annie Homasi and family, Tagisia and Huao Kilei and family, Kalahati and Oliula T. Kilei, Naama Maheu Latasi, Houati Iele, Eseta Pilikosi and family, Amasone and Taiafiafi Kilei and family, Sunema Rongorongo Makatui, Hon. Bikenibeu Paeniu, Saufatu Sopoaga, Dr. Alesana Seluka, Seve Lausaveve, Kokea Malua, Lagitupu Tuilimu, Pokia Tiihala, Lena Satalaka, Taukelina Finekaso, Rev. Iosia Taomia and the Tuvalu Language Board, Rev. Penitusi Taeia and his wife Taaliu Taeia, Manuila Tausi, Dr. Tiligaa Pulusi, James Conway, Vavae Katalake, Hilia Vavae, Makaleta Haulagi, Kilateli Saulo, William Halm, Nelson Anciano, Fr. Camille DesRosiers, Joyce Manoa, and Joseph Kim.

*Nanumea*: Noa Monise and his wife Selepa, Pou Monise, Laina and Line Teuea, Tie and Emalia Maheu, Fetai and Fotu, Siniva and Teoti, Sosemea (Lolesi) and Tinamoe, Soke, Tevesi, Palota, Apiseka, Neimeli, Patiale, Lepa, Falaile, Siitia, Tavita, Katagi, Siata Alefaio, Mita and Maaloo.

For their special interest in our work and concern that we "get it right," we are grateful to Maheu, Rongorongo, Samuelu, Malulu, Tepou, Taulialia, Manuao, Kauapa, Haleti, Sue, and Venu.

We also are thankful to the many other Tuvaluans who have befriended and helped us, as well as to colonial and local government officials, expatriate advisors and our anthropological colleagues. Their insights and the information they shared with us have greatly enriched our understanding and, we hope, this book. We want particularly to thank the following for their critical reading of our book in draft and the many helpful suggestions they offered: Michael Lieber, Peter McQuarrie, James Conway, Tagisia Kilei and members of his family, Julian and Connie Battaile, Diane Schaeffer and Brian Frink, and several "generations" of Anne's anthropology students.

Financial and logistical support has been vital to much of the work lying behind this book. Our parents, Peg and Frank Vonnegut, and Oleta and Keith Chambers provided essential help when needed, and the Vonnegut home in Honolulu was an important refuge for us and our children on many occasions. Our original sponsors were The Victoria University of Wellington Rural Socio-Economic Survey of the Gilbert and Ellice Islands Colony and its co-directors, Professors Ray Watters (Geography) and Nancy Pollock (Anthropology). The University of California, Berkeley supported Keith with a US National Institutes of Health graduate fellowship (special thanks to Professor George Foster and Ms. Gerry Moos). Additional institutional support has come from the University of Trondheim Institute for Social Anthropology (esp. Professor Jan Brogger and his staff and students), the University of Auckland (particularly the Department of Anthropology, Professor Ralph Bulmer, and Associate Professor Judith Huntsman), and the New Zealand Medical Research Council. Southern Oregon University, our current academic home, has also provided support for our research.

Tom Curtin and Jeni Ogilvie at Waveland Press provided editorial guidance, for which we are grateful. We also deeply appreciate Holly Ambler-Jones' thoughtful development of the study guide. Many thanks to Claire Chambers for her cover design.

Finally, we would like to thank Nancy and John Mairs and family who made a regular place in their home for our son, David.

Anne Chambers
Keith Chambers
Ashland, Oregon
August 1, 2000

# ❧ 1

# Encountering Nanumea

Through the tropic darkness came the sounds of singing, inter-spersed with laughter. We stopped on the village path to listen, peer-ing quietly from behind some bushes. The members of a women's group sat crowded together in a small cookhouse, practicing songs for their coming feast day, thoroughly enjoying themselves.

"They're practicing your song!", whispered our friend Sunema. With her help we made out the words: "Kiti from America, Ane from Hawaii. How many hundreds of miles have they come. . . ."

Suddenly, a raucous female voice broke into the melody. "Yes! They've come so far, so far to ask us . . ." She paused and then shrieked triumphantly, "How many fish we eat! How many sewing machines we have!" The group of women convulsed in laughter. The voice went on, "How many coconuts! How many canoes!" The laugh-ter swelled as each item was named. The speaker herself could now barely talk, bent double with mirth. "How many coconut shells of toddy!", she managed to shriek finally. The women were beside them-selves. How ridiculous it seemed, our coming from so far away, only to ask endlessly about trivia!

Outside in the darkness, we had to laugh at ourselves too.

Field Journal<br>September 1973

When we arrived in Nanumea in June 1973, we could say no more than a few polite memorized phrases in the local language. Even these probably were mispronounced. Since only a handful of community members spoke English, a key part of our research would be to learn Nanumean, and we consciously made this our first fieldwork goal. Nanumean, one of the distinct dialects of Tuvaluan, differs in intonation, vocabulary, and phonology from the other dialects, especially from the more widely spoken "southern" version of Tuvaluan. For this reason, our learning to speak Nanumean was important beyond its practical utility. It came to symbolize our distinctive connection to the Nanumean community as well.

かん

## LEARNING TO SPEAK

Our learning strategy was one of immersion. With Nanumean spoken around us continuously, it was natural to attune our ears to its sounds and rhythms. After a few days we could begin to pick out, occasionally, a word or two that we knew. We tape-recorded short conversations and sat for hours with our English-speaking research assistant, Sunema Rongorongo, transcribing the tapes word for word, making literal translations and asking about the grammatical usages that puzzled us. We learned the useful phrase "What is this in Nanumean?" and used it often, writing down lists of words and their translations in our field notebooks. We listened to the evening English language radio news broadcasts, and then to the Tuvaluan version, straining for glimpses of meaning in the latter. We went to church regularly and heard insistent sermons, to island meetings and heard gracious welcomes as well as passionate speeches of persuasion. Throughout these first few months, Sunema accompanied us almost everywhere, and we had to rely on her to interpret for us. Except when we were directly involved with just one or two people, we usually had to be content with short summaries of what they had said, which often left us feeling disappointed and annoyed.

There is nothing more frustrating than the early stages of learning a language. The few words known are dwarfed by the hundreds that are not. Every carefully pieced-together grammatical pattern seems to have exceptions. Mispronounced words, it seems, are often profane! The sheer immensity of what needs to be learned is overwhelming, and faced with this challenge, human memory seems to operate only slowly and with embarrassing inefficiency. People, of course, are anxious for results and with every greeting or question, they test the new speaker's abilities, offering new words and more new words. All this is utterly exhausting. Already struggling with the challenge of adapting to a new way of life, you want to sleep late, go to bed early, and nap in between. But in Nanumea, at least, no able-bodied person is still in bed after dawn, and there is scant privacy for napping in an open-sided village house.

Luckily, determination and perseverance pay off eventually. Our vocabularies grew and soon we were able to converse in simple, childlike sentences, focusing on concrete topics. Philosophical discussions and abstract matters were much more difficult and remained beyond our grasp for some time. As the months passed, however, we found that we could understand more and more of what people said directly to us and could ask people to explain anything that was unclear. Communicating better all the time, we made speeches at community feasts and began to go about the village independently in pursuit of the cultural information that interested each of us. It was a happy day when we realized that we could understand many of the casual conversations that we heard around us. With the help of the entire community and six months of very careful listening and observing, we had learned to speak some Nanumean at last. We had finally met the most important precondition for our research.

ぶ

## FIELDWORK METHODS

Both of us shared the goal of understanding the basic features of Nanu-mean culture. We needed to learn about village life. Why, for example, did some households have nearly twenty members and others have only a few? Which social groups were important in which contexts and who belonged? How did the community make decisions, and to what extent did the traditional chiefs still play leadership roles? What values were con-sidered crucial to living "as a Nanumean," *faka Nanumea?* How did peo-ple prepare for birth, choose a spouse, become an adult, or mourn a death? What subtle pressures, rewards, and punishments did people con-sider in making the innumerable decisions of daily life? Answers to such questions informed the overall pattern of life in Nanumea, as they do in all human societies. We worked to piece together and understand these cultural patterns, pooling our research notes and discussing endlessly what we had learned.

The first systematic survey we undertook, some three months after we arrived, was a village census that had several related goals. First, we wanted to have an accurate profile of the people living on Nanumea, including information on their age, gender, and household composition. Second, we also wanted to know how many people were considered to be community members even though they were temporarily absent over-seas, how long they had been gone, and where they were. Third, we hoped to compile background information on the community as a whole, regarding incomes, land holdings, work, educational experience, and household possessions. And finally, we wanted an opportunity to formally meet each family and ask their help with our research.

The rules of Nanumean hospitality, we soon learned, make it impossible to move quickly and efficiently from house to house, counting people and asking questions. Instead, this should be a time to become acquainted, to show interest and respect—and that is best done by sharing food. The timetable of our census inevitably had to expand to accommodate local ideas of politeness. We began making appointments to visit only two or three households each day. We asked that insofar as possible all the household residents stay home to meet us, but that people not go to any other trouble for our visit. Each family nonetheless made the preparations customary for important guests. After our questions were answered and our papers were put away, each household gave us a small feast, complete with a basket of food to carry home afterward. In this most hospitable way, day by day, we ate and talked our way through the main village, north along the sandy point to the clinic, and over to the few households scattered along the far side of the lagoon. At last, we made a

*Sunema and Anne returning home with gifts after a census visit (1973)*

several-days-trip to the small village on Lakena, the islet where the starchy taro roots are grown, at the northernmost end of the atoll.

Our census of the island's nearly 150 households took us several months to complete. We had to make adjustments for the departures and arrivals that occurred at each ship's visit and for movements between households of people we had already enumerated. But by the time we finished, we had met virtually all of the thousand people on the island and had developed a stable foundation on which to build a better understanding of Nanumean life.

It was at this point that we each began to pursue our own special areas of interest. Anne, as one of the five researchers in the "Rural Socio-Economic Survey of the Gilbert and Ellice Islands" project, was to focus especially on social organization and economics. The four other project members in the survey team had each been assigned to an island in the Gilberts (now Kiribati), and, like them, Anne was to document the way local people made a living and what hopes they held for the future, both individually and as a community. She needed to find out how people used their time; what land resources were available to different households; what sources of income they had; how much fish was caught and by what methods; how many coconuts were fed to pigs, how many were eaten by people, and how many were dried into copra. The list of topics included in the official research protocol was so comprehensive that we sometimes wondered whether it was more of a wish list than a plan of action. In either case, though, information gathered by the five researchers would be used to help the Islanders and their overseas advisors make decisions toward independence and nationhood. Because Anne was interested in ecological relationships, we had brought equipment to press and dry plant specimens, and she planned to investigate local plant classifications, names, and uses.

Keith, with research funding from a graduate fellowship at the University of California, Berkeley, shared an interest in many of the project topics but also wished to focus on how the community viewed itself in relation to its history. What were the narratives and perceptions of the past that were most valued? How did recollections of early contact with the West relate to records kept by explorers, missionaries, and other outsiders? He hoped to explore the ways in which family histories and genealogies were important in contemporary politics and the extent to which traditional knowledge was still important to the community.

We both wanted to learn as much as possible about being Nanumean, and we discovered that we were best working as a team. Between us, we tried to attend (and take detailed notes on) every significant community meeting. In this tightly organized village, the frequency of these meetings was as overwhelming as the number of their sponsoring groups: the Island Council, the community elders, the five women's groups, the deacons, the Land Court, the civil court, the village divisions, plus various church groups. Because the fishing economy was largely the domain of young men, Keith hired Laina Teuea, an active fisherman, to record the fish caught by each of the canoes that fished regularly most evenings. Keith carried out a canoe census and documented and photographed canoe construction techniques and traditional lore. We worked together to measure and map over one hundred land plots and taro pits, the land resources used by four households. Both of us recorded the comings and goings of island residents each time a ship visited. We interviewed key island elders and with their help charted genealogies for the whole community, a precious resource for all time.

In the second year of our initial stay on Nanumea, Anne began to gather detailed information about household economics. Using the census data we had compiled earlier, a sample of twenty households (representative of the community in terms of membership, wealth, and subsistence orientation) was selected for a systematic survey. This sample included 13 percent of the island households, the largest number that a single researcher could visit and interview in a working day. After securing the cooperation of the households, Anne spent one week out of each of the next eight months visiting the sample households, asking about each family's life during the previous day and recording pages of answers. The questions were standardized and exhaustive. Who lived in the household yesterday? What did each person do, hour by hour? What food was prepared, using what specific ingredients, and what else was eaten at each meal? What income was received? What was bought at the store, or elsewhere? What was given as gifts and what was received, either as a gift or a solicitation, from whom and why? From this survey, encompassing eight week-long survey periods spread over eight consecutive months, we gained detailed insights into the flow of village life—why people move from household to household, how important it is to share food, how rest alternates with work. Of course, making the round of twenty households spread throughout the village and to the far side of the lagoon was a challenge. Most days Anne barely managed to reach home, exhausted, as the bell for evening prayers sounded through the dusk, putting a stop to the day's tasks. Though some of the questions were so basic that people found them trivial, domestic economics is intimately connected to prestige and social solidarity, issues too sensitive to delegate to an assistant.

We also made a point of seeking specialized knowledge from experts and of talking privately to individual members of the community. Having heard one version of a dispute, for example, we would seek out

*Conversations with Taumili, Pae, and Peo (1974)*

other points of view. Keith spent many hours with elderly men, family spokesmen who were repositories of local knowledge. There were formal and informal experts of all kinds in the village, and we sought out traditional healers, song composers, retired civil servants, political leaders, and others as occasion demanded. Sometimes groups of older men working at rolling sennit cord, the endless occupation of the gray-haired, were a willing discussion group. Members of the women's clubs gathered to make thatch or bake bread for a fund-raiser were equally helpful sources of information. Often, it was more useful to talk privately with people. We assured those who wished it anonymity.

Our constant research method, however, was *participant observation*. This technique combines paying close attention to what is going on with taking a part in it (though usually only as follower). It gives a sensitive outsider the closest possible experience of what it is to live as a community member. Participant observation is exciting and unpredictable, and it can be done as effectively in our own society as in exotic settings. In our Tuvalu context, we discovered that a morning trip to the bush to gather coconuts with friends, for instance, might turn into a lesson in starting a fire with a fire plow or an opportunity to ask about a recent sorcery dispute. This methodology leads a fieldworker on paths of inquiry that she or he might never have thought to choose and opens up the possibility of chance encounters and serendipity. It is minimally disruptive and so there is often less of an "observer effect" than in some other methods of research, but the researcher also usually has little control over what transpires. The key is to flow with events as they occur. Often it is impossible to ask for explanations or to clarify information on the spot, and focused interviews are necessary later to yield real understanding. Sometimes it is possible to jot notes documenting conversations, mannerisms, and events. At other times, the prudent course is to be "all eyes and ears," waiting until later to write up notes. In either case, going around with many different people, pitching in with daily chores (however ineptly), and witnessing the significant events of community life all help the anthropological fieldworker become a "real person."

The intensity of such work can be overwhelming. Sometimes we wished that village life would simply stop so that we could catch up with our field notes and take time to analyze some of the information we were amassing. Both to renew our perspective and to accomplish some research-related tasks, we took several short trips away. In January 1974, after we had lived on Nanumea for six months, we spent a month in Suva, Fiji, working through historical and administrative documents held at the Western Pacific High Commission archives and conferring with colleagues. Before returning to our work, we visited anthropologist friends who were similarly engaged in their first extended fieldwork in Vanuatu (then New Hebrides). This pleasant break enabled us to compare our work with theirs and enlarge our points of view. On the way back to Nanumea a shipping delay kept us in Funafuti, the colonial district center, for three weeks. We took this opportunity to observe and participate in life in the administrative center, to meet with government officials, and to read through official files. On the voyages out and back to Nanumea, the ship stopped for half a day or so at other Tuvalu islands and time ashore helped us understand the similarities and differences among Tuvalu communities.

Even more useful was the opportunity we had in October 1974 to travel with the United Nations party observing the Tuvalu referendum regarding separation from the Gilbert Islands. On this seventeen-day voyage through the entire Ellice archipelago, conveniently starting at Nanumea, we spent one or two full days on each of the nine islands and were able to experience firsthand their social and environmental differences as well as to gather comparative information on such topics as income received from telegraphic money orders, copra production, handicraft sales, and the number and kinds of canoes available to the community. As far as we were able to, we attended the meetings that the referendum officials and United Nations observers held with each community and through these gained insights into local aspirations. As the ship moved between islands, deck-side conversations with the members of the United Nations delegation and local government officials helped us see the bigger picture from their perspectives.

For most of our first stay on Nanumea we lived in the main village on a plot of communally owned land that had been built up from lagoon fill during World War II. The community built us a wonderful two-story house on this site looking out on the lagoon. It was constructed entirely of local materials, including hand-sawn coconut timber and traditional pandanus thatching, the nearly universal roofing material at that time. Located on the boundary line separating the two "sides" of the village, the house was within sight of the island meeting hall, church, and school. This was a good location, not only because it was central but also because we were not automatically classified as members of one village side simply because we lived in its territory. We knew that it was important to the community that we belonged to the community as a whole, rather than to one particular group, family, or other faction. This was also a main reason why we had established our own household rather than living with the pastor or a village family as we had graciously been invited to do. We did finally accept an invitation to join one of the four village work groups, but otherwise we alternated our participation among the various competitive groupings on different occasions. Our closest relationships were with our neighbors, the families of our research assistants and the twenty sample households, and with some of the members of the "Hawaiian group" (*Kau Hawaii*), who generously included Anne as a relative on account of their common "homeland." We were involved in a wide cross-section of the community and were not restricted to any one faction in our participation in island life or in our collection of data.

At what point does a fieldworker know enough to write authoritatively about a way of life? Reaching the stage of knowing everything is an impossibility, of course. But one common rule of thumb in anthropology is to look for the point where information consistently begins to repeat itself, and you can accurately anticipate the answers to the questions you ask. By this guideline, we eventually reached the point where we could justify the end of our initial fieldwork. We knew what a proper wedding or funeral should consist of and we had seen many variations on the same theme. We virtually knew by heart the flowery opening phrases that were part of every island speech. We knew which offenses were heard regularly each month by the Island Court and could appreciate the significance of those that were unusual. But we also could not help noticing that in this community of a thousand people, despite these regularities and our carefully drawn expectations about them, there was always something new going on.

There were countless matters that we still wanted to ask about, shades of opinion to plumb further, personal stories to hear and mull over.

We left Nanumea in January 1975, twenty-two months after we had first arrived in the colony. Our first stop was the colonial capital, Tarawa, where we conferred with government officials and took a last look at official files. By this time, the political situation in the colony had solidified considerably. The referendum we had been privileged to observe had shown the overwhelming desire of the Ellice Islanders to separate from their Micronesian neighbors. Preparations were now underway for the division of the Gilbert and Ellice Islands into separate nations, each with its own government. Decisions were being made about the assets each nation was to have, the relationship between them, and what sorts of development the future might hold. Exciting times indeed! Leaving Tarawa, we went to Nauru for a few days and visited the small Nanumean community of phosphate mine employees there, and also stopped briefly in Majuro, capital of the Marshall Islands, to see what the American-influenced Pacific was like.

ॐ

## A SECOND CHANCE

Ten years were to pass before we had an opportunity to return to Nanumea. By this time we were living in Auckland, New Zealand, and had two young daughters. Keith was teaching anthropology at the University of Auckland and had become eligible for a sabbatical. He wanted to develop further his understanding of the role that oral tradition played in Nanumean politics. Anne had written a research proposal focusing on the pre-eminent female domain: fertility and birth. She wanted to talk with women about their life experiences and to relate them to cultural expectations and the values that guided reproductive decision making. We also knew that developing an effective family planning program was a national goal. We hoped that Anne's research would be useful, especially to the overseas consultants who were brought in by aid agencies to design the programs. Her project received funding jointly from the New Zealand Medical Research Council and New Zealand's Social Science Research Fund Committee. Our girls were enthusiastic about visiting the place they had heard so much about, and we left New Zealand for Fiji early in December 1983, laden with supplies and gifts.

Travel is never predictable in the Central Pacific, and it took us an entire month to get to Nanumea. The small airplane that flew twice weekly from Fiji to the Tuvalu capital of Funafuti was fully booked for weeks with students returning home for the Christmas holidays and with government officials. Luckily, however, the national ship was in Suva, due to leave soon for Tuvalu. We secured passage on it and arrived in Funafuti five days later, the ship limping into port in need of engine repairs. The changes that nationhood had brought were fascinating to see, and we enjoyed renewing our ties with many people in the capital. We stayed with Fuafua and Peter McQuarrie, attending the local Christmas celebrations and waiting daily for news that repairs to the ship's engine had been completed and that its scheduled voyage to the outer islands would resume.

How glad we were, after three days of voyaging, to see the low outline of Nanumea's palms and church steeple on the distant horizon! We were tired of traveling and eager to take up the socially intense but slow-paced life on Nanumea. With the other passengers, we clambered into the ship's work boats and were expertly taken through the surf into the reef channel, to the quiet waters of the lagoon. In a warm welcome at the shore, the girls were swooped up by would-be "volunteer mothers" and men helped carry our boxes to our house.

During this visit, which lasted about six months, we again lived as much as possible as members of the community, participating in many of the daily activities of village life. As in the past, people's kindness was overwhelming. The community had refurbished a local style thatched house for our arrival, lavishly furnished with mats. Our former house, located near Nanumea's primary school, had been assigned to the head teacher when we left Nanumea in 1975 and was still being used as his dwelling. This time we lived on the government station, an acre or two of land on the lagoon shore where local government employee housing was located, as well as the Island Council offices. It was just after Christmas and the festive season known as Big Days was in full swing. Games of *ano*, a traditional ball game, were played daily from dawn to dusk and community members ate together in the community hall each noon. After our ten-year absence, these leisurely festivities provided the ideal context for renewing friendships, for becoming acquainted with people we did not yet know, and for hearing about recent changes and community concerns. By the time the holiday season ended a month later, most people had heard that Anne wanted to focus her work this time primarily on women's lives while Keith would concentrate his on traditional customs, working mainly with older men. Approval and support were widely shown for these plans.

Once again, we began our formal fieldwork with a full house-to-house census. We visited all of the island's households, noting the births, deaths, marriages, and changes that had taken place in schooling, jobs, and so on. Some people had returned home from overseas in the ensuing decade, and we sought more detailed information from these households. We each then began to work intensively on our own projects, very conscious of the quickly passing days and our limited time on the island. Our language ability (which we had worked to keep alive by listening to tape-recorded interviews and conversation and through contacts with Tuvaluans in Auckland) came back quickly and we were able to work without interpreters or assistants this time.

Anne's goal was to talk with each woman about her reproductive history and to use these detailed case studies to document persistent themes relating to fertility patterns and local life cycles. She became particularly interested in women's attitudes to marriage, since this seemed to be an area of ambivalence. Talking with women as they worked alone at domestic tasks was a good strategy since some conversations became very personal and would be impossible to have in front of others. Anne also conferred with midwives, nurses, and pregnant women to learn about pre- and postnatal care.

The questions that most intrigued Keith on this visit involved influences that the myths of Nanumea's founding and settlement still had on contemporary politics and efforts to maintain family influence. Although the traditional chiefs had no formal role in island leadership, most were active as individuals in local politics. Several other islands had recently reinstated their chiefly systems, and there was growing sentiment, after nearly a decade's independence from Britain, that this could also be done in Nanumea. Realizing that different families had significantly different versions of the "charter" myths, Keith spent long hours with the older men hearing and rehearing these stories and discussing their meanings. He also updated and augmented the genealogies we had painstakingly gathered during the 1970s.

Our daughters' presence probably made us seem a more normal couple to the community than we had seemed a decade earlier. Lorien, who was six, attended the village school from 7:30 to 12:30 each day along with the other children. Friendly and self-confident by nature, she made friends widely and took pride in being able to help the other children with English, one of their hardest subjects. By the time we left the island, she was a proficient speaker of Nanumean and felt quite at home there. Claire, our shy three-year-old, was initially overwhelmed. She sometimes went out interviewing with Anne, but more often she stayed home, looked after by a young woman whose little sister was a natural playmate.

On our first trip, Anne had developed a nominal daughter relationship with an older woman from the Hawaiian group. Salailoto's great grandfather had been a Hawaiian, and since Anne, too, was from Hawaii, there seemed to be a natural basis for a special connection. On this second visit, Salailoto lived nearby and took solicitous care of us, helping carry water from the cisterns and attending to small domestic matters in the manner of a caring relative. Our deepening relationship with her was special to us all.

It was hard for us to leave in late June, as we had arranged, after less than six months on the island. As always, some of our research plans remained unfinished, and it was painful to think that while life in Nanumea would go on, we would soon be far distant. Inevitably, some of the people we had come to love would die before we could return again. Our expectation, though, was that we would return in some three or four years to continue our work. With this in mind, we even packed most of our household utensils (kerosene stove, pots and pans, buckets and basins, etc.) in a large wooden crate and asked Salailoto to store it for us. As it turned out, the box (but not its contents) would be devoured by termites before we could manage to return.

ê

## A THIRD VISIT

Twelve years passed before we saw Nanumea again. During that time we had moved from New Zealand to Ashland, Oregon. Getting established in our new community took time, as did the need to reinvent our academic careers. A third child came along, and our oldest daughter graduated from high school and began university. We wanted to return to Nanumea again as a family, but it was difficult to find a time when we were all free to make the trip. Anne's nine-month teaching schedule conflicted with Keith's need to be at the university during midsummer, and there were our children's school and university schedules to consider, too. At last, a small window of opportunity opened up: mid-May through July 1996. It would be a short trip, but after an absence of twelve years, any time at all in Nanumea seemed like a gift.

Imagine our delight, as we emerged from immigration formalities at the Funafuti airport into the hot, humid afternoon, to be warmly greeted by leaders of the Nanumean community in the capital. To hear the distinctive Nanumean version of Tuvaluan spoken again! To recognize some familiar faces! Before we knew it, the five of us together with our baggage were transported to a guest house for the night. By the next day, we were settled with a Nanumean family while we waited for the next ship departure for the northern islands. Around us, the capital bustled. In the eighteen years since independence, people had flocked in from the outer islands, swelling Funafuti's population and extending its urban area. In fact, nearly 45 percent of Tuvalu's population of some ten thousand people now lived here. Many overseas experts advised government departments and worked on aid projects. The cooperative store now sold frozen goods, and both fresh bread and fresh fish were available from private businesses nearby. A new high school run by the Tuvalu Church was helping the government fulfill its recently announced goal of universal education through the tenth grade, complementing the long-established secondary school at Motufoua, on Vaitupu Island. More trucks, cars, and buses moved in procession up and down the sandy, unpaved roads. Every day of living in the capital increased our insights about the changes over the past decade, about Tuvaluan hopes for the future, about the lives of former Nanumean neighbors and friends. Again, too many had died. But there were constant delights: finding that our language ability came back easily, that traditional *faatele* songs were still sung, that so many people remembered us warmly. Attempting to recall names to put to familiar faces was not as easy as we wished but became more manageable as we adjusted to the fact that everyone (including ourselves) was now twelve years older. As the weeks of our stay in Funafuti increased, so did our appreciation and gratitude to the capital's Nanumean community and to Kalahati Kilei and his wife Oliula, who shared their home with us, providing our children with a haven while they adjusted to living in a third-world environment.

After three weeks in Funafuti, we boarded the *Nivaga II* for the familiar sea leg of our journey: a three-day voyage to Nanumea, which

*With hosts Kalahati and Oliula, Funafuti (1996)*

would include a day's stopover on the island of Niutao. We were in good company on this visit. Nanumea's two members of parliament were traveling with us and would stay on Nanumea until the next ship visit. They offered to help us any way they could. It was with a sense of great expectation that we all watched the dawn bring our island's outline into view and boarded the ship's work boats, eager to be through the breakers and into the safe waters of the lagoon, ashore on what is for us the most beautiful island in the Pacific. On Nanumea, we were led to a newly built house on the government station, just a few feet from the house we had occupied in 1984. There was fresh paint on the cement block walls, a gleaming metal roof, and mats spread invitingly on the floor. Salailoto had loyally stored our household possessions for a dozen years, convinced that we would return. The few things we lacked we were able to borrow or buy. We were relieved to find that people still categorized us as "of the island," and took communal responsibility for our well-being. Constant kindnesses flooded in. As we walked through the village and began to reacquaint ourselves with the community, we learned that a rumor was circulating that we had come back to retire and build a house. We had not, of course, but this was a pleasant thought.

So much had happened here since our last visit. Men we had known as sons had now replaced their fathers as family heads. The traditional chieftainship had been reinstated and three men in succession had served the island as chief. The island's church had been completely renovated and a taller, more elaborate bell tower added. The community had purchased a tractor and trailer for hauling materials, as well as a catamaran for lagoon transport. Copra making, once a routine feature of village life, was no longer done, and only a handful of families still maintained large ocean-going canoes. As in Funafuti, the cooperative store often sold imported frozen meats from its freezers, themselves new and powered by gasoline generators. More people preferred slip-on sandals to going barefoot. The island had an aid-financed solar-powered telephone system and even a fax machine. People told us proudly that there were now more pigs than people—several times more pigs, we soon realized. Grass was encroaching on the wide, sandy village roads in some places, and village architecture was an ever more creative blend of old and new styles, making use increasingly of imported materials.

We hardly knew where to begin. Our goal on this trip was to assess the changes and continuities in Nanumean life and culture, an objective so broad that every conversation, every visit, every walk was potentially valuable. Unfortunately, our stay on the island this time would be too short to complete a census. We did spend several days mapping the Hauma/Matagi areas to get a better sense of changes in building materials and residence patterns, but we hired two research assistants to record the number of island households. We copied down data on income levels, store sales, taxes, births, and deaths. We tried to understand the extensive changes in fishing activity and canoe ownership, and how these impacted traditional sharing obligations, how much people bought from the store, whether they still gardened, and what young people did for entertainment. We talked with people all day and long into the night.

Meanwhile, our children were thoroughly enmeshed in school life. David, welcomed into the fourth grade with other children born in 1987, found that he could play with friends even though he couldn't speak Tuvaluan. Lorien and Claire had volunteered to help teach English at the primary school and were each given responsibility for four classes' daily lessons. After spending most of each day teaching, they also tutored in the afternoons and prepared lessons for the next day. Both also maintained a voluminous correspondence with friends at home. Through teaching, they soon got to know most of the children, and our regular swim in the lagoon turned into a party most evenings, as David and the girls played in the water with neighborhood children. Lorien found that her long-ago fluency in Nanumean made her language relearning faster, though Claire, with the language background of a former three-year old, had little apparent advantage. In any case, many of the young adults now spoke considerable English.

### ❧

## SEEKING FEEDBACK

In June 1998, Keith took a draft of this book and a long list of questions to Tuvalu. He spent a fortnight in the capital, participating in festivities connected with the ordination of two new ministers, consulting with Nanumeans about the book and current issues facing the community, and talking with old friends and government leaders about the problems and opportunities of contemporary Tuvaluan life. His visit made us even more aware of the dilemmas posed by the changes facing Tuvalu and its people, and how insistently the industrialized West encroaches on this island world.

### ❧

## LOOKING BACK OVER A QUARTER CENTURY

Looking back on these precious periods in Tuvalu, two themes seem to run as threads through our recollections. First, in uncountable instances over several decades, we have seen evidence of the increasing pace and magnitude of the changes confronting this island nation. Every realm of life now appears to be poised on the brink of vast cultural transformation. Many Tuvaluans, especially the urban elite, are eager to develop new business ventures and to experiment with new sociopolitical forms. Personal ambition is described in government planning documents as a valuable underpinning for national development goals, though it meshes uneasily with the traditional emphasis on group welfare. In many ways, the factional dispute that has afflicted the Nanumean community since 1994 encapsulates these tensions. This dispute, involving the island's major social groupings (the Tuvalu Church deacons, elderly family heads, the reigning chief and his council, the women from one village moiety), brings out the key dilemmas of the era. Must social unity be premised on religious unity? What limits should be put on communal goals so that family needs can be fully met? How are individuals to find personal satisfaction and still participate in a cohesive cultural tradition? Finding good answers to these questions will bring Nanumea into a future grounded in traditional wisdom but open to the opportunities of modern life.

A second theme concerns the increasing interest many Tuvaluans have in their traditional heritage. The generation of elders with whom we worked in the 1970s has passed away, taking with them a vast store of knowledge touching all areas of life, from ancient songs to political structure. Although all these elders were born long after contact with the West had begun (the oldest were born about 1890), they were widely perceived to be well versed in traditional culture. And while what is revered and "traditional" undergoes continual change, the early contact period was a time when Nanumea's familiarity with its pre-Christian past was fresh, simply part of the fabric of daily life. Much of the elders' knowledge was rooted in direct experience. Some things, especially genealogy, they transcribed into their family ledgers. They shared other knowledge verbally with us, and it became woven into our published cultural interpretations and materials preserved in the form of genealogies, tape recordings, transcriptions, and field notes. In 1996, spurred by many letters requesting genealogical information apparently no longer locally available, we gave the community several copies of the composite genealogical diagrams that we had compiled using interviews and family records: thirty-two newspaper-sized sheets in all. Will this be useful information? What other appropriate ways can we find to help Nanumeans remain knowledgeable about and connected to the information that the previous generation valued enough to share with us?

ॐ

## NOTES AND SUGGESTIONS FOR FURTHER READING

### Research Funding

Our initial work in Tuvalu was made possible by Anne's participation in the Victoria University of Wellington Rural Socio-Economic Survey of the Gilbert and Ellice Islands, which took place from 1972 to 1976. This interdisciplinary project, directed from Victoria University in Wellington, New Zealand, combined the skills of anthropologists and geographers and was funded as Research Aid Scheme no. R2625A and B by the United Kingdom's Ministry of Overseas Development. Resulting publications included Anne's *Nanumea Report: A Socio-Economic Survey of Nanumea Atoll, Tuvalu* (1984, originally 1975), and four similar reports for the Kiribati (formerly Gilbert Islands) communities of Butaritari, Tabiteuea North, Abemama, and Tamana. An analytical comparison of all five studies was published as Geddes et al. (1979), *Rural Socio-Economic Change in the Gilbert and Ellice Islands: Team Report*. Keith was supported in our initial fieldwork through funds from a U.S. National Institutes of Health Graduate Traineeship (GM 1224) administered through the Department of Anthropology, University of California, Berkeley.

### The Tuvalu Language

Nanumean is a distinct dialect of Tuvaluan, which is itself one of the approximately fifty languages of Polynesia, and thus related to Samoan, Tongan, Hawaiian, and the other languages of the Polynesian triangle. Nanumean differs from the more widely spoken southern version of Tuvaluan in vocabulary and in some of its grammatical features. Like neighboring Nanumaga, Nanumeans use the phoneme [h] in place of the [s] common in the south. All varieties of Tuvaluan are mutually intelligible, though the Nui community speaks a dialect of Micronesian Gilbertese (Kiribati). The Tuvalu language has been written using the English alphabet since the first missionary presence in the 1860s. Literacy in Tuvalu is close to 100 percent. Useful material on the Tuvaluan language includes Ranby's lexicon (1973, 1980), Besnier's dictionary and lesson book (1981a and 1981b), dictionaries by Noricks (1981) and Jackson (1994), and a brief introduction to Tuvaluan (Jackson and Jackson 1999). These latter two works are a good starting place for language learners. The Tuvalu Language Board, based in Funafuti, is currently working on a Tuvalu language dictionary.

## Participant Observation

Participant observation is the hallmark method of sociocultural anthropology and has been used by most fieldworkers since Bronislaw Malinowski's pioneering work in the Trobriand Islands in the early years of this century. Because of the accurate and complex information they provide, qualitative methods like participant observation are drawing increasing interest from other social scientists, even in disciplines with a heavily quantitative tradition. Useful descriptions of qualitative methods in anthropology include Ellen's *Ethnographic Research* (1984), Agar's *The Professional Stranger* (1996), and Crane and Angrosino's *Field Projects in Anthropology: A Student Handbook* (1992). To see how participant observation fits with other research methods used by anthropologists, consult H. Russell Bernard's (1995) *Research Methods in Anthropology.*

## The Ellice Islands Referendum

The referendum process that decided the postcolonial political organization of the Ellice Islands and the separation of the colony into Tuvalu and Kiribati has been described by historian Barrie Macdonald (1975a, 1975b) and by Tito Isala, the government's official translator on the referendum voyage (1983a). We also published our own short comment on the referendum (Chambers and Chambers 1975).

# ❧ 2

# "Of the Island"

We awakened instantly to the sudden silence. The ship's diesel engines had been shut off and the void left by their silence was startling. M.V. *Nivanga* lifted and rolled to meet the swells and we could hear the crisp swish as waves slid past, their phosphorescent crests like lace spread on a dark velvet background.

Beyond the deck railing, sea and sky blended in a seamless expanse of darkness. Out there somewhere, less than a mile away, was our invisible destination: Nanumea atoll, the northernmost community in the Tuvaluan chain of nine atolls and reef islands. Or so we assumed. None of it could be seen, not even a pinpoint of light in the black void surrounding us.

Field Journal aboard *Nivanga*
Wednesday, June 20, 1973

Though we had prepared ourselves for fieldwork in Nanumea as well as we could, we couldn't help but feel apprehension, as well as anticipation, as the ship drifted and we waited through the darkness for dawn. In a few hours we would enter an island world we had never seen before, where we knew no one and could not communicate in the local language. People had been informed we were coming, of course, but how would they respond to having a pair of anthropologists around for months, once the excitement of our arrival had worn off? Our minds felt dull, unready to begin the struggle of hearing and remembering streams of new words. The difficulty of encountering a thousand new people, of keeping their names and faces straight, seemed overwhelming. Judging from the people we had seen on the ship, everyone seemed to look vaguely the same. We found ourselves realizing, with some surprise, that we would have to overcome our natural reserve if we were to "do anthropology" successfully. Going ashore as strangers, even on the glorious mission of fieldwork, was going to be stressful and hard. Now that Nanumea lay just hours away, we wanted to postpone being there.

The horizon was just beginning to take form, separating the steely gray ocean from the visibly lightening monuments of clouds, when the winches creaked into life. The work boats were being lifted from atop the *Nivanga*'s central hatches and lowered into the water. The ship's motors resumed their throbbing and, with the smaller work boats now launched and in tow, we moved slowly toward Nanumea (see fig. 2). Floating between sea and sky, a dark line broken into two parts was just becoming visible. The island, we saw, was separated from the deeper ocean by a sur-

*Nanumea village from the ocean reef (1974)*

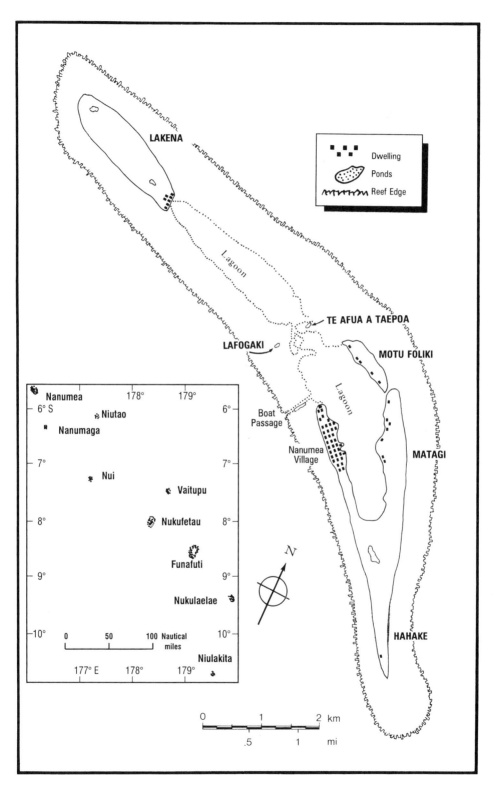

Figure 2  Nanumea Atoll, Tuvalu (with Tuvalu inset).

rounding reef, and it was this barrier that caught the swells of the ocean and turned them into breaking waves. Beyond this line of rough white foam along the reef's edge, a calmer and shallower stretch of water lapped against the atoll's sandy beach. The land itself rose only eight or ten feet higher than the reef, a frail barrier to the power of the sea. As the daylight increased, we could pick out some details: tall palms that defined the limits of the tree line, brown-thatched houses, a large, white cement building whose gleaming red-roofed tower stood taller than the rise of palms. The beach looked wide, smooth, and clean, but surprisingly we could see no people gathering to watch the ship approach. Wasn't the arrival of the ship important in this isolated community?, we wondered.

As we stood at the upper deck railing, drawing what knowledge we could from this distant view of the island, we realized what limited understanding the early European explorers must have been able to develop about life ashore from their distant views of islands. Usually shipbound, explorers sought to chart island positions and draw sketch maps. But it is difficult to accurately assess an island's shape and dimension from a sea-level perspective, especially for atolls that are broken into islets spaced around an irregularly shaped reef. Only if local canoes ventured out to meet the visitors did the explorers normally see any of the inhabitants. Even these encounters were usually limited to brief off-shore trading contacts. The language barrier, as well as general apprehension on both sides, worked against any meaningful social interaction. With a few notable exceptions, the early explorers were mainly interested in charting and claiming new territory. Even the whalers, who followed them in the nineteenth century, seldom came ashore on small central Pacific atolls like Nanumea. The possibility of securing fresh provisions always had to be weighed against the danger of running aground on uncharted reefs and of negotiating narrow passages.

We knew that the boat passage into the atoll's lagoon lay at the northern end of the village peninsula. On the aerial maps of Nanumea that we had seen during our fieldwork preparation, the passage had stood out clearly: a line of deep water, perhaps forty feet wide and several hundred feet long. Along one side lay a sparsely vegetated strip composed of the reef rubble that had been blasted and dredged out of the shallow passage. Leaning out now as far as we could over the railing, we could see this low mound, but there appeared to be no opening in the chain of waves breaking all along the reef. We remembered that early visitors to Nanumea had simply gone ashore over the reef itself, just inland from where we now drifted. The boat or canoe would ride a wave inland, as fishermen still sometimes do today, using the wave's momentum to cushion the impact and to propel the boat shoreward in shallow water.

Our thoughts on the relative merits of this landing method were interrupted by the noise of an outboard motor being coaxed into life. The engine caught and the lightly laden first boat moved off toward the passage, keeping just outside the line of breaking waves. Now that the work boats were in the water, the waves on the reef seemed suddenly larger by comparison. Even the swells near the ship seemed more substantial. Another wooden work boat, larger than the first, was being loaded with cargo: tins of cabin crackers, sacks of rice, boxes of canned and dry goods. The single cooperative store on the island would soon be restocked, except for flour and kerosene, which had not arrived in the capital on the last cargo ship from Fiji. Riding low in the water, this first load of store goods finally headed slowly for the passage, and another work boat was made ready for passengers.

People began to move down toward the stairs that led to the cargo hatch and then over the side to the waiting boats. Children, parcels, and woven bags were handed down to a crewman who stood amidships, helping people into the boat. At the stern, a man in his early twenties sat with one hand on the outboard engine throttle, ready to head for shore. The boat's benches filled quickly with passengers, and it was clear that several trips would be needed to bring everyone ashore. Finally the engine sputtered to life and the boat swung forward into the swells. Everyone's eyes were on the island and the waves that lay ahead; none of the passengers waved back to those of us still standing by the rail.

On the deck, we resigned ourselves to a half-hour wait until the boat could return for another load, and chatted with Sunema, our newly hired assistant, about her homecoming expectations. We had first met Sunema a month earlier on the island of Tabiteuea North in the Gilbert Islands, when we visited a colleague working there. Hearing the broadcast announcement on Radio Tarawa of our desire to hire an interpreter/assistant to work with us on Nanumea, Sunema had phoned on the radio-telephone to offer her services. We arranged to visit Tabiteuea, and Sunema had presented herself early one morning: a cheerful young woman, perhaps twenty years old. She spoke four languages, including English and Tuvaluan. Sunema was Nanumean but her mother had been from Tabiteuea. In typical island fashion, Sunema had come to visit her relatives on Tabiteuea a year earlier and then stayed to marry a local man. The marriage evidently had not endured, for now she was eager to return to her father's household on Nanumea. In addition to being free to travel with us, she was intelligent, vibrant, and had a compelling sense of humor. We felt that she would do a good job of interpreting for us until we could learn enough Nanumean to speak for ourselves, and being a Nanumean herself, she could advise us on local customs and personalities. As we later realized, meeting Sunema was an example of the serendipity that sometimes graces fieldwork. Her patience, tact, and advice were to help us immensely for the next twenty-one months. But on the boat deck that morning, we knew Sunema only as a pleasant acquaintance. We could only hope that her social connections within the community would be an asset to our research and that she would be loyal and honest in her dealings with us.

When our turn did come, Anne went ashore with Sunema and our cabin luggage while Keith waited to see that none of our other supplies were left behind in the hold. Our boat, like the others before, powered along the reef edge toward the passage. Its momentum seemed to be little affected by the swells that, just a few feet inland, split open on the reef. None of the other passengers seemed particularly tense or apprehensive, but Anne remembers a breath-stopping moment while the boat paused in the passage mouth, waiting while the next swell built ominously higher, cutting off sight of the waiting ship. Then the work boat was rising up and moving fast with the wall of water, almost surfing, its outboard motor racing, sliding past the reef edge and into the waveless calm of the passage. With the elation of relief, Anne found herself recalling assurances that, despite its drama, no one had ever drowned in the Nanumea passage. Even on the boats that capsize, strong swimmers always seem available to help the less able. As our boat motored through the calm water of the passage, striped iridescent fish could be seen hovering in the crevices made by the blocks of reef coral that formed the small islet alongside the passage—and then suddenly there was nothing but the green depths of the lagoon.

Within minutes, the work boat rounded the tip of the village peninsula and moved along the lagoon shore toward the broad landing beach at the government station. It passed just a few yards away from a thatched house—a compound of houses, actually: a steep-roofed sleeping house closest to the lagoon and inland from this a cooking shelter with a hearth, and a roofless bath enclosure. The open sides of the house let the lagoon breeze blow freely through and the only furniture to be seen was a row of trunks along one wall. As the boat coasted toward the main part of the village, we could see houses clustered more closely together and thatched roofs interspersed among the tree trunks for some distance inland. The gray light of dawn was made heavy by gathering rain clouds, and the shore looked greenish gray and damp. More numerous than the houses were the canoes, drawn up above the high-tide line, tucked at odd angles under the spreading *kanava* trees lining the water's edge. Coconut frond panels draped the canoe hulls, overlaid sometimes with tattered pandanus matting, outriggers protruding delicately from this protective sheathing.

*Boat day brings people down to the lagoon beach (1973)*

Suddenly the boat was abreast of a long, narrow beach bordered by grass and palms and thronged with people. They stood in groups, talking and watching the boat approach, with an air of anticipation and festivity—women and children mostly, some older people, a few dogs—a sea of flowered prints, brown faces and bodies, bare feet. Piles of boxes and rolled mats dotted the length of the beach, evidence of the successful landing of previous boats.

The boat motor died and seconds later its bottom scraped on the sand. With the other passengers, Anne swung her legs over the side and stepped into the tepid lagoon water. A tall, white-haired man, wearing a tailored *lavalava* wraparound, came toward Anne. "Mrs. Chambers?", he asked hesitantly. Anne felt herself wanting to smile, half expecting him to add Stanley's famous "I presume" to his greeting, but instead she assented solemnly. Surrounded by curiosity and hubbub, he went on to explain that he was Ioane, the Island Executive Officer, the IEO. He served, we knew, as the colonial government administrator on the island. He collected license fees and taxes payable by all the community adults, helped the elected Island Council run its affairs, and assisted the official visitors who came to the island. Where was Keith?, he wanted to know. He had received the telegram we had sent from Tarawa, and he naturally expected to see the two of us together. Were these things still in the boat ours? Ioane spoke English well. He offered to have our boxes carried to an empty house on the government station and beckoned to several men.

Sunema's relatives had already taken her suitcase and bundles of mats, and she had disappeared into the crowd.

People watched Anne without meeting her gaze, but no one else came forward to offer a greeting. It was embarrassing to be the object of so much covert attention. Our pile of supplies seemed mountainous. Boxes of tinned food, everything from canned corn to peanut butter. A case of toilet paper. People in Tarawa had insisted that the local store inventory would be meager and only sporadically replenished. Two trunks of fieldwork supplies: notebooks, tape recorders and tapes, film, typewriters, pens. In a separate box, newsprint and cardboard for drying plant specimens. A suitcase of clothing and bedding. A large mosquito net, purchased in Fiji. Two bicycles. And most incongruous of all, an enormous packing crate containing a kerosene-powered refrigerator—standard equipment for each of the researchers on Anne's project.

By the time Ioane returned to the shore, Keith had arrived. In the distance, across the palm-dotted green field just beyond the beach, a jumble of boxes and crates was piling up beside a thatched house. We walked inland with Ioane as he told us, "This will be your house. It is really for the radio operator but he lives with his family in the village and doesn't need it."

The house was the last in a line of four thatched buildings. It was rectangular, perhaps thirty feet long and eighteen wide, divided by an internal wall into two rooms. The room toward us was obviously the public area of the house, surrounded by a low wall and interrupted by doorway gaps on two sides. Higher walls enclosed the back room entirely, making it quite dark inside. All the walls were made of sticks cut from coconut midribs, tied with sennit cord to a light framework, gray weathered segments interspersed with brown new areas. On the roof, too, some clumps of new thatch contrasted with the older, weathered pandanus leaves. The house had been well prepared for our arrival. Ioane was pointing to the house at the opposite end of the row, telling us that it was his and that we could find him there if we needed anything. As he turned to go, he added that we could meet the Island Council later, if we liked.

Ioane's parting words highlighted a concern that had been nagging since we had first stepped ashore. Where were the Island Council members, and why had they not been the ones to welcome us to their island? The telegram announcing our arrival had been sent to them and we had understood from the other members of Anne's research team and officials in Tarawa that the council was the government of the island. Did their absence mean that we were not welcome visitors? Had we somehow already offended the community? Aware from reading other anthropologists' fieldwork accounts that welcome formalities are often an indicator of local attitudes toward researchers, we were a little worried. We also realized that we had no way of knowing whether the house we had been assigned was, in fact, a socially appropriate place to begin our relationship with the people of Nanumea. Did living there have implications that might harm our ability to interact freely with all segments of the community? These worries recalled the fate of a fellow graduate student who had become adopted by a clan on another Pacific island. When a factional dispute broke out in the community, he was forbidden by the more powerful group even to leave his house. Sunema was an obvious source of advice about our own situation, but she had not yet returned from greeting her family.

Fortunately for our peace of mind, the isolation that had prevailed as we stood on the beach was broken by our movement inland. A crowd of curious children surrounded us, keeping just out of touching range, waiting to see what we would do next. As they whispered together, we heard the word *paalagi* (foreigner) again and again. They clearly hoped for something extraordinary from such exotic visitors. As we hesitated, looking around, a short, heavyset man walked briskly by and, in passing, spoke gruffly to the children. Perhaps he reminded them that it was time for school, because most of them, dressed in blue with notebooks in hand, dutifully moved off down the path. Feeling relieved of some of their curiosity, we entered the house. The white coral pebbles comprising the floor seemed clean, and along one wall was a stack of plaited coco-nut-leaf mats. Wordlessly, we sat down on these and, half hidden from view by our low walls, looked at each other with the same unspoken question: What should we do now?

It was still early morning, gray and overcast, with rain not far off. A light wind played in the palms overhead, producing a continuous rustling sound. Through this, we could hear the steady scratching of brooms on sandy soil as the night's fall of leaves was swept from around the neighborhood's houses. This morning serenade would later come to be a dependable alarm clock, bringing us guiltily awake on the few occasions that daylight found us still asleep. Other sounds vaguely infused the morning air: voices singing, accompanied by a strummed guitar. Looking inland through the jumble of half-cleared vegetation, we could see a group of people moving in our direction, following the broad, unpaved road that appeared to come from the direction of the village. The remaining children were already heading toward the procession, and we quickly followed them, camera and notebooks in hand, glad of a diversion that would give us a reason to interact with someone.

Reaching the road, we saw a curious sight: a young woman, dressed in an elaborate white wedding dress, was being escorted by a group of girls and children. They were in high spirits, singing as they went, talking and laughing between the songs. There was no sign of a bridegroom, and the absence of any adults made the procession seem more of an outing than a ritual. We watched, mystified, as the group advanced, totally unsure of what our response should be. The singers gathered voice and enthusiasm when they saw us but then the song petered away as the guitar player stopped her strumming and spoke insistently to us, motioning toward the camera Keith held in his hand. A photograph was being requested. As Keith arranged the camera settings, the group crowded closely around the bride. We noticed that one of the older girls, perhaps a companion to the bride, wore a wreath of leaves and flowers and, over her bright print dress, had tied a belt from which hung long black and red streamers. Everyone stood solemnly while the picture was taken. Then the guitar player strummed a chord, a song was begun, and the group moved off up the road, leaving us staring after them, wondering about the meaning of our first ethnographic encounter.

Returning to our house, we saw that we had visitors. Sunema and a middle-aged woman she identified as her "auntie" had brought us food and some tea. While we ate and talked with Sunema about people's reactions to our arrival, Sunema's uncle arrived. He thought we might like to walk down to the end of the village near the boat passage, see the medical clinic and meet the doctor, a suggestion that we readily accepted (see the village map in fig. 3). Dr. Tiligaa proved to be extremely pleasant and knowledgeable about the health situation on the island and in Tuvalu generally. As he showed us his small white dispensary building, the adjacent two-roomed maternity clinic, and the cluster of thatched houses in which hospital patients lived under the care of their relatives, he regaled us proudly in English with statistics of the community's declining birth rate and praised the local women's commitment to improving the quality of maternal and child health.

Returning home again, we found visitors: Ioane and a short, muscular, older man introduced as Monise, one of the Island Councilors, had been waiting to escort us to lunch at Ioane's house. The meal was a small feast: roast pork, raw slabs of kingfish, rice, bananas, and a dark, sweet pudding that seemed to be the focus of appetite for our hosts. The procession we photographed had been followed by a wedding earlier this morning, it turned out, and food had been sent over from the marriage feast. As delicately as we could, we copied our hosts and ate with our fingers, though Ioane's wife had thoughtfully given us each a spoon. No one seemed particularly interested in talking and, in the best Polynesian tradition, it was a quiet meal. When we all had finished, a girl brought us a bowl of water, in which a small piece of soap floated, so we could wash our hands.

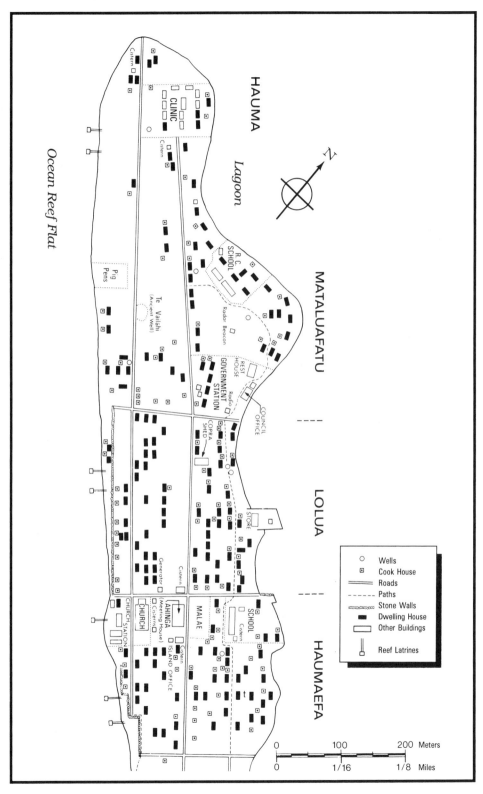

Figure 3    Village Area in Nanumea, 1974.

Monise excused himself to go home for a rest, and we seized the opportunity to ask Ioane about meeting the other council members. Since the next scheduled council meeting was a week away, should we visit the president and vice president of the Island Council? We wanted to explain the work we hoped to do on the island and ask for the council's cooperation. Ioane agreed that impromptu visits would be permissible and suggested that since Sunema knew where the leaders were, she could take us there. A few minutes later, we were walking down the sandy road that ran through the center of the village, glad of the overcast sky that mitigated the heat of midday but apprehensive about our reception when we arrived unannounced at the homes of these important men. The council members, we knew, were elected by all the adults on the island. They were charged with budgeting and spending tax revenues, setting island policy, and serving as liaisons between Nanumea and the colony government. They received a few dollars a month in token compensation for the time they spent in meetings.

Neither of the two men was at home. The president's small, tidy house was deserted, and the vice president and his family were gone, too. Some children playing nearby told us that they were all away at the wedding. We stood for a while in the shade of a breadfruit tree, debating what to do. Sunema advised us to wait and let the men visit us. She would let them know that we wanted to meet them and probably they would come to see us tomorrow.

This advice proved to be sound and much more in tune with local conventions than stopping by unannounced would have been. By midmorning the next day, the two men were seated in our house. Venu, the president, looked younger and more vigorous than we had anticipated. In his early fifties, he had the muscular upper body of an active fisherman. His straight hair was cut very short and stood up in a sort of crew cut. He seemed interested in our plans but professed to speak no English, so we communicated mainly through Seselo, the vice president. Seselo was about the same age, with the manner and appearance of an intellectual. He had learned English through his years of working for the colony government, and now also served as the local magistrate. Conferring with Sunema, he translated what we said for Venu.

It was hard to strike a balance between describing the details of our planned research and the generalities that would make sense to people who knew little of the preoccupations of anthropology or academic life. We began by outlining the structure of the research project Anne was associated with: how there were other researchers assigned to four other communities in the Gilbert Islands, how the project was supported by the British government, how it aimed at a holistic understanding of island life, how the information gathered would hopefully be useful in planning for the future. We made it clear that Keith would join Anne in this work and that he also had a strong interest in learning about history, traditional life, and oral narratives. We stressed that we had come here to learn what it was like to live and think like a Nanumean and that this would require us to learn to speak their language and to move informally through the community. Finally, we asked for their support and also for an appropriate way to let the rest of the community know about our research plans.

Both men seemed receptive, and we were pleased with their invitation to present our plans at next week's meeting of the Island Council. A few days after that, they said, the council would call a meeting of the whole community in the big meeting hall at the center of the village so we could talk about our work. When the councilors had gone, we asked Sunema what she thought of the meeting. It had gone well, she advised, and there was nothing to do now but wait for next week.

Feeling cheerful and enthusiastic, we decided to walk over to the other side of the village to deliver a letter that we had hand-carried from Fiji. Fortunately, we asked Sunema to come with us. The letter was to a woman who had brought her children to visit their paternal relatives while her husband, who was a pastor, was attending a church meeting in Fiji. They were staying with Samuelu, her husband's father. Samuelu was a deacon in the local church and one of the most respected elders in Nanumea. He was descended from one of the two chiefly lineages that had traditionally alternated in ruling the island, and, even though the chiefs no longer played an official role in island government, the old man was a respected speaker at village meetings. We knew nothing of this, of course, as we approached Samuelu's house with the letter. In fact, it would take many hours of careful interviewing and over a year of observing community decision making to even begin to understand the complex role that the chiefs still played in local politics.

Focused as we were on the simple task of delivering the letter, we were surprised at the insistence with which Samuelu invited us to sit down and visit with him, and then even more surprised to find that he was intently questioning Sunema about our reception thus far. People, he said, were very curious about why we had come and there was some concern that we were not being taken care of properly. With only a few days' warning of our arrival, the community had not been able to prepare a welcome feast for us yesterday. Traditionally, the elders would have organized a reception for visitors such as ourselves, he explained, and decided whether to allow our research. The Island Council, instituted by the colony government to run the affairs of the island, now had these responsibilities. Samuelu was concerned that the arrangements that the council made should reflect well on the community. As he talked about these concerns, we gradually realized that Samuelu was giving us advice. Next week was too long to wait to explain our work, he was saying, and we needed to involve the elders as well as the council members. We should tell the council president to invite the "old men," the elders of the community, to the council meeting so that they could hear about our plans soon, directly from us. If the council refused to allow this, he added ominously, then we could always call a separate meeting of the village elders.

Samuelu was serious and persuasive. Our work, he said, was "of the island," not just the government. Therefore, it was a matter that concerned the community as a whole, not just the council. He also urged that we follow local protocol in dealing with officials. Newcomers such as ourselves should not just arrive on the president's doorstep with our questions. Instead, he advised, we must ask the constable to go and request that the president pay us a visit. He emphasized that people could not make any decisions about how we were to be received until they understood what our work entailed.

We felt dismayed. What we heard sounded like a dispute between the council members and the community elders, and it seemed that we might unwittingly have already been caught in the middle. Hesitantly, we agreed with Samuelu that his advice sounded good and that it seemed reasonable to ask the president to convene a special council meeting as soon as possible, with the elders as specifically invited guests. If Samuelu were any example, the "old men" of Nanumea clearly were a power to be reckoned with. Had we inadvertently offended them by dealing only with the Island Council? The phrases Samuelu had used, "of the island" and "of the government," stayed in our minds. This dichotomy was apparently the way that Nanumeans conceptualized the spheres of colony and local government. Did the old men still make important decisions locally, despite the formal authority of the elected council? What would it mean to our research to be classified as "of the government"? Should we (or even more pointedly, *could* we) try to influence our classification one way or the other? It sounded better to us to be "of the island," but what limitations did that involve? Sunema had no opinion about these questions. Deciding whether or not to follow Samuelu's advice, in whole or in part, was clearly going to be up to us.

After considerable discussion that afternoon, we finally decided to do as Samuelu had suggested. Catching sight of the constable as he passed nearby, we requested that he summon Venu to meet with us again, hoping as we did so that this wouldn't be seen as presumptuous. We then spent the rest of the afternoon distractedly listening to some tapes of Nanumean conversation we had made, trying to pick out a few familiar phrases from the stream of sounds. Luckily Sunema was still with us at dusk when the president arrived. With her help, we told Venu that we would like to have a meeting with the council soon, hopefully tomorrow, and that we wondered whether it would be possible to invite the old men to attend. Venu sat quietly thinking for a bit before he announced that the meeting could take place tomorrow morning. However, did we definitely want the old men there, he wondered. And what about the IEO? Keith responded that the old men were essential but that we didn't know about the IEO. After a pause that seemed like an eternity to us, Venu assented. A meeting of the old men, the council, and anyone else who cared to come would be arranged for tomorrow, and he would send someone to fetch us there. He added that because this was "island business," the IEO need not be requested to attend, though he could come if he wished.

Venu then went on to apologize for the lack of a proper welcome to the island for us. He simply didn't know what should be done, he said, because it wasn't clear at all whether we were on a government mission or whether we should be considered guests of the island. Relieved to hear that both Venu and Samuelu were thinking in terms of the same issues, we told Venu that we thought of ourselves as guests of the island. However, it was sobering to realize that, from the Nanumean point of view, our reception thus far had been only a "poor" one. That didn't seem to bode well for our research.

We were up early the next morning, wanting to be ready for the meeting whenever it had been scheduled. A little before eight, councilor Monise arrived to tell us that people were assembled in the meeting house, waiting to hear us. With Sunema and Monise, we walked down the broad shady street, through the village, to the meeting house in which some thirty-five older men (and the single councilwoman) had gathered. A mat was spread in front for us, and we took our places, sitting cross-legged on the floor. Keith, we had decided, should be the one to speak to this male gathering. Slowly, waiting for Sunema to translate, he reiterated the plans we had already described to the council officers and to Samuelu. The elders listened silently and afterward asked many questions. Some were insightful, showing that people had understood the general outline of our research plans. Other questions surprised us but were illuminating later as we mulled over the motivations that might have inspired them. How did we want them to help us with our work? Could we teach them some better ways to grow *pulaka*, their main root crop? Where were we from? How long would we stay? How would they know about the results of our research? Were we going to study old customs, too, or just those of the present day? Had we no children? One old man said ruefully that he had waited all his life for the British government to send someone to help the community, but now he was old and blind and could not see them! When the questions stopped, we thanked the elders and left the hall, leaving them to decide our fate in private, as Samuelu had advised.

We agreed, as we walked home, that the meeting had seemed to go well. What we found out later confirmed this feeling. Those at the meeting had decided that we were to be considered guests of the island. The community approved of our research and would help us insofar as they could. Because we were not affiliated with any particular family and thus had no right to use island land, we would be given food for the next few months. Each Tuesday and Saturday, families would take turns bringing us coconuts and some raw starchy food that we could cook for ourselves: breadfruit, taro, sprouted coconut. This hospitality was the traditional welcome that Nanumeans had long extended to outsiders, those "pitiable" people who were not integrated into the kinship web of the community. We were also to be given an official welcome feast midway through the following week. Samuelu's advice had indeed proven sound.

As the weeks of our stay on Nanumea turned into months, we learned more about island politics. Several times we heard criticism that the council was "sleeping" when active community leadership was required. People's dissatisfaction focused on the fact that the government-mandated council had usurped many of the traditional responsibilities of the elders, who had used decision making by consensus and social pressure to guide community life. As we attended island meetings and council meetings alike, we realized that the council members were caught between traditional expectations and the rules of the Western bureaucracy. At the time of our arrival, Venu had been council president for only a few weeks. He had been as unfamiliar with the president's role as he had been about our classification. The elders had the benefit of traditional precedents to follow in dealing with visitors and making decisions, but they had neither official status nor a formal leader. For decades, the colonial government had found it difficult and frustrating to deal with the "old men" and so had recently instituted elected councils throughout the Gilbert and Ellice Islands as a democratic and, it was hoped, more effective solution to the "problem" of local government.

It was into this mixture of old and new that we had unsuspectingly plunged. Because we had heard of the council's role from colleagues and from government officials before we even reached Nanumea, we assumed that we would need to ask its members for support for our research and work through them to establish rapport with the rest of the community. Nobody had said much about the "old men."

In retrospect, our welcome had two striking implications for our research. One of these was to warn us how thoroughly local political traditions and colonial impositions were entangled together. By insisting that being "of the island" was a fundamentally different category from being "of the government," and requiring that we state our allegiance, the community asserted the continuing local importance of elders' authority and political traditions. At that time, the Island Council system of local government was only a recent colonial imposition, though one of great importance to governmental administration. While council members played a mandated role in island life, Nanumea's traditional political institutions (the council of elders and the chiefly lineages) remained vitally (though covertly) important to both community dynamics and worldview. Encountering this dichotomy so early in our research was fortuitous. Years later, in the late 1980s, we could easily understand Nanumean eagerness to resume the traditional chieftainship as soon as independence made this possible. We could also appreciate how convoluted the community's political history had become during a century of colonial control and how difficult it might prove simply to return to "tradition."

The second implication concerned the tenor of our relationship with Nanumea. Our acceptance into the category "of the island" structured our understanding of Nanumean life in fundamental ways at the same time that it motivated the community to take collective responsibility for our welfare. With Nanumean assistance, we slipped naturally into a local category that made sense to the community. As pitiable strangers, lacking kin ties to particular Nanumeans, we would become a community responsibility and, equally, a community resource. For the first months of our stay on Nanumea, the village sides rostered their member households to provide us with staple foods every few days, and the community as a whole kept a careful vigil over our activities. We accepted our linkage with the community as a whole, scrupulously balancing our involvement with the island's many groups and being careful not to privilege any single family unduly. Though we only dimly understood how community-focused our orientation was, we did not find it unduly constraining. We gradually formed warm relationships with particular families and individuals, most often because our research put us in close contact, though these remained somehow private and subsidiary. Our connection to the community as a whole was dominant. By allowing us to be "of the island," the community had made a public claim that fit precisely the communal orientation pervasive in all other aspects of village life. Ever since those early days, we have tried hard to be worthy of the honor that being "of the island" conferred upon us.

At a more practical level, the important repercussions that flowed from these early decisions reminded us how important it is to be open to advice. We could see how useful it had been to solicit opinions from a wide circle of people. Clearly, we needed to expect contradictions and complexity even in this small and relatively homogeneous community. Making decisions consciously rather than acting tacitly on our assumptions would be imperative. Looking back on these experiences now, our encounter with Samuelu seems like an ocean swell that voyagers might encounter. Passing almost imperceptibly at first beneath the canoe, the swell's surge lifts the fragile vessel as it passes underneath, reminding the voyagers of the sea's power and their own fragile balance on it. The questions raised by our reception made us more aware that the ethnographic challenges that lay ahead would require a delicate approach. Our goal was to understand Nanumean life, from the local point of view as well as from our own. But we were beginning this task with only the most fragmentary knowledge of local categories, values, and options. Socially, we were mere infants, unable even to communicate properly. Like any baby we would have to watch the reactions of those around us, stumble and fall, and learn from the mistakes we would surely make.

è&

## Notes and Suggestions for Further Reading

### Fieldwork Relationships and Narratives

While our primary fieldwork relationship has been with the community of Nanumea as a whole, it is more common for researchers to become linked with a particular family, usually the people with whom they live. Our own situation conformed to Nanumea's strong communal orientation and to the local expectation that as a "scarce resource," we should be equally available to everyone.

Thoughtful accounts of fieldwork now constitute an established genre in anthropological writing. Some classics that we remember fondly from our early years in anthropology and that probably influenced our fieldwork in subtle ways include *Guests of the Sheik* by Elizabeth Fernea (1965), *The High Valley* by Kenneth Read (1965), and *Return to Laughter* by Elenore Smith Bowen (Laura Bohannan) (1964). *Stumbling Toward Truth: Anthropologists at Work* edited by Philip R. DeVita (2000) is an insightful collection of fieldwork accounts, many from the Pacific. Martha Ward's *Nest in the Wind* (1989) and Cathy Small's *Voyages* (1997) also evocatively convey the adventure of close involvement with a Pacific Island community. *Fieldwork and Families*, edited by Flinn, Marshall and Armstrong (1998), explores the reciprocal influences that family dynamics and Pacific Island fieldwork situations have on each other.

## Cultural Categories

Linguistically-marked categories structure peoples' views of the world and define decision-making options in all societies. Understanding the Sapir-Whorf hypothesis can help in appreciating the linkage between worldview and cultural categories. David Thomson (1997 [1975]) provides an interesting short overview. James Spradley's *The Ethnographic Interview* (1979) is a step-by-step guide to the process of documenting cultural categories and linking them to tacit and explicit meanings. Focusing especially on the southern island of Nukulaelae, Niko Besnier's *Literacy, Emotion and Authority* (1995) illustrates how local linguistic categories are used to demarcate nuances of meaning important to Tuvalu speakers.

# 3

# Tefolaha in
# the Cookhouse

There are various objects which the people hold sacred, the chief of
which seem to be the *skull* of one of their ancestors whom they call
Folasa, and the *seat* of one of the canoes in which their ancestors
came from Samoa. These appear to be held in great veneration.

Missionary A. W. Murray
Journal of visit to Nanumea in 1866

The village in which we lived was compact, centering on the meeting hall,
church, and open "plaza" area. Neat rows of thatched houses lined the
sandy roads on either side of this town center. Most of the rest of the atoll
was bush, uninhabited except for a few scattered houses. As we settled
into our work, we sought to gain some perspective on the island's history.
Was this village a new one, inspired by the colonial government? The
answer to this question was complex. As the elders explained to us, the
village area we saw had always been the focal point of community life.
But in the past, people lived in smaller household clusters, not in today's
neatly organized rows. We came to understand that the atoll's residents
had long lived congregated together, rather than sparsely scattered
around the atoll, though living patterns were not always exactly as we
now found them to be. Whaling captain Henry Pease, the first outsider to

41

describe in detail what he had seen ashore, characterized the settled area as a "town" after he spent several days on Nanumea in 1853. Though that term probably overemphasizes the density and size of the settlement, early visitor accounts and local traditions depict the atoll as socially and politically integrated. Nanumeans were clearly united into a single community with a well-defined political and religious leadership, living in named neighborhoods associated with specific extended family groups.

ॐ

## FAMILY CORPORATIONS

Understanding how the village had changed over the last century helped us to grasp the dynamics of contemporary life more clearly, because the past serves as the canvas on which the present is painted. Nanumeans told us that the basic social units in traditional life were extended family residential groups called *kopiti*, but since kopiti had not been functional residential groups since the turn of the century (or earlier) we had to piece together an understanding of how they functioned by talking to older people in the village. While these elders did not have experience of kopiti life as adults, they shared the stories they had heard from relatives as they were growing up and the diffuse cultural knowledge they had constructed over a lifetime. Many of them still used the term kopiti to describe their own extended families to us in 1973–74. In the 1970s, even middle-aged adults recalled that the community had assembled in kopiti groupings in 1953 for the ceremonial installation of Paitela as high chief, though few could remember their family's assigned place in the meeting hall. The location of kopiti neighborhoods was no longer common knowledge either, though elders believed that they were sited on the village land parcels still bearing the old kopiti names. The reconstructed kopiti locations correspond for the most part to the land names used for these parcels today in official land records. Significantly, all these old kopiti locations are within the "old village." Thus, the area where rows of nuclear family houses were constructed after the turn of the century under the direction of the church leaders (the "old village"), still the core of Nanumea village today, is essentially the same part of the atoll inhabited in precontact times.

Tantalized by the fragmentary nature of these local recollections, and concerned that this information could soon be forgotten as elders passed away, we talked extensively with older people about kopiti living arrangements and about the relationship of these groups to the chiefly lineages that provided political leadership in traditional times. Indeed, knowledge of precontact social organization has continued to erode since our first fieldwork. In 1996, we found that community leaders sometimes consulted our ethnographic writings to augment their own knowledge. For many people, the names of kopiti groups and chiefly lineages were becoming indistinguishable, further impeding our efforts to reconstruct Nanumea's traditional social organization. The most probable situation, however, seems to be as follows.

Elders told us that members of kopiti groups owned land collectively, in much the same way that kin groups do today. Kopiti had customary title not only to the neighborhood land on which they lived but also to a variety of other land holdings scattered the length of the atoll. These holdings included taro pits, coastal land dotted with coconut palms, and plots in the sheltered inland forests where large timber and canoe trees grow. Under the direction of the oldest capable male relative, kopiti residents worked to produce food and the other items they needed, and to contribute as required to community-wide feasts and activities.

Each cluster of extended family dwellings, we were told, probably included several sleeping houses, as well as smaller buildings used for work or informal socializing. Women needed sheltered places to work on

*Older-style house (1974)*

craft projects and mat weaving, men worked together on canoes and other building projects, and younger people congregated for leisure activities. These buildings were much like those that we saw throughout the atoll in 1973: thatched, open-sided houses with floors of coral gravel edged by a framework of coconut palm trunks. Henry Pease's description of the houses he slept in at Nanumea in 1853 is also identical. In elders' accounts, the several sleeping houses forming each neighborhood cluster probably accommodated one branch of the kopiti, perhaps a parental couple together with the families of their married sons. Each family branch probably had its own cookhouse, and members would have prepared food together, although resources were also shared more broadly within the extended family or corporation. Kopiti elders represented their family's interests in community decision making, and each named group had its designated place in the village meeting house, as exemplified in Paitela's installation to the chieftainship in 1953.

Family corporations had a patrilateral orientation, with leadership usually passing from a father to his eldest son, from that son to his eldest son. At marriage, sons brought their wives home to live in their own kopiti, and as the couples had children, they lived there, too. Daughters grew up as members in their father's kopiti, but once a woman joined her husband's family at marriage, her children would be raised as primary members of their father's group. However, kopiti membership was flexible because maintaining a wide circle of bilateral kin was also valued. People kept close ties with their maternal relatives, and it was possible for individuals to affiliate with their mother's kopiti if that group lacked enough members (or members of a particular sex) or if living in that group was more compatible. Nonetheless, Nanumean cultural ideals regarding family composition and residence stressed the male side, making living with one's father's paternal kin the "best" choice for most people most of the time. This preference continues today in the family estates that control land, even though, as will be described in chapter 5, Nanumea's cognatic (or bilateral) descent system allows people to affiliate with the estate of either of their parents.

Judging from what older people told us, there were probably seven or eight extended family corporations in Nanumea in the mid–nineteenth century. Each numbered no more than about a hundred persons, and most were probably smaller. These recollections match well with W. F. Newton's estimate (based on early missionary sources) that Nanumea's stable population was about six hundred fifty people in the early nineteenth century. The number and size of kopiti would have varied through time, of course, as groups expanded or perhaps even died out. When group members became too numerous to cooperate effectively, or if bad feelings arose between branches of a family, a kopiti could split, dividing its land and building another cluster of houses.

Kopiti corporations had distinctive names. Some names alluded to an aspect of family history, for example, the foreign origins of an ancestor (as in Kopiti Samoa, the "Samoan kopiti," or Kopiti Haa Tonga, "kopiti from Tonga") or a trio of founding brothers (as in Faletolu, "Three Houses"). These groups also sometimes referred to themselves by the name of their village land parcel (for example, Maheku), and some names related to community events in which the extended family had played a key role (for example, Kopiti Te Malie, which took its name from the peacemaking role of an early warrior ancestor). Other family names had become simply that, their origins lost in time.

Kopiti were of religious importance, too. The eldest man in each family was responsible for looking after the preserved skulls of the group's ancestors and maintaining contact with their spirits. The spirits could be asked for help in subsistence matters, in healing, and in disputes with other extended family groups. To keep the spirits contented and to show them the respect that their power warranted, ancestral skulls were kept in a small shrine inside the family sleeping house. Skulls were regularly anointed with coconut oil by elder family members and given offerings of food and coconuts. In addition to these household gods, other spiritual beings were recognized by everyone in the community. Magai, Telahi, and Maumau are some spirits whose names are still remembered today—the island's founding ancestor, Tefolaha, was also revered. Public shrines to these spirits as well as their "canoe landing places" (*afaga*) were reportedly located on village land owned by particular kopiti groups, suggesting that certain family elders may also have taken responsibility for looking after these spirits, their relics, and sacred sites on behalf of the whole community.

By 1973, as we documented this information, kopiti neighborhoods survived only as named land parcels, dotted with the huge breadfruit trees that had been planted when the first "new village" was rebuilt early this century. The established village area, with its orderly rows of village houses and straight sandy roads, housed most of Nanumea's population in 1973, but people were increasingly moving away in order to live on their own landholdings. Houses were being built between the government station and clinic, as well as across the lagoon, along the shoreline. As our later visits would make clear, this decentralization process has continued and even intensified in the 1980s and 1990s. We will return to consider the effects of recent changes in residence patterns in chapter 8.

The village center is dominated, as it probably was centuries ago, by an open-sided meeting hall. In the late 1800s, this was joined by a second large structure, an imposing whitewashed Protestant church. Today's church building features an elaborate bell tower, ornate leaded glass windows, and decorative elements high on its reddish brown corrugated metal roof. By contrast, the meeting hall (called the *aahiga*) is a broad, low building, roofed with gleaming aluminum (though until the 1960s it was thatched), painted inside in pastel green, yellow, and blue. These two impressive buildings have come to symbolize the unity of the Nanumea community. Grouped together next to an open plaza or playing field, they split the village physically and symbolically into two "sides," which have been used since early this century to organize most community-wide events. The northern side of the village is called Lolua, and the southern side Haumaefa. Membership in these "sides" (*feitu*) is ordinarily inherited from father to son. However, with the flexibility typical of kinship structure in this tightly organized society, household heads sometimes change sides, moving the family's seating place to the other end of the meeting house and contributing to that side's projects and feasts.

The village's division into competing sides was probably an innovation suggested by missionaries and accepted by government administrators. The missionaries wanted houses to center around the church, in symbolic affirmation of the prime place Christianity should play in the life of a godly community. They had no use for the old gods and ancestral skulls revered by kopiti elders, or for the extended family neighborhoods that symbolized the "darkness" (*pouliuli*) in which the pagan Islanders had lived before the coming of Christianity. British administrators were preoccupied with order and cleanliness. They encouraged raised house foundations, neat rows of houses, and straight roads. They preferred an open settlement, cleared of brush and "useless" vegetation, through which a healthful breeze could blow from the windward side of the island. Regular inspections and enforced communal work projects ensured compliance with this pattern throughout the first three-quarters of the twentieth century.

A walk through today's modern village discloses reminders of its past inhabitants and history. Most obvious is the "old village" itself, a dense grid of house sites immediately flanking the church and meeting hall, stretching north and south between the two main roads. These houses, built just after the turn of the century on eighteen-inch-high platforms edged with lime cement and floored with coral gravel, are only thirty to forty feet apart. Laboriously made with lime prepared by burning coral in shallow depressions, the cement platforms are cracked and pitted and have been often repaired. Many of the original house platforms are disintegrating, marked only by a low mound of coral debris. Others stand empty and dilapidated. Century-old breadfruit trees cast a deep shade, but there is little other vegetation. Inside occupied houses, pillows and sleeping mats are rolled into neat cylinders and stored in the rafters. The family's other possessions are tucked away in wooden trunks at one end of the house. Woven coconut frond shutters are tied up along the outside eaves except in bad weather and, if no one is at home, coconut frond undermats are stacked along one wall to protect them from fouling by chickens that forage through the village. The coral gravel that has spilled for decades from the house floors onto the surrounding earth is gray with the patina of human use. If you look down as you walk, odd-shaped bits of shell sometimes catch your eye, for mixed among this gravel is the debris of prehistory: chips of the cowrie lures that were used to catch octopus, pieces of shell borers and scrapers, and shell adze heads, remnants of the industry that produced canoes, house timber, and tools.

The adze heads are by far the most common. This tool was something like a hatchet, but with its cutting blade attached at a right angle to the handle, rather than parallel to it. Blades made from the thick hinged part of *tridacna* "giant clam" shells were the hardest cutting tools available to the early Tuvaluans. Some of the smaller adze heads, two or three inches long, are still whole, and even have fairly sharp cutting edges. The larger ones, five or six inches long, are usually found only in fragments. Nanumeans still regularly use adzes to make canoes, to carve the large wooden basins used to mix and display wedding food, and to smooth beams for houses and in other woodworking projects. However, contemporary adzes have steel heads that seldom break and that can be kept sharp with a few strokes on a whetstone. The broken shell tools that litter the old village, archaeological treasures and reminders of the past, are fragments from days gone by, abandoned because they are no longer useful.

Cookhouses provide another link with the island's past. Many are located on the old kopiti sites. Others stand on land that has long been associated with particular families, so that people today still cook and carry out subsistence chores in the same places that their ancestors did. During village reorganizations under British rule, sleeping house sites were apparently assigned randomly to nuclear family heads, and many people came to reside on land that had been donated by other family groups. Cookhouses, though, were built on the named plots that relatives had owned and used together for generations. Cookhouse sites of siblings and cousins clustered together, allowing relatives to interact with a closeness that their sleeping house locations did not always provide.

Cookhouses today continue to be the heart of family activities, the private "backstage" where intimacy and productivity coincide to give meaning to life. As in the past, cookhouses are the venue for gossip, for mundane chores, for family decision making, and for debates about pub-

lic politics and morality. People dress casually in cookhouses. In contrast
to the bright prints and carefully washed clothes in which people normally take such pride, cookhouse clothing is tattered and stained, its col-
ors dull from age and use. After all, most cooking here is dirty work: the
open fires smoke and smolder, fish scales scatter as they are scraped,
breadfruit peel exudes a sticky sap as its inedible skin is scraped off, and
coconut must be grated and then squeezed by hand to obtain the rich
coconut cream commonly used in cooking. Cookhouses are a place for
family privacy and informal interactions, not for public show. Foraging
chickens and the island's half-starved cats (and sometimes dogs too) hang
around them, eager to devour any shreds of grated coconut or other
scraps not saved for the pig bucket.

*Falai, Failelei, and Faatuu grating pulaka in cookhouse (1974)*

ॐ

## A COOKHOUSE ENCOUNTER

Given the importance of cookhouses in family life and their close linkage with the past, it was fitting that our own cookhouse was the site of our introduction to descent group politics and Nanumean history, topics that are mutually indistinguishable from a Nanumean point of view. This introduction took place on a remarkably clear and sunny morning in which the air had a purity that only follows a hard rain. We had been on Nanumea for less than two months and were beginning to settle into our fieldwork and into the community. On this day we planned a morning of language study, working with Sunema to transcribe taped conversations so we could grasp the construction of Nanumean sentences. She was late, and we sat with our coffee in the cookhouse, chatting while we waited. To our surprise, we suddenly realized that the elderly man slowly hobbling up the path was heading straight toward us, clearly intending a visit. Moments later, he was sitting in the cookhouse, having eased himself through the door with the help of his walking stick, and we greeted him as warmly as our feeble language ability allowed. We unrolled a sitting mat, trying to offer the hospitable welcome we had ourselves received a hundred times in the past weeks in other houses, and then fixed another cup of coffee, making the weak, milky-sweet mix that everyone but ourselves seemed to prefer. By the time the coffee was ready, we realized that Takitua had come on a serious visit. He had some questions for us, he said, and we would need Sunema to help as interpreter.

We knew that Takitua was the head of the *Kau Aliki*, the group of twelve "chiefs" that had nominal authority over traditional aspects of community affairs. The colonial government had long found these Tuvaluan elders difficult to deal with. Preferring to work with younger, English-speaking men, administrators had tended to denigrate and circumvent the chiefs' authority. The elected Island Council form of local government had finally been created in the 1960s as a more democratic form of community leadership. Still, in many Tuvalu communities, the traditional chiefs continued to have considerable influence in island affairs, although with no officially recognized or sanctioned powers. Government reports in the archives at Tarawa had led us to believe that Nanumea no longer had its chiefs—and yet here we were sitting with a recognized chief who had limped halfway across the village to talk to us about something important.

When Sunema finally arrived to interpret, we discovered the reason for Takitua's visit. He had come, he said, to tell us about the founding of Nanumea some twenty-six generations previously. Takitua began by relating the adventures of Tefolaha, the island's founder and cultural icon. Tefolaha was a Tongan warrior, Takitua said, whose exploits had gained renown in the era when Tonga, Fiji, and Samoa were continuously at war. With a group of other Tongan warriors, Tefolaha had been victorious in battles in both Fiji and Samoa. He married in Samoa and remained there awhile, eventually joining with his Samoan in-laws to fight a series of battles against the Tongans. With Tefolaha's help, the Tongan raiders were defeated. After these successes, Tefolaha left his Samoan wife, who had borne him no children, and sailed off alone on a quest for a new land. Coming at last to Nanumea, which at that time had no name and was just a barren spit of sand, he went ashore to inspect what appeared to be an uninhabited island.

Before long, however, he came upon the house of two women, who are said to have originally come from Hawaii. Tefolaha, bold and assertive, challenged them, demanding to know what they were doing on *his* island. Incredulously, Pai and Vau replied that this was their home and that he should leave. Tefolaha proposed a deal. If the two could guess his name, he would leave. But if he could discover theirs, they must go and the island would be his. The two women agreed and sat down inside their house, continuing to weave a mat. Thus far, Tefolaha had appeared to them in his ordinary human nature. Now he shifted to his spirit form, which rendered him invisible, and went up into the attic of the house above where the women were sitting. He first lowered down above Pai's head a small worm on a bit of web. Vau saw it and cried out, "Pai, watch out for that thing above your head!" Tefolaha repeated his trick above Vau's head and then returned to his human form. He approached the two women and said, "Well, what is my name?" "We don't know," they replied. "All right," he said, pointing, "you are Pai and you are Vau!" The two women, crestfallen and in tears, proceeded to leave the island as had been agreed.

Pai and Vau picked up the things they had originally brought with them, baskets of sand, and a long stick used for picking breadfruit and other produce from tall trees. As they left the island they had called "Namea" (a name that is still used to refer poetically to Nanumea), sand spilled from their baskets, creating the island of Lakena at the northwest end of the atoll. As they walked, their picking stick dragged behind them, making a long indentation on the windward reef flat that can be seen today. Some say that the two women went on north to the Gilbert Islands (some adding that they formed these islands much as they had Nanumea), while others say it is not known where they went. In any event, Pai and Vau did not return to the island they had made and named. Henceforth, it belonged to Tefolaha and his descendants.

Tefolaha voyaged back to Tonga, married a woman named Puleala, and sailed with her and her brother to Samoa to recruit a crew. Eventually, when Tefolaha's canoe had a full complement of men, along with his wife and her brother, and at least two other women, they set sail again, stopping at each island in the Tuvalu archipelago except tiny southernmost Niulakita. At each barren, unnamed sandbank, several men got off, taking coconuts ashore with them to plant. By the time the group arrived at northernmost Nanumea, there were just five people left: Tefolaha, his wife Puleala, her brother, and the two unnamed women. As Takitua recounted, these five people were the founders of today's Nanumea. Tefolaha and Puleala went on to have three sons, all of whom also had offspring. Takitua recited to us the names of the children, grandchildren, and great-grandchildren of Tefolaha and Puleala, finally stopping when he could recall no more. Twenty-three generations separated Tefolaha from himself, he said. All were recorded in his family ledger, inherited from his father's brother, a man who had been Nanumea's chief before the turn of the century when the British Protectorate was proclaimed.

ॐ

## COMMUNITY FOUNDATIONS

We had listened, entranced, as Takitua's story unfolded. Here were the elements of both myth and legend: demigod creator figures, a trickster, gullibility, and an epic voyage linking Nanumea to its neighboring islands. If, as Takitua claimed, he had the lineage of the founding family fully charted out in his ledger book, we would have access to an authoritative account of the founder's descendants down to the present, a direct connection between the island's chiefs and the founder, Tefolaha. We realized the old man was offering us a gift, and we were encouraged by the acceptance that his sharing of genealogy seemed to imply.

The story finished, Takitua sipped his coffee for a few minutes and then spoke again. We waited attentively for Sunema to translate. Takitua asked whether we could clarify any of this. How long ago had this happened? What sort of man was Tefolaha? He had already shared this information with two government officials, he said, once just after World War II, and once a decade later. Both times his listeners had noted down with interest some of the detail, but no information was ever returned.

Takitua's questions put us in an awkward position. What insights did he hope we could offer?, we wondered. Verification of Tefolaha's exploits in other places that would confirm his existence as a culture hero? Dates for the island's settlement? Archaeological confirmation of traditional history? Not able to give him any information immediately, we promised to do what research we could and to let him know anything we could find that might be relevant. In the meantime, wanting to make some return, we offered Takitua an approximate calculation of the island's span of settlement, using his genealogies as a base. Takitua seemed pleased with this response and, in reply to our question, named for us the other eleven chiefs in the current Council of Chiefs. Some we had already met. Samuelu, who had advised us to consult the island's "old men" about our work. Monise, the council member with whom we had eaten lunch on our first day on the island and who had subsequently organized the food gifts the Islanders were bringing us twice a week. Others we had heard of as fathers of people we knew. Some names were new to us.

Takitua soon departed for a meeting of the Land Court, leaving us to write detailed notes about his visit, the founding myth he had presented to us, and the organization of the island's chiefly system. We felt elated. Here we were, doing "real" anthropology at last, the worth of our field notes confirmed by the inclusion of concepts such as descent, myth, and traditional chieftainship, which had been important in the ethnographies we had read in graduate school. And to make it all the sweeter, the rich material had been a gift freely brought to us by an important member of the community.

❧

## MYTHS AND "REALITY"

While gifts may be given altruistically, it is impossible to separate them completely from the web of social relationships within which they take place. We soon began to realize that Takitua's gift probably had more complex meanings than we originally thought. A few days after his visit, Sunema was chatting with some neighboring women in the airy, over-the-reef latrine where people lingered in those days to gossip and discuss the doings of other community members. Talk focused on our fieldwork activities and on Takitua's social call. Sunema's neighbors complained, she later told us, that Takitua's version of the Tefolaha story was only partly true. They explained that the two "Hawaiian" women Tefolaha found living on Nanumea had themselves originally produced the atoll's land by spilling sand from their baskets into the sea. Thus, Pai and Vau's ownership of the barren sandbank was based not simply on their presence but on their powers of creation. The critics went on to say that George Holomoana, a Hawaiian sailor who had lived on Nanumea last century and is locally credited with helping prevent Nanumeans from being abducted by Peruvian slavers in the 1860s, had probably originally come to Nanumea in search of these two distant Hawaiian ancestors. Takitua, they said, should have told us these things, too.

When Sunema shared her neighbors' critique with us, we were puzzled. Why was Takitua portrayed as deceiving us rather than as having simply left out some details of a complicated series of events? How many other, somewhat different, versions were there of this founding myth?

Was contention lying just beneath the surface of this apparently peaceful community? Sunema couldn't answer these questions, and, distracted by other activities, we could not pursue them further right away. Work had begun on building our house, and the following day was taken up with preparations for the annual women's celebration, a day in which women take over the meeting house for a day of feasting and dancing.

But as time passed, we increasingly came to appreciate Tefolaha's importance to Nanumea as the root of the community's identity. We were often told the dramatic tale of how he had helped his later descendants overcome a Tongan raiding party led by the giant, Tulaapoupou. We were shown the impressive *Kaumaile*, a six-foot-long spear of dark, hard wood that did not grow locally, reputed to have belonged to Tefolaha himself. A drawing of the spear, used as an emblem by the community, graces the island's letterhead paper and was stamped on movie tickets sold by the Island Council. Kaumaile School is the name of Nanumea's primary school, and its two sports teams (and any other division into two groups as may be necessary at school) are invariably named Pai and Vau, Tefolaha's female adversaries in his conquest of Nanumea.

Early in January every year, Nanumeans fill the community hall for a night of feasting and dancing known as Tefolaha's Day. This celebration began, people say, in 1922 to mark the fiftieth anniversary of missionary activity on Nanumea and to affirm the community's commitment to the Protestant Church. The boisterous holiday has complex overtones: the "children of Tefolaha," who had once worshipped their ancestor as a god and used his blackened skull in important religious rituals, now gather for festivities bearing his name to raise funds for their Christian church. Despite Nanumea's conversion to Christianity, Tefolaha endures as the founding ancestor and symbol of identity in the community he pioneered. To tell and appreciate the story of Tefolaha (or to follow the old practice of pouring onto the ground the last sip in a drinking coconut as an offering to him) is one of the many small gestures that forge the common identity on which Nanumeans draw in their dealings with people from other places, both Westerners and fellow Tuvaluans alike. To recognize and value Tefolaha, we came to realize, was one key to being Nanumean.

The founding myth was also a cornerstone of island politics, with leading families contending over "their" version of the founding, particularly over genealogical issues that establish claims to the chieftainship and the traditional duties allocated to particular descent lines. The Tefolaha story (or stories) was not just a timeless tale of origins, a truth embodied in a single variant. Nanumean traditional narratives had not been compiled in an authoritative edition for people to consult. The founding narratives involved (some might say) fantastic adventures of culture heroes—dramatic, colorful, and rich in symbolism. While we expected to find differences in each telling of a particular tale, at the outset we naively thought the differences would involve minor details. Our approach to these "texts" at first was to search for the most authentic ones we could find, with the aim of assembling them into a whole that would represent Nanumean collective knowledge of its past. This approach fits the Western worldview, but it ignores the continually evolving nature of local histories and the intrinsic differences among different families' accounts. As we gradually discovered, stories of Tefolaha's doings were vital and active parts of community life, narrated and discussed (and continually disputed) precisely because they are fundamental to contemporary political issues.

Tefolaha's story also has sacred qualities. Accounts by early visitors make it clear that Tefolaha was revered in traditional times. Henry Pease, ashore in Nanumea in 1853, saw an ancient, blackened skull with jawbone still attached that, he was told, "was the head of the first king who ever ruled on this island." In rites Pease witnessed, this skull (certainly Tefolaha's) was sprinkled with water and chanted over. Godlike figures with names resembling Tefolaha's were also known in other Pacific Island societies: Samoans called him Folasa, the Gilbertese Borata, and he was famous in other Tuvaluan communities as well. Nanumeans acknowledge that their Tefolaha had indeed visited these other places. But they also know that only in Nanumea did the legendary warrior settle down to engage in ordinary social life, leaving aside his spirit nature, marrying a human wife, and producing children with her from whom contemporary Nanumeans descend.

Gradually, we realized that the people we thought of as Nanumeans thought of themselves as the "heirs of Tefolaha," *gaa tama a Tefolaha*. From this perspective, their claim to their atoll home depends on their ancestor's deeds. It is a heritage that makes them unique, separate in community organization, ideology, and history, not only from the other communities of Tuvalu but also from everyone else in the world.

### ≈

### NOTES AND SUGGESTIONS FOR FURTHER READING

### *Precontact Tuvalu Society*
Only fragmentary knowledge of traditional religious beliefs and practices remains. Early missionary descriptions, such as A. W. Murray's (1876) account of London Missionary Society (LMS) activities and its network of Pacific mission stations, provide some glimpses of information (though obviously filtered through missionary preconceptions). Murray visited Nanumea in 1866, six years before a Christian teacher was allowed to take

up residence. Some accounts indicate that Murray's life was in danger during this initial encounter. LMS journals and reports are available as Pacific Manuscripts Bureau microfilms at Australian National University and University of Hawaii, Manoa (originals housed at the School of Oriental and African Studies, University of London). The full account of Captain Henry Pease's Nanumea adventure was published in his hometown newspaper in Martha's Vineyard in 1854. Also see the edited volume by Hugh Laracy, *Tuvalu, a History* (1983), for writings by Tuvaluans themselves about traditional society and contact with outsiders. *Field Notes on the Culture of Vaitupu* by longtime colonial administrator and amateur anthropologist Donald Kennedy (1931) depicts Vaitupu as Kennedy knew it in the 1920s. Keith's doctoral dissertation (1984) provides information about early Nanumean social organization and the process we used to distinguish kopiti from the chiefly lineages.

### Traditional Material Culture
Gerd Koch's *Material Culture of Tuvalu* (1961 and 1984) provides detailed descriptions and line drawings of many traditional tools and household items, concentrating on the islands of Nukufetau and Niutao.

### Mythical Narratives
R. G. Roberts (1958), a colonial official in Tuvalu in the 1940s and 1950s, published a short collection of founding narratives that provide material comparable to the Nanumean account of Tefolaha. Creation of islands from sand or dirt dropped into the sea is a common motif in Polynesian myths, and tricksters (such as Naleau in Kiribati) often use ruses similar to Tefolaha's to learn opponent identities and to gain power over them. Basil Kirtley's *Motif Index of Traditional Polynesian Narratives* (1971) compares and analyzes such mythic themes. Two popular books by Arthur Grimble, who knew the Gilbert Islands in the early years of this century as a colonial administrator, show how mythology permeated all aspects of island life in the past: *A Pattern of Islands* (1952) and *Return to the Islands* (1957).

### A Hawaiian Connection?
In the Tefolaha narrative, Pai and Vau's supposed Hawaiian origins are intriguing. It seems unlikely that Nanumeans knew about Hawaii prior to European contact. Yet most Nanumeans know this story and agree that Pai and Vau were *faafine Haauai*, which is usually translated as "Hawaiian women." However, it is possible that the term *haauai* may have referred in the past to the women's nonhuman characteristics rather than to their Hawaiian origins. This possible interpretation is discussed further in Keith's *Heirs of Tefolaha* (1984:72).

# 4

# Emerging from the "Days of Darkness"

At about 3 P.M., all the inhabitants of the island assembled in a large square in the centre of town, fronting the shore—all the old chiefs sitting around the king, proposing questions, which he repeated in a slow, clear manner. . . . I pronounce these people to be the most quiet, peaceable, friendly and affectionate to children and hospitable toward strangers, of any people I have ever met with.

Captain Henry Pease
Whaling ship *Planter*, Nanumea, September 29, 1853

The people are all devil-worshippers, and have never suffered any missionaries to come amongst them . . . they have a bad reputation, so we persuaded some to come on board, and fired a few shots to give them an idea of the white man's power.

Captain John Moresby
H.M.S. *Basilisk*, Nanumea, July 21, 1872

Could whaler Henry Pease and naval captain John Moresby both have been chronicling visits to the same small Pacific island? Their recollections seem to contradict each other, even though their Nanumean encounters happened only twenty years apart. Pease was fascinated with the world he had found. He held philosophical discussions with the

57

island leaders, describing in his journal how he was made an honorary "citizen" at the end of his three-day stay. Captain Moresby's impatient ethnocentrism fit his role in extending Britain's Pacific empire in an era when the European powers were competing for control of the world's largest ocean. His bombardment showed Nanumeans that they had little chance of resisting Western demands, whether these involved acquiescing to a new religion or submitting to foreign political control.

The differences between these accounts tantalized us. We combed through microfilm copies of missionary journals and whaling log books, read notes from British colonial records in Fiji, Funafuti, and Tarawa, and corresponded with historians and newspaper archivists. Immersing ourselves in all the fragmented remains of Nanumea's encounter with the West that we could find, we hoped to learn how the process of Western contact had proceeded and how outside influences had affected Nanumean society.

Takitua had hoped that outsiders' knowledge might shed some light on his own concerns regarding Tefolaha. The earlier questions he had posed to us spurred us to pursue our own related quest to try to bridge two very different perspectives. Could local oral tradition, genealogies, recollections of colonial encounters, and selective memories of more recent events be related to the written records kept by Westerners?, we wondered. What common threads might unite traditional accounts and documented history? Could the process of contact with the West be reconstituted with any certainty? What shared images might emerge from both sources, and what perspectives might be missing entirely? These questions resonate in the events we describe below.

ઝ

## DATING TEFOLAHA

When he first introduced Tefolaha to us, Takitua had been seeking to understand Nanumean settlement history. He wondered if we could provide any information that would chronologically date Tefolaha's arrival. How long a settlement history was represented by his (and other Nanumean families') lists of ancestors and descendants? Especially for relatively recent events, where genealogy connects people alive today with ancestors living when the event occurred, it seems reasonable that some standard number of years could be assigned to each generation, thereby creating a roughly accurate dating system. For example, an invasion by Gilbertese warriors described below is believed to have occurred some ten generations ago. Since generations are constrained by biology, each generation could represent an average interval of about twenty-five years, dating the

Gilbertese invasion to about 250 years ago. Dates for several internal wars seem reconstructable in a similar way.

Genealogy-based time estimates for very distant events (such as initial settlement) become less certain, however. While Tefolaha's genealogy, preserved in oral accounts passed down through centuries in the precontact period, was among the first entries made in family ledger books once literacy became common in the late nineteenth century, politically important information such as this is not treated as impartial fact by Nanumeans. Elders have a protective interest in genealogies, which help support their claims to chieftainship, to land, and to influence in local affairs. As might be expected, differing versions of descent lines support the claims and counterclaims made by elders from different families. Competing versions can become topics for public debate. Sometimes, too, information from several generations coalesces together. This unintentional telescoping can easily occur when the same family names are reused generation after generation in order to keep them alive. Though tantalizingly rich with cultural information, genealogies and the stories attached to them are not simple equivalents to historical documents.

Takitua, born in 1903, had told us he was the twenty-third generation in descent from Tefolaha. He had been able to recite the intervening generations name by name. Assuming an average of twenty-five years per generation, the twenty-three generations in Takitua's genealogy could represent 675 years of settlement history, placing the estimated date for Tefolaha's establishment of Nanumean society at about A.D. 1325. This settlement date certainly is not implausible. Nanumean society was clearly well adapted to its island habitat at the time of Western contact, with a subsistence technology and sociopolitical structure finely tuned to the realities of atoll life. This degree of fit could be expected to have required centuries of local residence to develop. However, it is still possible that genealogy-based calculations of settlement time depth might err by being too shallow. As cultural constructions produced in response to historical realities, they could represent only part of a much longer depth of settlement. Recent archaeological work in the Pacific region suggests this latter possibility. Thus it is important to try to consider Takitua's question as related to a regional settlement context.

Westerners have been as curious as Takitua about the exploration and populating of the Pacific, creating a series of hypothetical reconstructions that have not been entirely free of their own ethnocentric assumptions. Many early explorers noted with surprise that on island after island, isolated places to which they had found their own ways with such difficulty, the existence of large populations with elaborate cultures indicated considerable settlement depth and seafaring abilities. By the end of the

Western era of "discovery," it had become apparent that the ancestors of contemporary Pacific peoples had indeed settled every single habitable island in the world's largest ocean. Where resource availability had permitted, systems of impressive social and political complexity had developed. Pacific cultures came to be synonymous with massive stone temples and statues, with elaborate public ceremonies and rituals, and with intensive marine and terrestrial systems of food production and storage. The high islands of Polynesia seemed especially remarkable to Westerners. Associating cultural complexity with civilization, they were surprised to find it in the middle of the Pacific Ocean, independent of European cultural influence.

Research in the last fifty years by archaeologists, linguists, and physical anthropologists now offers an overview of likely settlement patterns in the island Pacific, providing the context for answering Takitua's question. The earliest settlers of Australia, New Guinea, and nearby islands began arriving from Southeast Asia at least 60,000 years ago, possibly even earlier. Much later, perhaps around 12,000 years ago, another eastward population flow began out of Southeast Asia. Archaeological excavations show that these ancestral people shared a sophisticated maritime technology, spoke an Austronesian language, and made a distinctive style of decorated pottery. These "Lapita people" spread relatively quickly further eastward, moving beyond the high islands of Melanesia out into the remote Pacific where islands were separated by hundreds of miles of open ocean and where successful voyaging depended on navigational knowledge, sophisticated canoe technology, and well-organized expeditions. The determination and ingenuity typical of pioneers would have been essential too. These people pressed gradually eastward, century after century, reaching Samoa and Tonga in the heartland of western Polynesia about 3,500 years ago. Finally, even eastern Polynesia, the far-flung corners of the Polynesian triangle, and tiny, scattered reef islands and atolls were settled. In Polynesia, similarities in language and culture have offered tantalizing possibilities of reconstructing the dispersal process and mapping the "genealogical" relationships among island societies.

Tuvaluan settlement appears to have originated from the south (probably from the western Polynesian heartland of Samoa, Tonga, and Fiji), with the first settlers probably arriving about 2,000 years ago. Sea levels were probably too high to allow habitation of the central Pacific atolls much before 2,500–2,000 years ago, and it now seems likely that Nanumea and other remote atolls were settled not long after sea levels receded. Recent archaeological work conducted by Marshall Weisler in the Marshall Islands to the north (atolls that have built themselves on peaks of the same subsurface mountain range that underlies Tuvalu) shows settlement starting around 2,000 years ago. Dated animal remains there suggest that the Marshallese atoll environments offered early settlers rich resources, including sea birds, turtles and land crabs, as well as fish. Tuvalu atolls were probably equally inviting initially, though population increases would soon have made intensified crop production essential.

Although Tuvalu has not yet had any systematic archaeological exploration, there have been a few limited excavations and surface surveys. Test pits dug in 1984 on the atoll of Vaitupu by Jun Takayama revealed shell fishhooks of an archaic type as well as pottery pieces apparently originating from Fiji, the nearest high island group, some six hundred miles to the south (the clay and sand found in these items does not occur naturally in Tuvalu). One bone fishhook, excavated from the same sediment layer as the pottery, was radiocarbon dated to about A.D. 1080. Takayama and his co-workers did not conduct a thorough survey nor did they apparently locate the island's earliest sites. It seems certain that initial settlement of Vaitupu occurred well before this date. Thus, we believe a settlement date of about 2,000 years ago seems likely for all of Tuvalu.

Though the intentions and circumstances of the initial discoverers remain obscured by time, it is clear that intentional voyages were essential in the settlement of the Pacific. Geoff Irwin and others have shown that settlement eastward into the island Pacific would have required an ability to sail against prevailing winds and currents, indicating that these voyages would have been well planned and well equipped expeditions. Indeed, the sophistication and efficiency of traditional sailing vessels, as well as extensive local navigational knowledge, indicate that early Pacific Islanders were technologically able to undertake intentional voyages across hundreds of miles of open ocean thousands of years before Europeans embarked on their own voyages of discovery. Tefolaha's journey to Nanumea from the vicinity of Tonga (or Samoa or Fiji) would have required sailing close to the wind at most times of year—not a simple downwind drift. On the other hand, as traditional Nanumean stories document, accidental drifting between island groups was a fact of atoll life. Fortuitous landings (and occasional tragedies) continue even today.

ﻉﺍ

## PRECONTACT SOCIETY

Similarities in language and culture throughout Tuvalu indicate that the islands were probably settled within a relatively short period of time and that interisland canoe voyaging between the nearer islands kept them in frequent contact. Around A.D. 1800, the archipelago probably contained a series of small chiefdoms, each its own ministate with a population of 350 to 550 people per island. Traditional accounts, supported by analysis of linguistic similarities, show a division into northern and southern clusters. The northern islands of Nanumea, Nanumaga, and Niutao (and perhaps Nui as well) probably were in regular contact. To the south, Vaitupu, Funafuti, Nukufetau, and Nukulaelac probably formed another cluster linked by sporadic interisland voyaging contact. Southernmost Niulakita was probably too small to support a permanent population.

What can we reconstruct of precontact political and social life? The general outlines are clear: as was common in Polynesia, the traditional chieftainship that came to exist on Nanumea and in Tuvalu was an intriguing blend of egalitarian and hierarchical elements. Descent from a founding line of rulers, traced ideally through male links, was the core principle of political life. On Nanumea, the reigning chief was drawn from two descent groups whose special prerogative was to provide the island's leader. These two favored lineages usually alternated the chieftainship between them. They were supported by five other descent groups (also "chiefly," in Nanumean ideology), each of which had charge of a particular domain: the sea, division of communal foods, peacekeeping, service to the reigning chief, and so on. While family traditions differ in details, all Nanumeans agree that only descendants of Tefolaha had, and continue to have, rights to membership in the chiefly lines. By one well-accepted (but not universal) account, Tefolaha originally appointed his youngest son, Laavega, as ruling *aliki*. The seven chiefly lineages known today trace their descent from him. His brothers Tuutaki and Fiaola were charged with protecting and assisting Laavega's rule, in much the same way that nonruling chiefly branches still support the chief. Tuutaki, the eldest, is said to have been given Tefolaha's powerful spear, the Kaumaile. This is said to have passed down through his descendants and is still kept safe by them on Nanumea today.

The difficulty of understanding another political system can be compounded by ethnocentrism and preconceptions, as well as by difficulties in translating local terminology. Early Western visitors to Tuvalu typically used words like chief and king to describe the political leaders they encountered. The English connotations of these words do not match those of the Tuvaluan word *aliki*, encouraging missionary and colonial visitors to overestimate the actual powers of the reigning chiefs. Outsiders often later became critical of the "weak" nature of the chieftainship, failing to see limitations as essential in maintaining the egalitarian aspects of local political systems. Both because they tended to see the world from the Eurocentric perspective of hereditary monarchy and because they stayed only a short time on any given island, many early observers probably never realized that Tuvaluan "kings" typically served only short terms and were regularly replaced when natural disasters or other untoward events occurred. In Nanumea, chiefly families worked for a living like everyone else and their lifestyles were essentially similar to those of non-chiefly families. Their role was one of public service rather than of power.

The Tuvaluan notion of chieftainship saw rank and status as derived from male descent, a pattern shared throughout Polynesia. But it had a more egalitarian emphasis than was typical of stratified Polynesian chiefdoms, which developed in larger islands, where a rich resource base and relatively dense population made substantial surplus production and stored wealth possible. In more marginal habitats such as Tuvalu, the basic Polynesian chiefly structure was overlaid with a strong egalitarian ethos. Nanumea thus provides an example of the more egalitarian style of Polynesian chieftainship, contrasting with societies like Hawaii and Tahiti whose nearly deified chiefs wielded true authoritarian power.

ào

## THEMES IN NANUMEAN TRADITIONAL HISTORY

Takitua was one of the first Nanumean elders with whom we discussed issues of traditional history and genealogy. Over the course of our work we also learned from many others: Taulialia, widely respected for his phenomenal memory and seemingly endless stock of historical anecdotes and genealogical connections; Tepou, descended from warriors who defended the island in the late nineteenth century; Malulu, eldest spokesperson for a main chiefly lineage; Samuelu, head of his chiefly lineage and leading deacon in the church, and his son Sosemea; Venu, council president, master canoe maker, and fishing master. We are indebted to them and to the scores of other remarkable individuals who shared their stories of community history and origins with us, endeavoring to help us comprehend traditional society. We heard (and tape-recorded) many tales of beginnings, adventures, feuds, and wars. We spent many hours listening to accounts of recent events and discussing the context of elders' memories of the past. Two broad themes seem apparent in these local accounts of the community's earlier life.

### Overseas Raids, Invasions, and Adventures

Once Tefolaha and his descendants had discovered and settled Nanumea, other visitors also made their way to the atoll. The first outsider to arrive, at least the first of whom a story is recalled, is said to have been a Tongan prince. Lupo's canoe was wrecked on the reef and he was killed by Nanumeans when he tried to come ashore. His body, with a Nanumean spear still protruding from his eye socket, drifted back to Tonga, where his relatives used magic to determine the place of his death. A long period of sporadic warfare between Nanumea and avenging Tongan raiders resulted. One raid was led by the Tongan giant, Tulaapoupou. Said to stand taller than the coconut palms and to brush them aside like grass when he walked, Tulaapoupou terrorized Nanumea until he was finally undone by the valiant local hero, Lapi. Lapi was able to defeat Tulaapoupou because he called on the spirit of founder Tefolaha and used as his weapon the spear that Tefolaha had brought to his initial settlement of the atoll. Today when the tide is low, Tulaapoupou's foot and knee prints still mark the reef where he fell.

The next fleet of Tongan war canoes was destroyed by the combined magic of several powerful Nanumean guardian sea gods. Later, another invading group included Laukava, son of a Nanumean woman kidnapped by the first Tongan raiders. His war party was defeated, but Laukava himself was spared when he was able to prove his Nanumean ancestry. Allowing him to remain in Nanumea proved a fortuitous decision. When Tongan warriors returned to Nanumea a generation later, Laukava defeated them single-handedly. He was able to persuade the survivors that a Tongan victory would never be possible, and they promised never to return. Thus ended the generations of intermittent Tongan raiding that had killed many Nanumeans and regularly disrupted island peace.

Nanumeans also recall more recent invasion attempts from the Gilbert Islands to the north. Gilbertese warriors Kaitu and Uakeia, believed to have conquered the neighboring Tuvalu island of Nui (which today speaks a dialect of the Gilbertese language), are said to have passed through Nanumea too. At first, Nanumean magic made currents too strong for them to land but eventually Taitai and several other warriors from the fleet managed to get ashore. Taitai, his sister Teputi and a fellow warrior, Temotu, all were adopted by Nanumean families, with both Taitai and Teputi marrying on Nanumea.

Gradually, however, Taitai began to scheme to dominate the island, secretly killing Nanumean men as they worked alone on their bush lands. Eventually, he terrorized the island's chiefs into fleeing to Niutao so that he could rule Nanumea himself. One young chief, Logotau, stayed behind, hiding himself in the bush and plotting with Maatio, the island's remaining warrior, to kill the usurpers. They lured Taitai into helping dig a posthole for a new community hall and managed to stab him fatally. Temotu, whom they had distracted with a party of dancing girls, was subsequently killed as he tried to escape. Taitai's sister Teputi and the children of the Gilbertese invaders were spared. Meanwhile, the exiled chiefs were using magical vision to keep abreast of developments at home. With the Gilbertese warriors vanquished, the chiefs decided to return, agreeing

*Seselo holds Kaumaile spear (1974)*

that the first one home would rule. Logotau, who had never fled, was there to greet them when they arrived and ridiculed their cowardice. Though the chiefs urged Logotau to rule as high chief, he refused. Instead, he pledged to uphold the authority of whomever was selected as chief, providing continuity as the ruling chief changed through time. Logotau's descendants today are members of the Tuumau lineage of chiefs. Their ancestor's "steadfastness" (*tuumau*) is commemorated in the lineage's name and in its role of overseeing chiefly selection procedures and installation ceremonies. Takitua was this lineage's leading spokesman during our initial work in Nanumea.

Another event associated with the Gilbertese visitors concerns Poepoe, grandson of the warrior Taitai. Wanting to avenge his grandfather's killing, but forbidden to do so by his father, Poepoe was unable to endure his family's shame. He and his mother's brother, Piikia, set out to *folau*, putting out to the open sea in a canoe to near-certain death. On Nanumea, these men were never heard of again and were presumed drowned. Some two hundred years later, in the 1960s, Tuvaluans living in the Solomon Islands heard a local story about Poepoe's safe arrival at tiny Anuta Island. Anuta accounts of Poepoe's voyage were recorded by anthropologists Raymond Firth in 1929 and Rick Feinberg in the 1980s. Descendants of Taitai and Logotau still live in Nanumea today and keep alive these stories. In some cases, people are able to trace their genealogical path back to the main characters with some certainty. Taulialia's "family tree," for instance, lists eight generations between himself and Taitai, placing Taitai's arrival on the island about 1700–1750. Of course, this group was probably just one of many who arrived in Nanumea, with great or little drama, subtly altering the course of island history with their personalities and ideas.

### Internal Feuds and Wars

One aspect of Christianity's influence throughout the Pacific was an end to wars and violent quarreling. Nanumeans characterize the "days of darkness" (*pouliuli*, i.e., the pre-Christian pagan past) as times of interfamily feuding, with force often the main determinant of power. Oral accounts of these local conflicts provide clues about the issues that occupied island society in premissionary times and about the social organization of the community.

A major war, called the *Taua Lahi* (great war) or *Taua i Talo* (taro pit war), took place about thirteen generations ago, perhaps two hundred fifty to three hundred years in the past. Possibly to cope with prolonged drought, the island had split into two groups, with some people living on Lakena Islet and the rest on Nanumea proper. Then, as today, there were no root gardens on the main island of Nanumea. The Nanumean group came to resent this lack and decided to break the ban on digging taro pits there, even if this meant having to put up with night-flying mosquitoes. They secretly raided Lakena to get shoots to plant, then returned to Nanumea and began digging their pit. Outraged, the Lakena people ambushed the Nanumeans as they dug. Each side retreated to positions at rock outcrops (*pae*) along the lagoon shore, the Lakena people at Pae a Kamuu and the Nanumean people at Pae Hoopuu. The pae provided each side with a home base (*nohoga*) as well as a supply of ammunition, since rocks and spears carved painstakingly out of coconut wood were the main weapons used. The names of the participants in these skirmishes are forgotten today, but the Lakena people evidently were victorious because taro pits remained restricted to that islet. Indeed, a landowner who recently built a house on the Pae a Kamuu site found skulls and bones when digging the foundation, which he believed were from this war.

Another war, called *Taua i haa Keli*, the war of Keli's family, is the last battle believed to have occurred between sizable groups of Nanumeans. The altercation involved two extended family groups, one led by Keli and the other by Laukava. People today can trace genealogical connections to both leaders and place the skirmishes about six generations prior to the birth of our elderly informants, approximately 1840 by our estimate. Laukava, avenging the attempted abduction of his wife by another man, was stabbed with a spear by Taamole, a warrior who took the side of Laukava's rival. Despite his wounds, Laukava survived and he and his relatives planned blood revenge, *taui toto*. Nanumeans say that in the ensuing battle, about half of the ten men who fought on each side were killed.

Stories like these provide insights into precontact society and illustrate how this largely egalitarian community exerted social control. Men described as *hotahota*, *fakamafi*, and *fakatagata* (troublemakers, bullies, showoffs) were usually either killed outright by the island's leading warriors (*toa*) or were bound and set adrift in leaky canoes to die at sea. Their wives and children were usually not harmed unless they interfered. A man's mother's brothers and sister's sons (*tuaatina*) traditionally were obliged to come to his defense, and their collective strength would have been shrewdly assessed by the warriors before they acted. Stories are told about the defeats of recent troublemakers such as Lavalua, Kafika, and Nakaola, but the story of Kalihi, the last man known to die by warrior intervention, is especially well known. Kalihi was killed about 1875 by a pair of brothers known as Tepou and Moulogo. The island's first pastor, Tuilouaa, tried to prevent this act of customary justice but was not powerful enough, though he was later able to persuade these two warriors to give up their "peacemaking" activities to other Christian toa, whom he was able to influence. By the time Moulogo died in the 1890s, he had accepted Christianity and had become a deacon in the Protestant Church.

Troublemakers like Kalihi were dispatched probably because they threatened the established social order. While pre-Christian Nanumea did not have formalized legal institutions, the young men of chiefly families, especially the reigning chief's tuaatina (his sister's sons) would naturally have been expected to assist the chief in enforcing his decisions. They would also have protected the island from external attacks. Within the community, Nanumeans say, warriors would have attacked only widely recognized troublemakers, only taking action when they had public support. They seem to have filled the role of an informal police force.

As we will see in later chapters, the tension between community well-being and family goals is a recurrent theme in Nanumean affairs. Perhaps it is not surprising that the threat of social disruption runs as a common thread through all these stories of long ago. New arrivals are potentially as problematic as rebellious insiders. They breach the community's boundaries, bringing new ways and novel desires. Marriage and adoption are time-honored ways to make newcomers "of the island," a good solution when the visitors are few in number or not bent on conquest. But even as Nanumeans were dealing with invasion attempts from neighboring societies and dissension within their own community, an infinitely more unsettling source of change was looming on the horizon. Westerners, driven by fundamentally acquisitive and ethnocentric notions of their place in the world, had discovered that new continents lay behind the horizon. The Pacific Ocean, offering sea routes to Asia and the "new world," was not simply home to a multitude of intriguing island societies. It was soon to become an arena for trade, political rivalry, and missionary endeavor.

### EXPLORERS AND WHALERS

The earliest known European contact with Tuvalu took place on 16 January 1568 when two ships under the command of Alvaro de Mendaña encountered the island of Nui. This expedition had been sent to extend Spanish influence in the south Pacific and "to convert all infidels to Christianity." Setting out from Peru, Mendaña's party had already traversed half the Pacific without sighting land. At Nui, by Mendaña's account, five canoes came out to meet his ships, but they turned suddenly back to shore after getting within calling distance, and Mendaña was unable to induce them to return. When an overnight storm prevented any further landing efforts, his vessels continued on westward, christening the island "Isla de Jesus."

Two hundred years would pass before the next recorded interaction between Western explorers and Tuvaluans would occur. Spain was still a major naval power and its ships maintained regular contact between the territories it had colonized. One such voyage began late in 1780 when the frigate *La Princesa*, captained by Francisco Maurelle, sailed from Manila with dispatches bound for Mexico. This was a difficult, poorly provisioned voyage, and Maurelle's journal shows that he had stopped in Tonga to replenish supplies before heading northward. He then sailed through uncharted Tuvalu, inadvertently missing all the southern islands but eventually happening on Niutao on May 5, 1781. He wrote that the inhabitants, painted strikingly in black, gave him a friendly reception, came aboard his ship, and even struggled for six hours to tow it toward shore with their canoes, since the water was too deep to anchor. Despite these efforts, Maurelle was unable to land and eventually had to sail on. The next day he sighted Nanumea, naming it "San Augustin," but made no contact with its inhabitants. Over the next half century similarly sporadic and superficial contacts were made by a handful of other explorers with one or another island in the Tuvalu group. Their "discoveries" were named and charted with varying degrees of accuracy, sometimes leading to an island's being "rediscovered," recharted, and renamed by the next explorer. Intent on mapping and claiming new territory for their respective governments, and wary of unpleasant incidents with natives, most of these early visitors avoided contact with local people.

What must these several centuries of European exploration have been like in Nanumea and the other Tuvalu islands? As we have seen, local oral accounts and genealogies preserve some memory of early invaders, but all these newcomers were Pacific Island peoples not too unlike Nanumeans themselves. Tongan raiders, whether actually from Tonga or from other larger Pacific societies, would have sailed in voyaging canoes similar to those known in Tuvalu and would have seemed familiar in appearance and language. While vessels from the Micronesian societies to the north where the Gilbert Islands lie would have differed somewhat from those of Polynesia, and the Gilbertese language would probably have been unintelligible, these societies were distantly related and shared some parallel adaptations to atoll life. By contrast with these oral traditions, local stories about contact with early European intruders are lacking, apparently nonexistent. An intriguing silence.

Nevertheless, it is impossible not to wonder what thoughts passed through the minds of Tuvaluans who saw unusual square-shaped sails and the unfamiliar bulk of European sailing vessels beginning to appear at long intervals off the coast. What changes in local worldview occurred as evidence mounted that vastly different societies existed over the horizon? What information and impressions were accumulating over the decades and centuries of intermittent contact? Was interaction with visitors from over the seas seen as fraught with danger? An opportunity to acquire trade goods? Or simply a recurrent happening, to be dealt with as each situation demanded?

We are unlikely ever to be sure. What we do know is that the frequency of sightings of European sails began to increase significantly in the nineteenth century. By 1820, whaling ships were combing the Pacific for sperm whales to provide oil for heating, lighting, and lubrication. Whalers would be a substantial presence in the Pacific for the next fifty years, transforming the ports where they wintered, distributing trade items in return for provisions, and frequently employing Islanders as crew. But Tuvalu waters attracted few whaling vessels compared to areas further from the equator, and most islands had little more contact with whalers than they had with early explorers. Whalers had good reason for avoiding these small islands, too. In the age of sail, landing at most of them was hazardous (or, as Mendaña had discovered, impossible). Without protected anchorages or sandy shallows in which to set an anchor and to get ashore, whalers had to allow their ship to drift in the lee of an island, row through treacherous waves, and then drag a small boat in over the reef. Fresh water, a constant need, was rare on atolls, and little local produce other than coconuts was available. Equally problematic, crew members sometimes deserted if they were allowed ashore. In the northern and least visited portion of Tuvalu, rumors about the unwelcoming intentions of the Islanders made whaling captains even more hesitant to land.

In this context, Captain Henry Pease's decision to spend three days ashore in Nanumea late in September 1853 was remarkable. Fortunately, he was both a sensitive guest and good observer, and his journal provides the only premissionary description of Nanumean life. Curious about local customs, Pease patiently underwent a day-long ritual demanded of newcomers, was feted and entertained, and engaged in serious discussions (using a Tongan member of his crew as interpreter) with Nanumean leaders about the nature of the outside world. He was told that his was only the second European ship to visit Nanumea. The unidentified first visitors, people told him, had attempted a landing many years before but had shot and killed several Nanumeans who approached them on the shore, then fled to their ship and departed. This unfortunate event probably occurred in the 1830s or 1840s, though we have not been able to link it to any of the historically documented whaling encounters. Pease's account provides rich insights into Nanumean life, and we have drawn repeatedly on his description of the village for information about life in the kopiti era. But while Pease was impressed enough by his Nanumean encounter to publish a twenty-page description of it in his local New England newspaper, Nanumean oral tradition no longer recalls his arrival at all. Why is this? Was Pease's visit, and possibly those of other Westerners, too, simply not memorable from the local point of view? Or was the significance of these visitors dwarfed by the impact of the next arrivals?

### ❧
### MISSIONARIES

Oral tradition accords missionaries a key role in transforming Tuvaluan life. The Congregationalist London Missionary Society (referred to today both by scholars and by Tuvaluans as the LMS) began to place Samoan pastors on the southern islands in 1865, after a convert accidentally drifted to Tuvalu. The apocryphal story as it is told in Tuvalu goes like this. Elekana, a deacon from Manihiki in the northern Cook Islands, was traveling in a small open boat with several others in 1861 when they were blown off course. Over several weeks the boat drifted some twelve hundred miles westward, finally washing ashore with its nearly dead passengers at Nukulaelae atoll. Though not formally trained as a missionary, Elekana was apparently welcomed as a teacher by the Nukulaelae people, who were reportedly eager for the new religion and for the skills of reading and writing. Elekana and his companions remained in Nukulaelae for several months before they were able to return to Samoa. Quick to see opportunity in this adventure, the LMS gave Elekana religious training and sent him back to Tuvalu in 1865 as a resident pastor.

Christian conversion of southern Tuvalu was accomplished within just a few years of Elekana's landing, but the northern islands proved stubbornly resistant. Though missionary A. W. Murray, heading the first LMS voyage in 1865 to these "north-west outstations," had heard that the northern Tuvalu islands had given up their old religion, he soon found that this was not true. He was forcibly ejected from Nanumea in 1866, and in the years that followed both Nanumea and Nanumaga put up stiff resistance to missionary efforts. LMS attempts to put a teacher ashore were unsuccessful until 1871 in Nanumaga and 1872 in Nanumea. Political and cultural allies, the two islands both demanded that strangers undergo an elaborate ritual at the water's edge before coming ashore. Numerous accounts make it clear that the rites, which Pease called "a period of naturalization," could last up to five days. Even a truncated day-long process drew such indignant protests from early missionary visitors that Nanumeans obligingly provided stools for them to sit upon on the exposed reef flat and even erected temporary sun shades overhead.

Nanumeans and Nanumagans apparently believed that unless these observances were carried out, island populations would be in danger of death. Were these rituals, which some missionary accounts refer to as "devilling," religious in nature? Were they designed to satisfy local gods or somehow maintain the purity of the community? They were applied, early reports indicate, to all visitors, European and non-European alike. Did the rites transform newcomers in some way that made them "of the island"? Nanumean accounts shed no light on these questions, unfortunately. The ceremonies did serve as a visible gauge of Islanders' adherence to traditional practices and were mentioned derisively in missionary diaries for many years. That these rituals continued until 1874 in Nanumea and 1875 in Nanumaga indicates that these Islanders successfully resisted missionary overtures for a decade.

The differences between local and missionary versions of the island's final religious capitulation provide insights into their respective worldviews. Nanumeans stress their fear that refusing to cooperate with foreigners' demands would be forcibly punished. They saw Captain Moresby's 1872 bombardment of the island (discussed more fully later in this chapter) as threatening them: "accept a missionary, or else!" Nanumeans also accord Temumuni, a Nanumean who had converted to Christianity while visiting the island of Nui, the honor of actually bringing the new religion to Nanumea. By converting his powerful warrior brother, Teuhie, Temumuni and his relatives were able to influence the reigning chief, Lie, into accepting a resident missionary. These political maneuverings may have been unknown to the missionaries or they may simply not have chosen to describe them. Journal accounts and official reports alike say only that Tuilouaa, the first Samoan teacher, was on the island when Turner led the annual LMS visit in 1874. Tuilouaa himself had apparently arrived in Nanumea with his wife on a nonmissionary ship late in 1872.

Resistance against LMS efforts at conversion in the northern Tuvalu islands should not be seen, as the missionaries maintained, as stubborn clinging to unenlightened customs. In both Nanumea and neighboring Nanumaga the missionaries encountered stable and self-sufficient societies. Traditional religious beliefs were intrinsic parts of local sociopolitical organization, and ritual practices connected to family and island-wide deities would have given meaning to daily life. Islanders apparently did not feel a need for new spiritual ideas or substantial religious change. They also reportedly feared that accepting a missionary teacher might bring harm to their society. They could not have been fully aware, of course, that missionary overtures would be just one aspect of an inclusive Westernization process or that, cumulatively, these new influences would alter local life fundamentally and forever. Unlike the situations of many other Pacific island societies, where guns as well as alcohol had preceded missionary arrival, the LMS movement into northern Tuvalu found a still-intact society whose members apparently saw no immediate advantage to be gained by trading a familiar religion for a new one. In islands such as New Zealand, Tahiti, and the Marquesas, rivalry among traditional political factions had been made much more deadly with the use of guns, creating levels of social disruption in which new belief systems may have been more attractive. In northern Tuvalu, the mission faced the difficult task of proving the inadequacy of local culture and the superiority of its own.

Six years after the first missionary landing at Nanumea in 1866, when a "teacher" (the roles of teacher and missionary were combined, then as now) was finally allowed to take up residence, converts followed rapidly even though the new beliefs and associated social changes were not universally welcomed. What wider social, political, and economic forces provided support for missionary conversion efforts? Threats of retaliation by European warships for perceived mistreatment of missionaries no doubt assisted the process. So did the economic power of the mission, backed up by ships sent from Samoa once or twice a year, filled with supplies such as cloth, soap, Bibles, and writing materials that a Christian lifestyle required. These one- or two-day official visits, chronicled as high points in London Missionary Society journals, paved the way for Tuvalu's incorporation into the colonial world. High-status Europeans arrived regularly to look over mission progress, check account books, lecture the faithful, and upbraid those still perceived to be in "darkness." Nanumeans today still tell stories about these times, chuckling at their own amazement over the miracle of writing and reading and recalling their hunger to become literate. By the late 1870s, each island had its own pastor, most often a married Samoan, and local families rotated his care among themselves.

The latter part of the nineteenth century was marked by power struggles as the mission gained adherents and strength as well as economic and political influence. Both colonial and mission records show that some pastors assumed exaggerated power well beyond a religious role. In Nanumea, the pastor became the island's wealthiest person and took over the direction of many community activities to ensure they met Christian standards. Having always had a unified religious orientation, people seem to have reoriented themselves collectively to the new teachings and religious leadership. Interfamily feuding gave way to settlement of disputes by mediation under the mission's influence. The pastor and his wife ran local schools at which both children and adults were taught to read and write. Even the village layout was affected: The pastors, with support from secular authorities in the new colonial government,

directed the realignment and rebuilding of the village around an imposing central church. By the turn of the century, Nanumea and the other
Tuvalu communities were largely Christian and literate. In just a few
decades, within the experience of a single generation, the islands had
been transformed physically as well as spiritually into communities
whose layout and lifestyle centered on the church.

ટ

## Traders, Beachcombers, and Sailors

Tuvalu was also becoming home to traders and beachcombers. In 1865,
missionary leader A. W. Murray had found Europeans living on a number
of the islands and noted approvingly in his journal that they often helped
prepare the way for the acceptance of Christianity. Most of these men
were traders, dealing in coconut oil at first and later in copra (sun-dried
coconut). Working from small, makeshift stores, they bartered items like
cloth and other hard goods for coconut products, contracting with trade
ships to pick up their profits at intervals. Many traders were transients,
moving from island to island. The writer Louis Becke, who spent nearly a
year on Nanumaga in the 1880s, had traveled widely in the Pacific in this
role before he arrived in Tuvalu. Others such as Jack O'Brien on Funafuti,
Martin Kleis on Nui, and Alfred Restieaux on Nukufetau chose a particular
community as a permanent home and founded extensive families. Such
traders functioned as agents of Westernization, too, with roles that over-
lapped those of missionaries. As the missionary A. W. Murray scathingly
commented about a trader who had departed Nui island for the Gilbert
Islands: "Bob was a dealer in coconut oil and he found that to set up as a
missionary was the readiest way to get his casks filled."

Up to the turn of the century, while world demand for coconut oil
remained strong, each Tuvalu community usually supported several traders. LMS missionary S. H. Davies, who visited in 1880, found three stores
belonging to three competing trading companies on Funafuti, as well as
five stores on Nanumea. Altogether, Davies tallied thirty-seven trading
stores in the sixteen islands he visited on his missionary circuit through
the Tokelau, Ellice, and Gilbert Islands that year, noting that trading vessels called in from as far away as Sydney and California. He complained
about the trader-as-missionary phenomenon, too, writing that the three
traders on Funafuti were professing "to hold services in English and . . .
wanting land from the natives on which to build chapels." Recurrent
quarrels between pastors and traders, which take up considerable space
in missionary accounts, arose from their competition for trading opportunities. Even by the 1870s, most copra and coconut oil was reaching trad-

ers through the pastors' hands, as pious Tuvaluans contributed to the material welfare of their new churches. One example of the wealth controlled by pastors is given in Davies's journal for 1882: in three years between 1879 and 1882, Nanumea's pastor had sold the island's trader $257 worth of copra, a huge sum in that era.

Some traders were honest, while others were greedy and unscrupulous. Still others simply may have misunderstood the local point of view. Nanumeans remember a trader on their island who forced about ten men and their families to work on Samoan plantations to repay a debt he claimed they owed. Apparently the trader had left trade goods with a Nanumean named Tuupau who succumbed to pressure to share the goods with relatives rather than selling them. Niutao traditions also recall a trader debt, but it is the Vaitupu people who seem to have suffered most from trader trickery. Missionary journals substantiate that in 1883, Vaitupuans were saddled with repaying $13,000, a relative fortune, to the same German trading firm responsible for Tuupau's debt in Nanumea. The Vaitupu community ultimately paid off the debt and the episode has assumed legendary status today, celebrated annually with a pageant. The most reprehensible behavior of all was shown by trader Tom Rose, who allegedly assisted Peruvian slavers in imprisoning and taking to South America virtually the entire adult population of the island of Nukulaelae in 1863. Most of these unfortunate individuals died on the voyage or in Peru.

Not all foreigners behaved so despicably, however. In Nanumea, George Holomoana, a native Hawaiian sailor and long-term resident, is remembered as a hero. According to local oral accounts, George arrived in Nanumea with a Tahitian named Ofati. Both men settled permanently on the island and have present-day descendants, though George played the more important role in island affairs. He is said to have warned Niutao Islanders and later Nanumeans about the Peruvian slavers' intentions. Largely due to his warnings, people say, few Nanumeans were carried off: Missionary accounts stated that twenty-one people were taken, though the names of only seven people can be recalled locally today. George may also have advised Nanumeans in their initial rejection of missionary Murray in 1866.

The incident that most securely established Nanumean gratitude to Holomoana was his intervention to save the island from "destruction" by a British warship (this was the same Moresby incident described earlier). According to Nanumean memories, because the Islanders had driven away "Misi Male" (the missionary A. W. Murray), the British sent a warship to shoot up the island. Holomoana spoke some English and is said to have boarded the ship, persuading its captain to spare the village and to fire the ship's cannon harmlessly into the bush rather than bombarding the village. Greatly alarmed by what they perceived as a direct reprisal for their rejection of Christianity, Nanumeans allowed a Samoan teacher to take up residence and conversion followed quickly for many. George Holomoana lived out his life on Nanumea and is buried on one of the small lagoon islets, chosen to allow a clear view over the horizon to Hawaii. His descendants, still loosely united by the term *kau Hawaii*, "the Hawaiian group," number about two hundred today, some 20 percent of the resident population. They have a continuing interest in tracing Holomoana's Hawaiian ancestry and locating distant Hawaiian kin.

### UNDER COLONIAL ADMINISTRATION

The Church preceded the flag by several decades in Tuvalu. Rivalry between England, Germany, and the United States was intense in the Pacific in the late nineteenth century, and by 1892, Tuvalu had been claimed (as the Ellice Islands) as a British Protectorate. After a brief visit by Captain Davis in the HMS *Royalist* in 1892 to ascertain the initial reaction of Tuvaluan leaders, Captain Gibson of HMS *Curacoa* visited each island, read the declaration of "protection" to the assembled inhabitants, and raised the British flag. The following year colonial officials obtained signatures from each island's chief (or "king" as most early records put it) and council of elders on documents recognizing Britain's Protectorate and its right to levy taxes. On Nanumea, chief Vaetolo, Magistrate Tuupau, and nine councilors signed English and Samoan versions of these documents on November 15, 1893. Political linkage with Britain was further formalized in 1916 when Tuvalu was joined with the Gilbert Islands (the Tokelau Islands were included temporarily, too) to form the Gilbert and Ellice Islands Colony. With the colonial center for both island groups hundreds of miles to the north, at Tarawa in the Gilbert Islands, outer-island life was little affected by this change in political status. Visits to the outer islands by the resident commissioner were rare and administrative staff were few.

While colonial records largely focus on increasing administrative control over local life, Nanumean tradition emphasizes the strangers who came to live on the island and the communal work projects that were undertaken. Tofe, described as a "rich European," lived on Nanumea sometime before 1892. Reportedly neither a government official nor a trader, Tofe is remembered for directing the construction of a kilometer-long road that still runs down the ocean side of the main village peninsula. He eventually left Nanumea and nothing more is known about him locally. We wondered whether Tofe could have been Edmund Duffy, a man who was listed as a trader in British records and who acted as interpreter for Captain Gibson on his flag-raising visit to Nanumea in 1892. We visited Duffy's grave site in

Apia, Samoa, in the 1980s, met some of his descendants, and heard that he had given Nanumean names to several of his children. But two of the other traders recalled by some elders proved impossible to trace. George Carter and another Australian remembered only as Lopati (Robert) appear to have arrived in Nanumea about 1902. Lopati is said to have died shortly thereafter, but George Carter married and lived on Nanumea for about three years before moving his family to the Gilbert Islands. Unlike Tofe's involvement in island affairs, Carter reportedly confined his activities to collecting *hoopuu kula* (shellfish used for button manufacture) and minor trading, associating himself only with his wife's family.

Wage work was another powerful force for change in the late nineteenth and early twentieth centuries. Tuvaluans had been signing on as crew on whaling and trading ships since the middle of the nineteenth century, but these opportunities were limited and many deckhands who went away never returned. Around 1900, the discovery of phosphate on Banaba (Ocean Island) and Nauru to the west of the Gilberts offered a new, steady source of employment. Recruits to the phosphate diggings were hired for short-term contracts, a system that rotated employment opportunities through the community and was very enlightened for its time. Colonial records document that the first few overseas workers were given jobs in 1901 and that in 1906, thirty-five men followed to work on Ocean Island. Enthusiasm for off-island work was so strong in northern Tuvalu that Assistant High Commissioner Mahaffy limited the number of Nanumean men who could work overseas to twenty-five in 1909 and prohibited all recruiting from both Nui and Nanumaga for two years. He was concerned about the "deficiency of grown men" at home as well as the toll dysentery epidemics, brought by returning workers, took on the communities. A few Nanumeans were taken overseas for police training, and others continued to sign on as ship's crew, when the opportunity was offered. Many of these men eventually returned home, with stories of their overseas adventures that enriched Nanumean knowledge about other parts of the world.

Government and commercial infrastructures were increasing slowly in the colony, too. By 1916, a resident district administrator and a doctor were stationed in Funafuti to serve the group, though education remained in the hands of the Samoan LMS pastors on each island. Resident traders were gradually supplanted by trading visits by large firms based in Samoa or Fiji, whose ships called periodically to sell directly to the Islanders from well-stocked trade rooms. In 1926, a cooperative store was initiated on Vaitupu, and during the 1930s, the central government established locally run cooperatives on each island. The cooperative movement flourished and today is still the dominant commercial influence in the outer islands of Tuvalu. By this time, traditional chiefs, recognized in the 1894 Native Laws as the highest authority on each island, were being relegated to figurehead status within island government. A legal code was drafted, too, increasing in complexity decade by decade as customary rules were integrated with British legal ideals.

How did Nanumea fare during this first half-century of intensive Western contact? What subtle economic alterations were instigated by money flowing in from overseas? What changes in worldview were confirmed by interactions with expatriate colonial officers and Western-trained doctors? Full answers to such questions will never be known, though it seems that this era was one of optimism and cultural consolidation. Nanumeans themselves remember the 1920s as a time of intense community spirit and ambitious building projects. In 1922, following the celebrations marking the fiftieth anniversary of the arrival of a Christian teacher on Nanumea, village rebuilding began again. The residential area was leveled, breadfruit trees were planted near each house site, and lime-cement foundations were constructed in closely spaced parallel rows.

An even more elaborate project was the new church, begun in May 1931. This was actually Nanumea's third church built of "permanent" (i.e., not thatch and wood) materials. The first church of coral block was completed by 1880. In 1902, this was replaced by *Fetuu Ao*, "Morning Star," a lime-cement building with imported stained glass windows. Now in 1931, an ambitiously larger structure was envisioned. Named *Loto Lelei*, "Virtuous Heart," the new building was designed by Valo, a Nanumean sailor who had seen large churches in overseas ports but who had no formal architectural or engineering training. Using funds contributed for thirty years by Islanders working on Ocean Island, the community ordered building materials from Australia and reestablished the communal work groups that had been used before on smaller projects, naming them Vakalele, Usitai, Kalofia, and Lesili, names that are still in use today. The whole village turned out to dance in the foundation to pack the soil. Building Loto Lelei is recalled as a monumental undertaking, with Valo's demanding supervision ensuring that any sloppy workmanship be redone. The finished church—with massively thick concrete walls, a red iron roof with several cupolas, and a bell tower reaching high above the tallest palms—was viewed as a tribute to community cooperation. Fifty years later, this accomplishment has come to have familiar overtones. The foundation and walls of Loto Lelei were renovated yet again in 1987, the bell tower was heightened and new leaded glass windows were added. The supervising engineer was Valo's son, Truman, summoned from Australia to undertake the work.

In the 1930s, the colonial government was preoccupied with a demanding project of its own: devising a workable land code. Land law had proved a particular challenge to the colonial administration because traditional practices were based on shared tenure and flexible cognatic affiliation. Land disputes were consuming considerable amounts of administrative effort, and rules based in customary practices were needed to guide decisions. Donald Kennedy, an experienced administrator and teacher who spoke Tuvaluan, was put in charge of a commission that would travel in turn to each island. The commission had a dual goal: to register landowners and their land holdings and to document the traditional land tenure systems of each community so that future disputes could be adjudicated by local courts. Cases of contested land ownership were analyzed so that the resulting legal ordinances would fit local custom.

In Nanumea, Kennedy selected twenty-six respected older men to form the local land commission and heard cases together with this group from August to December 1936. Kennedy publicly read out a previously prepared list of the lands "owned" by each family head while clerks took note of any contrary claims. Each of these was then heard in turn and final decisions were entered into official land registers, one copy of which remained on Nanumea and the second taken to the administrative center in Funafuti for safekeeping. Kennedy also drew up rules to guide local government in deciding subsequent land cases and tried to persuade Nanumeans whose houses were located on other people's lands to make written agreements with those owners for use or ownership of the nearby trees.

Kennedy reported that as a result of the Commission's decisions, 25 percent of all lands on Nanumea changed hands, a much higher figure than for any other Tuvalu island. This was because he had found it necessary to reverse a decision allegedly made by his predecessor, commissioner Smith-Rewse, some twenty years earlier. Kennedy and the Nanumean commissioners decided that the ruling attributed to Smith-Rewse, that "all lands willed to persons outside the *gafa* (descent line) must be returned to the survivors of the line" was erroneous and that the rule had actually been manufactured by Smith-Rewse's Nanumean interpreter. Kennedy noted that the earlier decision had caused an "economic and social upheaval," forcing reexamination of very old wills and resulting in major adjustments in land ownership. Now, under Kennedy, a similar upheaval returned these lands to their former owners. The outbreak of World War II interrupted the Land Commission proceedings, but Kennedy had been able to complete its work on Nanumea before the war began. When the postwar Commission later reconvened under Commissioner Lake, only a few appeals needed settlement on Nanumea.

ᴓ
## THE WAR YEARS

Early in 1943, the Ellice Islands were designated by Allied forces as a forward operations base for bombing raids against Japanese positions in the Gilbert Islands. Nanumea, northernmost of the Ellice Islands and closest to the Gilberts, became the site of a bomber airfield and American troop base, as did both Funafuti and Nukufetau. In August 1943, landing craft of the 16th Naval Construction Battalion brought 128 Seabees plus construction equipment and supplies to the island. A month later, the number of American Seabees and Marines there had grown to nearly 900 and would eventually increase to over 2,000, more than double the local population. By all accounts, Nanumeans accepted this invasion graciously, although they had never had more than one or two Europeans on the island at any time before this. Nanumea's location just to the south of the Japanese-held Gilbert Islands made its airfield a vital part of the war effort.

The U.S. forces lived in tent villages throughout the Nanumea village area; all their food and other necessities were brought in from outside. Nanumeans themselves were relocated to Lakena Islet, several miles away. All the village houses were disassembled and moved, a monumental undertaking. Contact with the troops was strictly limited. Able-bodied Nanumean men were picked up in motor launches each morning and taken to work with the soldiers in land clearing, stevedoring, and blasting. Women, children, and older men remained at Lakena, which was off limits to U.S. personnel. Despite these restrictions, a severe flu epidemic broke out shortly after the arrival of the first troops, causing eight Nanumean deaths in three months, despite treatment by local medical personnel and U.S. doctors. A whooping cough epidemic swept the island soon after. Island records show that during a two-year period in 1943–1944, sixty-three Nanumeans died (forty-nine of these in 1944 alone), more than twice the usual death rate. Nanumeans say that not a single child was fathered by the soldiers but that most people had special friends for whom they washed clothes and made handcrafted gifts, receiving clothing, GI gear, and food in return. They remember with pleasure occasional holiday visits to the main islet, where the Americans treated them to jeep and boat rides and feasted them on new delicacies such as butter, fresh meat, and tinned tongue and tuna fish. Nanumeans also recall their initial surprise at the friendliness of the American GIs and contrasted the easy camaraderie possible with the soldiers to the aloof formality of British administrators. The traffic of planes and ships, plus the wartime urgency, created a sense of excitement unknown in the quiet days before the war. Local cash flow increased dramatically, too. By December 1945, after sixteen months of American presence, Nanumeans at home had amassed some £700 in savings (about U.S.$3,500), most of it banked.

The occupation left the atoll heavily scarred, however. A Y-shaped bomber and fighter runway, 2,000 meters long, still cuts a swath through the bush despite postwar efforts to replant the thousands of trees destroyed in its making. Dredging and blasting work cleared coral heads in the lagoon, and a small boat passage, dynamited through the leeward barrier reef, permitted boats to enter directly into Nanumea's lagoon for the first time. Wrecked machinery, vehicles, and airplanes still dot the bush and reef, overgrown with creepers, inhabited by crabs and steadily cannibalized for their usable materials. The most spectacular war reminder is the rusting wreck of a 275-foot-long landing ship, which still adorns Nanumea's leeward reef just beyond the village.

The island suffered three bombings by Japanese planes, including a direct hit on the church, which made a large hole in the roof and started a fire. The last Japanese raid, a nighttime mission on November 11, 1943, dropped forty to sixty bombs, killing one American and wounding two others. Several American B-24 Liberators and a Douglas Dauntless dive bomber crashed in various landing attempts during the occupation. No Nanumeans were hurt in any of these actions, though people remember that one local man was shot in the arm as he tried to escape after raiding the soldiers' food stockpiles, a retaliation that they view as fair.

The greatest damage from the wartime occupation was to the atoll's vegetation. British District Officer A. R. Hill noted in his traveling diary for 1945 that:

> [Nanumea] island has suffered considerable loss as a result of army occupation. Over 40,000 trees have been cut down (including practically all suitable building timber), gardens have been destroyed. The old village will have to be completely rebuilt. . . . The church has been badly damaged by enemy action and requires a complete new roof.

Shortly after this visit, District Officer R. G. Roberts amended the tree loss estimates to nearly 32,000 coconut trees, more than 1,000 breadfruit trees, and nearly 2,000 "other trees." He noted that the island's population density was high and that Nanumeans were "hard put to find sufficient food." After his visit the following year, District Officer A. G. Lake estimated that one hundred eighty acres of trees (about 20 percent of the island's total land area) were war-damaged, much of this comprising the now-abandoned airstrip. Replanting assistance had been authorized in October 1946 and by August 1950, nearly £8,000 had been paid in government war compensation to Nanumean landowners. Nanumeans contemplated using this money to purchase an island, asking the British

Western Pacific High Commission to investigate this possibility for them. Several islands, including Laucala (owned currently by wealthy publisher and sometime U.S. presidential candidate Stephen Forbes) and Wakaya in Fiji were considered, but the prices quoted were prohibitive and no action was ever taken.

Harder to gauge today than the war's physical effects are the changes in outlook that came about through Islanders' wartime encounters with thousands of outsiders and complex military technology. Consider the effects of constructing the Nanumean military base, as depicted in Peter McQuarrie's history of the war (1994:83):

> [Construction] proceeded at a fast pace, tents went up, offices, chapel, post office, barber shop. A small town developed in a few weeks, where there had previously been nothing more than thatched huts and coconut palms. The Islanders were thus shown an example of what could be achieved where there was no restriction on resources and enthusiasm. There were 24 kilometres of graded roads, 450,000 litres of water storage and an evaporator plant capable of producing 157,000 litres of fresh water daily. Electricity generation exceeded 100 kilowatts, for lighting, refrigeration, workshops, and to power the water evaporators. All this on an island a mere three kilometers in length and less than one kilometre wide.

Aftereffects from the American occupation were obvious to colonial officials, whose postwar reports deplored Islanders' ostensible lack of industry and disobedience to local government, their "cocksure, sophisticated" attitudes, and possession of "too much money." However, Nanumeans recall the occupation period as a time of excitement and plenty, and seem to have accepted its dislocations with little resentment, despite having to evacuate their homes and totally rebuild their village after the war.

❧

## PASSAGE TO INDEPENDENCE

The American troops and the bustling lifestyle they had brought to Nanumea were fading memories by 1950. The village stood again in its original location, and the local economy geared down once more. Copra again provided the main source of income, though off-island work opportunities were still eagerly sought, and Nanumeans comprised nearly a quarter of the Tuvaluan labor force employed on Ocean Island. A slow-paced outer-island lifestyle resumed, punctuated by occasional visits from colonial officials or Congregational missionaries. Not until the late 1960s did more frequent ship visits, two-way radio linkages, and greater access to overseas universities increase contact with the outside world.

By the early 1970s, Britain's declining economic fortunes, coupled with world distaste for overt colonialism, made it necessary to return the Gilbert and Ellice Islands Colony to independence. A House of Representatives on the British parliamentary model was established in Tarawa, as a first step to self-government, and each island sent one representative. Ellice Islanders were becoming increasingly apprehensive about their future, however. They worried that after independence they would be politically, economically, and culturally marginalized (as well as out-voted) by their Gilbertese neighbors who outnumbered them five to one. A United Nations–monitored referendum in 1974 showed that Ellice Islanders overwhelmingly wished to dissolve their political linkage with the Gilbert Islands despite the economic consequences of being one of the world's smallest nations: a country that would have fewer than ten thousand people and only ten square miles of land. In 1975, as the first step toward independence, a separate legislature and an administrative structure were established in Funafuti, the Tuvalu capital. Out of the former colony's assets, Tuvalu received just one ship. Tuvaluans, nonetheless, decided to push ahead toward independent status. On October 1, 1978, Tuvalu was granted full independence and accorded a nonvoting "special membership" status in the Commonwealth, an association of over 50 countries worldwide, most of which have had a colonial association with Britain. Tuvalu's application for full Commonwealth membership was approved September 1, 2000. Like the other island communities, constituting the "eight standing together," as the name Tuvalu translates, Nanumeans faced an uncertain future with high hopes.

In the two decades since independence, Tuvalu's decision for autonomy has proven a sound choice. With overseas help, a national trust fund was established in 1987. This has grown substantially in recent years and now provides a small but stable basis for government expenditures. The national economy still depends on remittances sent home by workers abroad and on overseas aid. But this is not unusual among small, resource-poor Pacific countries, dubbed MIRAB economies (since their defining constraints include migration, remittances, aid, and bureaucracy). Recent studies indicate that MIRAB economies appear sustainable for small Pacific countries and that this model may be an improvement over the balanced export/import model commonly used in development planning. Nonetheless, small countries like Tuvalu have struggled to find a viable niche in the world economy. Tuvalu's philatelic bureau profitably marketed stamps in the 1970s and 1980s, but this income source is now modest. With hundreds of thousands of square miles of ocean within its exclusive economic zone, the country has successfully sold fishing rights worth millions of dollars annually to companies from several nations, including the United States. Poaching within Tuvalu's exclusive economic zone is a major problem, however, and enforcement is difficult despite the recent gift of a high-speed, military-style naval patrol boat by Australia. Handicraft exports provide a token amount of earnings, and copra income waxes to a modest level, then wanes to insignificance. New export earnings continually must be sought.

Tuvalu's economic future has brightened considerably in the last few years, however. New income sources based on contemporary information technologies, namely direct telephone and Internet communications, hold promise that was undreamed of even a decade ago. Ironically, Tuvalu's small size and its own lack of technology creates these commercial possibilities. International convention allocates each nation a unique country code. With few telephones, Tuvalu can lease its country code and associated international accounting rate. Despite local concern over the uses some overseas companies have found for the country code, leasing has proved to be a significant income source, generating between A$1.56 and A$2.76 million each year since 1996.

Tuvalu's designation, .tv, under the international convention establishing domain names for the World Wide Web, is another source of high-tech revenue that involves marketing the country's assigned Internet suffix. In the mid-1990s overseas entrepreneurs realized that "dot tv" offered commercial potential since a simple, eye-catching Web address (such as BBC.tv, CNN.tv) might be attractive to the communications industry. Indeed, several overseas companies vied energetically to purchase rights to market the suffix. Projected earnings in some of the bids were put at $100 million a year, ten times Tuvalu's gross domestic product. In 1998, a contract was signed with a Canadian information marketing firm, but this company defaulted several times on promised payments, leading the government to restructure the contract and resume negotiations with a group of Los Angles–based Internet venture capitalists. In late 1999 a deal was struck, which promises substantial new revenue for the country as well as 20 percent stock ownership in the dot tv corporation. An energetic sales campaign was undertaken on the Internet, resulting in considerable interest in (and purchase of) dot tv domain names via on-line auction.

Economic ventures such as these, as well as one hundred fifty years of intensive acculturation through interaction with traders, administrators, and missionaries, have built firm connections between Tuvalu and the wider world. The opportunities and challenges that now face Nanumeans (and all Tuvaluans) are far beyond the wildest imaginings of Lapi or Logotau, Pease or Moresby. But to understand more fully the shaping of these connections we must return to Nanumea itself, to explore the atoll's environment and to sketch in greater detail the social fabric in which island life is grounded.

ૐ

## NOTES AND SUGGESTIONS FOR FURTHER READING

### Genealogy and History

Jan Vansina's *Oral Tradition as History* (1985) is the classic source on the use of genealogies and oral materials in historical reconstruction. Following the lead of our Nanumean hosts, we accept Tefolaha's founding role in Nanumea and the authenticity of the Kaumaile spear, though there is no proof of his historicity apart from genealogies and oral tradition and the spear's age has not been tested by any scientific means. Comparative material relevant to settlement dating is available from some other Tuvalu islands. Lands Commissioner A. G. Lake's (1949) genealogical information for Nui suggested to him that that atoll had been settled about 1600 (using twenty-five years per generation). He also estimated that Nukulaelae might have been settled from Funafuti as recently as 1740 (computing *twenty-eight* years per generation)—though genealogies from this island would certainly have been affected by the community's decimation in the 1860s. D. G. Kennedy's (1931) ethnohistorical research led him to conclude that Vaitupu was settled in the 1600s. All of these estimates provide more recent dates than those obtained through radiocarbon dating.

### Archaeology in Tuvalu

The high islands of the Pacific were generally settled before the low-lying atolls, with occupation dates for larger Polynesian islands going back 5,000–6,000 years (New Guinea and Australia 40,000 to 100,000 years ago). The atolls offered a more precarious subsistence base, may not have been sustainably habitable until about 2,000 years ago, and were certainly harder for voyagers to locate. Geoff Irwin (1992, 1998) provides an overview of archaeological findings from the Pacific region related to settlement issues; Kirch and Weisler's (1994) appraisal of recent research in the Pacific is valuable, as is Kirch's earlier survey (1989). The surface surveys and test excavations undertaken on Funafuti and Vaitupu are described in Takayama (1987), Takayama, Eritaia, and Saito (1987), Takayama and Saito (1987), and Igarashi et al. (1987). Pottery, an important source of data for Pacific settlement dates and origins, cannot be made on atolls since clay and rock-based sand is not available in these environments. The Fijian origin of sand in the pottery artifacts is discussed in Dickinson, Takayama, Snow, and Shutler (1990). Sinoto (1966) described and illustrated several pre-European burial sites excavated at Funafuti. Though he arranged to have charcoal from the sites radiocarbon dated, the results are not included in his short manuscript.

Weisler's work in the atolls of the Marshall Islands, demonstrating evidence of about two thousand years of habitation, is reported in Weisler (1999a). Dating the sands immediately below *Cyrtosperma* pits in Maloelap in the Marshalls, "yielded a date of 3000 B.P., suggesting that it may take a thousand years or so after first emergence to build an [atoll] islet large and stable enough for full-time human occupation" (Weisler, personal communication, February 2000; also Weisler 1999b:640). Thus, early voyagers may well have found proto-atolls in Tuvalu and other parts of the central Pacific in this early period (prior to 2000 B.P.) that may have been too marginal for sustained settlement. The Nanumean view that Pai and Vau found a relatively barren sandbank and nurtured it to support life may not be far off.

### Pacific Settlement

Developing and testing theories about the "origins of the Polynesians" has sparked a great deal of public interest. Primary settlement of the remote (eastern) Pacific from either South America (Thor Heyerdahl 1952) or from Micronesia (Peter Buck 1959) now seems unlikely. The Polynesians seem to have developed their distinctive cultural characteristics and identity through the very process of voyaging eastward, probably beginning in the Bismark archipelago in eastern Melanesia. A useful summary of these settlement processes is *Prehistoric Settlement of the Pacific* edited by Ward Goodenough (1996). Also see Kirch (1984), Kirch and Green (1987), and Bellwood (1987, 1989). Geoff Irwin's research (1992, 1998), as well as earlier computer simulations by Levison, Ward, and Webb (1973), have convincingly shown that Pacific settlement was early, largely intentional, and consistently (with a few exceptions like New Zealand) in a west to east direction.

In fact, as New Zealand historian James Bellich (1996:17) recently argued, Polynesian voyaging was so much earlier, more sophisticated, and more extensive than that of the Vikings, that instead of referring to the Polynesians as "Vikings of the Sunrise" (as Buck did in his 1938 classic work), it would be more accurate to describe the Vikings as "Polynesians of the Sunset." Firth (1954) mentions Poepoe's drift voyage to Anuta, and a lengthy Anutan text mentioning this Nanumean canoe is included in Feinberg's collection (1998:205–16).

### Canoe Voyaging

A renaissance in canoe voyaging and navigation currently supports renewed pride among Pacific peoples and their increasing collaboration around indigenous sovereignty issues. See Ben Finney's (1994) *Voyage of*

*Rediscovery* or his recent account (Finney 1999) of a five canoe reconciliation ritual at Ra'iatea in 1995 uniting representatives from many eastern Polynesian societies. As is obvious from Edward Dodd's well-illustrated *Polynesian Seafaring* (1972) and Haddon and Hornell's *Canoes of Oceania* (1975, originally 1936–38), Pacific voyaging craft were immense, sophisticated sailing vessels—not simply "canoes." Navigational knowledge and techniques are described in David Lewis's *We the Navigators* (1972), Ben Finney's *Polynesian Navigation and Voyaging* (1976), Thomas Gladwin's *East Is a Big Bird* (1970), and Richard Feinberg's *Polynesian Seafaring and Navigation* (1988). A readable popular account is Stephen Thomas's *The Last Navigator* (1987).

## Precontact Political Alliances

Tuvalu's precontact name for itself, Te Atu Tuvalu ("archipelago of eight"), asserts a collective sense of identity although most Tuvalu islands seemed to be independent entities when Westerners first encountered them. Community distinctiveness is stressed in the local accounts compiled as *Tuvalu: A History* (Laracy 1983). Some political domination or alliances may have existed, however. When whaler Henry Pease called at Nanumaga in 1853 (Pease 1854), he was asked to take two Nanumean men back home and was told that the Islanders "quite often pass from one island to the other in canoes, when the weather is pleasant, the people on this island [Nanumaga] being subject to the king of Augustine [Nanumea]." Later, after visiting Nanumea, Pease noted in his journal that the high chiefs of Nanumea "awarded me all the rights and privileges possessed by the king or any of his chiefs, at either or both islands—St. Augustine [Nanumea] and Hudson's [Nanumaga]." Nanumagans today reject the idea that Nanumea may have once had political control of their island.

## Contact History

The "discovery" by Mendaña of Nui, and of Niutao and Nanumea by Maurelle is discussed in Maude (1968:53–56 and 93–94), Maurelle (1799), and Chambers and Munro (1980). Munro (1982) provides the best overview of whaling visits to Tuvalu. The only direct contact with Nanumeans we have found in whaling records is that of Henry Pease (1854, abridged and reprinted, 1962).

As social organization has increasingly come to be understood as a dynamic process, ethnographers have explored varying perspectives and differences in the way knowledge is constructed. Juxtaposing Western historical accounts and local traditions has been particularly productive in the Pacific. The classic work on the impact of the South Seas on European imagination is Smith (1960). A useful assessment of the early contact period and ways of knowing about it is provided by Borofsky and Howard (1989). More specifically, see Greg Dening (1980) for the Marquesas, Marshall Sahlins for Hawaii (1981, 1985), and Anne Salmond (1991, 1997) for New Zealand. An interesting example of contested interpretation of Captain Cook's reception in Hawaii in the eighteenth century is the exchange between Gananath Obeyesekere (1992) and Sahlins (1995), discussed by Borofsky (1997). Borofsky's *Making History* (1987) provides an insightful analysis of changing social institutions on the atoll of Pukapuka and their implications for understanding that community's history. See also the comprehensive overview of Pacific history edited by Donald Denoon (1997), which considers the differences between the more particularistic focus of oral tradition and the "objective" goals of history.

### *Missionary Endeavors*

The establishment of Christianity in Tuvalu by the London Missionary Society is a critical "moment" in local history and in the encounter between island and metropolitan worlds. For an overview see Munro (1982:80ff.), Goldsmith (1989:125–71), and Goldsmith and Munro (1992a). Elekana is the focus of Goldsmith and Munro's interesting paper (1992b), and that of Goldsmith (1995:5–14). Laumua Kofe (1976:40–48) provides a Tuvaluan perspective on Nanumean conversion, noting the roles of Temumuni, Teuhie, and Moulogo and also the assistance of another early Nanumean Christian convert, Fagota. A. W. Murray's (1866) journal described his early mission work in the northern islands (including his skepticism about traders as religious men); his book (1876) covers work in Tuvalu as well as throughout the Pacific. Davies's 1880 information on traders in Tuvalu and in the Gilbert Islands, as well as their missionary roles, is from Phillips (1881). See Macdonald (1982), Munro (1982), K. Chambers (1984), Brady (1975), and Goldsmith (1989) on the growth and decline of pastoral involvement in Tuvalu politics.

In the 1890s, many Nanumeans were still committed to traditional religious beliefs, and even as late as the 1920s, a small traditionalist group still remained. According to Nanumeans, this faction capitulated en masse in 1922 for the fifty-year jubilee of the founding of the LMS church. That day, now celebrated annually on January 8, has become *Po o Tefolaha*, Nanumea's most important holiday.

### *Traders, Beachcombers, and Sailors*

Louis Becke's (1967) short stories faithfully depict the lifestyle and worldview of south seas traders, drawing on his own experiences as storekeeper in Nanumaga in the Ellice Islands in the 1880s. One story tells of a voyage to Nanumea by sailing canoe, a dangerous passage made feasible by lighting huge bonfires on both islands. See also Day's (1966) biography. Vaitupu's trader debt is analyzed in Isala and Munro (1987), and Harry Maude (1981) provides a history of the Peruvian slave trade. On Nukulaelae, 250 people (79 percent of the population) were taken, leaving just 65 people remaining (Maude 1981:74–77; also Goldsmith and Munro 1992b). Nanumea escaped more lightly. LMS missionary George Turner (1876) was told that 21 Nanumeans had been carried off by the slavers (Captain Moresby had put the number at 17 in his 1872 investigation). According to Maude, the ship responsible was probably the Peruvian bark *Adelante*.

George Holomoana, credited locally for alerting Nanumeans to the slavers' intentions, was probably put ashore by Captain Pease of the whaler *Planter* in 1853. According to his journal, Pease provisioned George with supplies, animals, and a U.S. flag before leaving him on the island. We suspect that George was also the "Hawaiian" who gave his name as Tom Coffin when he went aboard the missionary vessel *John Williams* on its prosletization visit to Nanumea in 1871.

## Becoming a British Colony and Moving on to Independence

Moresby's account of firing his cannons to intimidate Nanumea is from his description of his Pacific voyages (Moresby 1876:80) The journal kept by Moresby's lieutenant Francis Hayter (1871–73) offers further detail on the July 21, 1872 incident: "Captain could not land owing to surf but an Englishman named Day came off with a Hawaiian. Captain fired two guns (blanks) for the benefit of the chief, whom Day said had threatened to kill him. . . . No missionaries here as they won't let them land, and the natives are armed with long spears."

The British flag-raising process is described in Gibson (1892), as well as in other original sources (see Tuvalu National Archives 1893). Land Court development is covered in Kennedy (1953). Notable sources on the British colonial empire in the Pacific include Deryck Scarr's *Fragments of Empire* (1968), Austin Coates's *Western Pacific Islands* (1970), which has an interesting chapter on Tuvalu (chapter 5, "Mother Earth Preferred"), and Ernest Dodge's *Islands and Empires* (1976). Tuvalu and its colonial background are discussed in Macdonald (1971a and 1971b) and Brady (1974). Macdonald's *Cinderellas of the Empire* (1982) is a readable description of the colonial context out of which independent Tuvalu and Kiribati developed. His other shorter works (1970, 1975a, 1975b) are also useful for this topic, as are Chambers and Chambers (1975), and Isala (1983a, 1983b). Doug Munro (1982), drawing extensively on original manuscript sources, provides a detailed overview of the development of colonial and mission control in Tuvalu.

### The War Years

The best and only complete source is Peter McQuarrie's *Strategic Atolls: Tuvalu and the Second World War* (1994). Geoffrey White and Lamont Lindstrom's *The Pacific Theater* (1989) describes wartime experiences in other Pacific communities. Our information on postwar damage and compensation is drawn from Hill (1945), Roberts (1946), Lake (1947, 1950), and Western Pacific High Commission (1947–48).

### Economic Development Issues

An economic model distinctive of small Pacific islands, dubbed MIRAB by Bertram and Watters (1985) in their original description, features migration, remittances, aid, and bureaucracy as key economic determinants. Bertram's (1999) recent reassessment finds that this type of economy has proven relatively sustainable and secure over the last two decades. The particular conditions that constrain classic export-based economic development in small, isolated, resource-limited Pacific Island countries such as Tuvalu have been extensively described and theorized about. Some recent analyses include Connell (1980 and 1991), Pollard (1989), Munro (1990), Ward (1993), and Hooper and James (1993), but there are many others as well.

For preliminary information on the national income potential offered by the satellite telephone system see Waqa and Keith-Reid (1996). Raskin (1998) reports on the "dot tv" Internet domain opportunity.

# ॐ 5

# Coral and Sand

It is impossible to behold these waves without feeling a conviction that an island, though built of the hardest rock . . . would ultimately yield and be demolished by such an irresistible power. Yet these low, insignificant coral islets stand and are victorious: for here another power, as an antagonist, takes part in the contest. . . . Let the hurricane tear up its thousand huge fragments; yet what will that tell against the accumulated labour of myriads of architects at work night and day, month after month? Thus do we see the soft and gelatinous body of a polypus . . . conquering the great mechanical power of the waves. . . .

Charles Darwin, ship's naturalist
Aboard the *Beagle*, April 6, 1836

Standing on the sandy ocean beach of Nanumea, looking out toward the distant line of pounding surf, we often felt grateful for the atoll's surrounding reef, furled out around its edges like a spreading skirt. At high tide there is little to see of this protective reef—just a line of breaking waves several hundred yards away and, beyond that, the heaving sea, huge Pacific rollers stretching unmarked to the horizon. At low tide, the reef shows itself, a yellowish surface laced with small fissures and shallow

91

pools, walkable but too jagged to be inviting. Without the protecting acres of reef, there would be no island, no place for plants to lodge a foothold or for people to settle and live for thousands of years. The atoll itself is a fragile sanctuary against which the ocean pounds ceaselessly. Waves constantly push against the reef and erode the atoll's sandy shoreline.

❧

## A MARGINAL HUMAN HABITAT

Nanumea provides a very limited foothold for human life. Belying the stereotype of a lush, tropical paradise, atolls like Nanumea are actually one of earth's more marginally human habitats. Only the most knowledgeable and careful use of resources enables their inhabitants to claim a living from these small islands composed, quite literally, of coral rubble and sand. A story told in the Agriculture Department in Tarawa shows how limited atoll soils are. The department had sent some soil samples overseas for testing as part of an agricultural project, the staff told us. Identifying the chemical makeup of the soil would clarify what fertilizer or mineral supplement could be added to allow a wider diversity of plants to be grown. A German soil lab did the tests and eventually sent back a terse reply: the substance they had tested was pure calcium carbonate rock and sand, "unsuitable" for growing anything at all! The agricultural officers were ruefully amused. Atoll soils have, after all, supported human populations for some two thousand years. They even offer a potential for intensive horticulture, provided work is put into composting, garden sites are carefully selected, and suitable plant species are grown. Resignedly, the Agriculture Department staff resumed their trials of coconut palms, which produce remarkably well in atoll sand and rocks and whose nuts contribute hugely to subsistence living and export.

Like all atolls, as Darwin theorized over 150 years ago, Nanumea is a coral reef that has grown upward from a subsiding volcanic mountain base over hundreds of thousands of years. Despite periodic rises in sea level during interglacial periods, the reef's tiny coral polyps have prospered in these warm tropical waters, building on the dead skeletons left by previous generations even as the ocean floor gradually sank. Storms buffet the reef from time to time, devastating exposed sections but also depositing more coral rubble, which the storm waves sweep upward from the reef's apron. Fissures and pools on the reef surface trap sand and coral debris, which gradually begins to emerge above the waves. The atoll's sandy shoulders become a depository for floating seeds, driftwood, and the refuse of birds—and finally enough flora develops to support human life in combination with the bounty of the sea.

This atoll-building process still continues. We sometimes came upon a solitary coconut seedling just above the high tide level on a sandy islet or rocky bank of debris. A few leaves jutting upwards, roots tenuously in place. Depending on future storms and patterns of sand erosion and accretion, a seedling like this might endure, eventually producing shade and a foothold for other vegetation. More likely, it will be swept away in the next storm. The strength and direction of prevailing winds and local ocean currents, as well as storm histories, all affect an atoll's emerging shape and its vegetation, determining the islets that form on the original volcanic base. As a result, there is a wonderful variety in atoll shapes and sizes worldwide. In Tuvalu, small reef islands such as Nanumaga and Niutao were probably once tiny atolls whose former lagoons have filled in through accretion, forming landlocked swamps. Vaitupu, with the largest land area in Tuvalu, now has a virtually landlocked lagoon, which is gradually filling in.

Nanumea is smaller and narrower than many other Pacific atolls, only eight miles long and less than two miles across at its widest point, fringing reef included. Unlike the narrow ribbon of land typical of atolls, where both lagoon and ocean are often visible from the middle of an islet, parts of Nanumea's islands are wide enough to offer protected niches where more delicate plants can flourish. Tucked away in the center of its two larger islands are small patches of junglelike forest, where tow-

*Canoes heading down the lagoon to Lakena islet (1973)*

ering soft- and hardwood trees shelter clumps of birds-nest fern and other humidity-loving ground cover. Of course, to call any of these plants really "delicate" is as laughable a description by continental standards as the term *atoll soil*.

Nanumea has fewer than one hundred species of vascular plants, half of which are insignificant grasses and small herbs. This is an extremely low level of plant diversity compared to continental or even high island environments. In the southern Oregon county where we live, for example, nearly two thousand taxa have been identified. Few Nanumean plants produce edible food either, though many have uses as medicines, handicraft materials, or building sources. In fact, the atoll's significant food resources come from only about ten plant species, with coconut, pandanus, breadfruit, bananas, taro, and pulaka roots being the most important. Showy flowers, always featured in South Pacific stereotypes, are rare, though a few tropical ornamentals (such as plumeria, hibiscus, and spider lily) now grow in the village. Atoll vegetation must be drought tolerant and able to survive salty wind-borne spray and saline groundwater.

Nanumea's total area of dry land above the high-tide line comprises only one and a half square miles (3.9 sq. km.), about 956 acres. This averages out to little more than one acre per resident, only half that much if Nanumeans living overseas all returned home. Given the atoll's high population density and its limited land resources, Nanumean attention to land rights is not surprising. Fortunately, the sea's rich bounty is available for subsistence, too. The healthy, strong people we came to know in Nanumea had access to miles of reef flats, a calm lagoon as well as open ocean. As we talked with people about their daily activities and their household menus, and heard leading fishermen praised for their prowess, we began to realize how essential ocean resources were for the community's long-term survival. While food from the land was obviously very limited, the surrounding ocean offered a virtual "seafood marketplace" that surpassed local subsistence needs. We increasingly came to think of Nanumea's economy and lifestyle as ocean based. How wrong we were.

As often happens in fieldwork, assumptions require constant attention and revision. After all, these assumptions only form the basis for working hypotheses; simplifications based on trial-and-error efforts to make sense of an unknown culture. How many images must be discarded and how many hypotheses unraveled until an approximation of "reality" emerges? How long will that "final" picture last? How to be sure that gradually emerging conclusions have taken accurate account of the million subtleties influencing human society? Asking the right questions, a skill that ethnographers cultivate and gradually develop through fieldwork, is a necessary tool. So, too, is learning to listen, to leave openings

in conversations that can elicit local versions of reality and invite people to comment on, contradict, or overturn one's assumptions. Local people can tell you the way things really are for them. They have been making inferences and drawing culturally valid conclusions since infancy. They can also tell you what you want to hear. Making the distinction is the hardest part.

*Coconut bush land (1974)*

୨ଈ

## "WHAT DO WE RELY ON FOR LIFE?"

Venu, Nanumea's Island Council president during our 1973–75 residence on the island, helped us move closer to understanding the local view of atoll subsistence. We had been discussing our research goals with him one afternoon, trying to explain as clearly as we could exactly what we hoped to accomplish. We had been in the community only a couple of weeks and could not yet speak Nanumean ourselves. Sunema was translating for us.

Venu listened attentively to her words, staring down at the mat on which we all sat. Suddenly he interrupted her translation with a question of his own: "Do you know how we live here—what we rely on for life?" As this was interpreted, he waited for a reply, looking intently at both of us in turn. We thought quickly, sorting through vague memories of atoll resource statistics, recollections of the island ethnographies we had read, and impressions drawn from our few short weeks on Nanumea. We were lost.

"Fish, I suppose," said Anne at last, guessing with hopeful confidence. "You live from fishing." Sunema translated, and Venu looked pleased. Anne felt that her answer was right. But when Venu replied, his manner was intense and authoritative. His answer surprised us.

"No! It is the coconut. Fish come and go. Sometimes there are none, even though we try for them. It is the coconut from which we live. Even in drought it sustains us."

Venu went on to explain that while fish from the sea were usually plentiful, land food (which coconuts epitomize) provides a more fundamental basis for Nanumean life. From this perspective, land-use patterns and the social relationships that determine land ownership were going to be of central importance to our research. But to understand how Nanumeans use and relate to land, we found we first had to understand kinship and descent.

ॐ

## SHARED ESTATES

All of Nanumea above the beach line is divided into named parcels that, except for approximately thirty acres that are communally owned, belong to individuals and family groups. These parcels have been handed down through generations as the basis for family subsistence. Land sales are not allowed on Nanumea, so people can obtain land only through inheritance from their parents or, more rarely, as a gift connected to adoption, paternity disputes, or a special caretaking relationship. The land code recognizes two types of land tenure: shared (*kaitahi*, literally "eat as one") and individual (*vaevae*, literally "divided"). Most parcels are held in shared tenure, but there is constant shifting back and forth between these two categories. Individually owned plots inevitably become shared parcels as they are passed down to the owner's descendants, just as shared parcels are sometimes allocated to an individual owner.

Massive leather-bound registers kept in the local government office list all the island's land parcels and their owners. Most of the listed owners are deceased, some many years ago, and their living descendants now share the estate through informal arrangements that divide up usage of particular parcels. These take into account the subsistence needs of family members living in Nanumea as well as the overseas relatives who might return someday. Land-owning corporations like these should seem familiar: They are the remnants of kopiti residential groups, which formerly structured Nanumean life as far back as we have been able to document.

Despite the best intentions, family members in shared estates periodically reach a point where informal understandings become unworkable and it becomes necessary to divide the landholdings. Figure 4 shows a hypothetical estate group at this point of division. The elderly woman to the far right is second generation, the last living member of her sibling group. She is listed in the land registers as the head of the corporation, controlling the land she and her siblings received from their parents. But daily use of the estate's twenty land parcels scattered throughout the atoll is actually directed by the third generation man to the far left in the figure. Other relatives in his generation are not using the family's lands, even though they have rights to do so, because they are overseas or living with their spouses' families. Under current land law, when the elderly second generation woman dies, her descendants and those of her siblings must formally register an estate division in the Land Court. Details of this division should be decided through consensus by the family members themselves, producing three new shared kaitahi estates "owned" by the three siblings in the second generation who had heirs.

Families are often able to come to a decision quickly and without difficulty, using a written will or verbal instructions from the older generation, but occasionally, relatives are unable to agree. If their deadlock per-

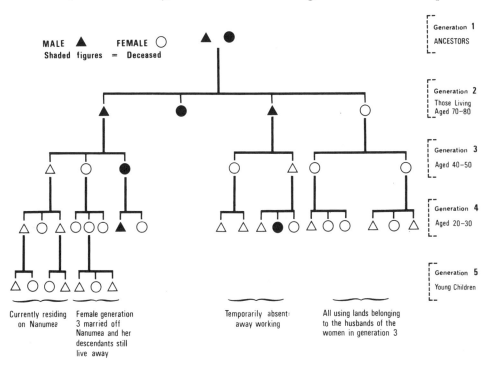

Figure 4   Land Inheritance in Kaitahi System.

sists for several years or is acrimonious, they turn to the Land Court for help. To prevent such difficulties, elderly estate heads usually leave a written will or a deathbed statement if they can. Existing wills are legally binding and though natural or adopted children cannot be disinherited completely, the share given to a child who has neglected his parents can be made quite small. This possibility reinforces the obedience, respect, and help that younger relatives should give to their elders.

Nanumeans inherit land-use rights from both parents. This allows people to choose among several potential living situations. At any point in time, however, a person's primary affiliation is determined by his or her residence. By living with other relatives (whether these are from the mother's or father's side) and contributing labor to group projects, a person demonstrates which potential affiliation has been chosen. Eligibility may depend on descent, but actual use rights depend on cooperation with other relatives and a demonstrated commitment to group efforts. If someone cannot get along with one group of kin, another side of the family can be sought out. Being able to choose among several potential kin groups tempers the authority of the family leaders in directing day-to-day resource use, too, since an elder who makes life too unpleasant for younger family members may lose them to another household.

The flexibility of this inheritance system, a feature of cognatic descent, allows people to maximize resources for themselves and their children. While people are active members of only one descent group, they retain rights to affiliate with other groups through links traced through ancestors of either their father or mother (and adoptive parents, too). Moving to another related household activates membership in that group. When older people leave the island for overseas work or an extended visit, they ask a close relative who shares the same estate to caretake the land they were using. For example, if a departing family had been using land shared with the mother's relatives, caretaking responsibility should revert to someone from her own estate. The husband would not normally ask one of his relatives to do the caretaking. Ideally, the caretaker will maintain the land's long-term productivity by keeping underbrush cleared and taro pits planted. Cognatic systems of inheritance encourage people to distribute themselves evenly over available resources, an effective adaptation in communities that emphasize collective well-being.

Decisions about where to live and which land to use are actually decisions about relationships. Being connected to a wide circle of relatives on both one's maternal and paternal sides provides social and economic security in a kin-based society like Nanumea. Marriage restrictions among close kin and respect behavior between specific kin categories both help to bind relatives together. At birth, wedding, and funeral celebrations, members of family corporations show their unified strength. Sharing expectations encourage people to show their connections with each other, too. But cultural ideals of widespread kinship and flexible cognatic group membership face practical limitations: People can live with only one subgroup of their many relatives.

Nanumeans often drew our attention to differences in past and contemporary inheritance practices. They reminded us that everyone's survival once depended on their family's access to local resources—there were no store goods, no buying and selling, and no government-financed ships to bring emergency supplies. Ample amounts of local produce and diligent work by all members of the family were critical to survival. For a kopiti to be strong, all its potential members had to be retained as residents, especially given customary limitations on numbers of children. As a traditional ideal, they said, people would inherit land from their fathers, and only sons would pass a share of the family estate on to their own children. Unmarried daughters continued to live in their father's household or joined that of a married brother, freely able to use the produce of their birth family's lands. A married woman was expected to join her husband's family and her children would inherit land rights from their father's estate. Children born outside marriage should be claimed by their fathers' families, too. These patrilateral expectations were not always followed, however.

Donald Kennedy's Land Commission, which recorded local land titles and inheritance customs in the 1930s, found that even seventy years ago Nanumeans did not always follow a strictly father-to-son principle in listing registered land owners. Instead, flexible inheritance patterns allowed families to use other strategies to maximize their members' access to land. Families with several sons usually listed only sons of their male members as eligible inheritors, but other families often included their sons and daughters equally. Local land law today gives all children a right to share in their parents' lands. How much of a share, however, continues to depend on a host of situational factors, and land tenure practices continue to be pragmatic and flexible.

Nanumea's cultural preference for patrilocal residence does help men keep greater control over land than do women. Women typically have less land registered in their names than their brothers, less jurisdiction over resource use, and less ability to pass land on to their children. Because most married women live with their husband's family, their children grow up as part of their father's extended family group, living and working on his family's shared estate. As the generations pass, daughters and granddaughters follow this same residence expectation. Routinely incorporating children into their father's estate group, unless some compelling reason exists for them to join their mother's family, contributes a consistent patrilineal bias to Nanumea's system of cognatic descent and supports men's roles in coordinating land use.

When the estate group depicted in figure 4 formally divides its shared land holdings, the Generation 3 man (far left) whose descendants all currently live on Nanumea will probably argue that the estate should be split mainly between descendents of the two brothers of Generation 2, with only a token amount going to descendents of the sister. Her daughters, he will probably emphasize, have both been relying on their husbands' lands for all their married lives. These daughters, however, might seek to maximize their children's options by claiming that their mother deserves an equal share in the division. Since all descendants of one of the brothers now live overseas, the Generation 3 man to the far left will probably continue to care for his cousins' land until they, or their children, return.

Paradoxically, the great respect that brothers owe their sisters supports this cultural emphasis on male inheritance, too. Participants in estate divisions understand that women and their descendants have special rights to family resources, in that they may always return to live in the family homesite and use estate resources if they wish. Families with few or no sons, or whose married daughters have brought their husbands home to join their own estate group, use this principle to include their daughters more fully in inheritance. Residence with the wife's family may be a good choice for a couple if her estate group has few residents or her side of the family can offer more resources to the next generation.

Individually owned lands are subject to the same inheritance rules as shared estates. The owner's children become collective owners of the parcel and eventually pass shared rights on to their own descendants. In this same way, through parents' and grandparents' marriages to members of other Tuvalu communities, many Nanumeans have come to share rights to land on other islands. But unless these are actively used, such land rights will lapse just as will shares in any kaitahi estate. Owning land in Nanumea or another island in Tuvalu in any enduring sense requires using it for subsistence or residence. "Use it or lose it" is the first rule of land tenure here.

Such flexible inheritance rules can result in disputed estate divisions, just as arguments always lurk in the background of family solidarity. Resentment over an "unfair" division may fester unresolved for decades, amidst hope that the tension will be forgotten eventually and an amicable relationship will be restored. Though the Land Court can arbitrate disputes, people are often reluctant to ask for a court decision because of the airing this will give to family contention. Public display of a dispute would be shameful and damaging to a family's reputation. For this reason, only urgent and intractable disputes are usually brought to court. Of twenty-four cases heard by the Land Court on Nanumea during our field-work period in 1973–75, only half were actual disputes. (The others involved undisputed transactions concerning adoption, paternity, or estate division.) All but three of the disputed cases concerned estate divisions whose principal claimants had died over fifty years previously.

Distinguishing responsible estate management from greedy self-interest can be difficult. Nanumeans are keenly aware that atoll land is finite and that land received in an estate division will be the basis of descendants' well-being far into the future. They also realize that continued fragmentation of landholdings is economically inefficient and that all but the largest land parcels are better left intact. Parceling out whole plots is the only way around fragmentation—but the size and productivity of each plot can vary considerably, and people must be willing to accept somewhat unequal shares. Where families are united by generosity and goodwill, as ideally they should be, amicable estate divisions usually can be achieved. But when compassion for other relatives is lacking, each elder will feel obliged to maximize the assets of his or her own descendants at the expense of the family as a whole.

଼ଅ

## WORKING THE LANDS

One of the goals of Anne's project in 1973–75 was to document local subsistence strategies since understanding how households used land resources was essential to economic planning for independence. We puzzled over how to research this. What data could encompass the complex realities of atoll land use: limited resources, complicated cognatic descent rules, several possible sources of access to land, and residence as the main criteria for actual land use? Clearly, simple calculations based on the per capita ratio of land to people would obscure any variation in people's access to land. We needed to make sure our data revealed the full diversity of subsistence situations on Nanumea. After mulling over several schemes, we decided to focus on households as land-using groups and to map the land parcels that were used by a representative sample of island households.

Until the mid-1980s, when a cadastral survey of Tuvalu was completed, no one (including Nanumeans) knew exactly how many land parcels jigsawed across the islets of Nanumea. Though every square foot of the atoll is included in one or another named parcel, owners rely on informal markers to outline each plot: large rocks, clumps of bushes, or marks on selected palm trunks. Boundary knowledge includes the history of estate divisions and the connections that particular plots have with specific

*Manuao's newly planted taro (1974)*

ancestors. Such information is continually refreshed and taught to the next generation as family members move about their properties, collecting fallen coconuts and other resources. Though people know the boundaries of their own landholdings, owners of adjacent parcels do not always use identical markers. Boundaries were relative until the cadastral survey and no overview of the community's landholdings existed. A set of maps now precisely demarcates the boundaries of 1,399 named land and taro pit plots. (Since many taro pits are informally subdivided, the functional number of plots at the time of mapping was actually probably closer to 1,500.) Most parcels shown on the maps are roughly rectangular in shape, though many have sides of different length and some are even five- or six-sided.

The useful resources on each land plot or taro pit vary widely, as do productivity and size. These variations are important for taxation purposes. An official system of land sizing, based on the number of ten-foot by twenty-foot parcels each plot is estimated to contain, is combined with a rating system of each plot's productive potential, using categories of good, fair, or poor. Size 15 or 16 lands (about half an acre) are most common, though parcels range from size 40 down to size 1. The agricultural pits on Lakena Islet have never been included in this system of size and productivity estimation, perhaps because many pits are so small. This rating system determines the land tax owed annually by the estate owners, but people usually do not characterize their land in terms of its assigned rating. This information can become important in estate divisions, however.

Our land-mapping project, which predated the cadastral survey by a decade, took weeks of our time. We arranged expeditions to the atoll hinterlands accompanied by a household elder who knew the land boundaries. We traveled by canoe to Lakena Islet and walked or bicycled over the network of inland paths. For days on end we stumbled through rocky underbrush and peered around palm trees, sighting boundary lines and angles with a hand-held compass and pacing out the length of each side. As we worked our way around the edges of each plot with the owner, we counted palms to estimate their density, noted other plants in the understory, and asked about each family's land use practices. We began to appreciate how dividing the island into many small parcels enabled every family corporation to have access to all of the atoll's ecological zones. The complicated inheritance links through which household members claimed rights to use each parcel surprised us. Gradually we came to realize that the land resources available to a household reflected its membership at any point in time. Each of the surveyed households had access to a core of lands derived from the shared estate of its household head, but land rights of spouses or other long-term residents often added additional resources as well. When someone with primary use rights to a land parcel moved to another local household, their rights often went with them. And, of course, many households were caretaking land for absent relatives.

The land survey gave us a fascinating view of the atoll's ecology. We saw plots on the old World War II airstrip where roots of yellowing palms spilled from shallow planting holes still encased in cementlike lagoon mud. After thirty years, these palms were still only head high. We learned to recognize the difference between scrubby wasteland and the more productive coconut bush that covers 60 percent of the atoll. There, palms are the tallest trees, shading a varied tangle of shrubs, herbs, creepers, and grasses, interspersed with self-sown palm seedlings of various heights. The big canoe trees, *fetau* (*Calophyllum inophyllum*) and *pukavai* (*Hernandia peltata*), grow only in the protected interior of the main islets. We could see how their scarcity made them valuable and why a family might designate a fine specimen of slow-growing fetau as a future canoe hull for a young son or nephew. Compared to the effort it took to map the bush plots, mapping of smaller, less overgrown taro pits and village lands went much more easily. We usually saved these for last.

Our original plan called for measuring all the land parcels used by the twenty households in the economic sample. This goal proved to be naïvely optimistic. After spending the best part of a month tramping the island, we finally had to call our surveying to a halt. We had mapped only four households' land holdings: a total of 113 parcels dispersed over the atoll. Using this survey information plus data from our initial census, later discussions with household members about their land resources, and information gleaned from participant observation, we compiled a comparative assessment of these four households' land situations. We found that two households (A and B) were locally regarded as having access to average amounts of land. Household C had a reputation for being relatively land-poor, while Household D was talked about as land-wealthy.

This mapping work taught us several interesting things about Nanumean land-use patterns. First, the resource reputations associated with local households appeared to be quite realistic. Though the members of Household A, for example, had somewhat better access to land than we had been led to think, the other households all conformed quite closely to their reputations. To earn a reputation as land-poor or land-rich, a household apparently had to have quite a markedly different people/resource ratio than most of its neighbors. Land-wealthy Household D, for example, proved to have about 85,000 square feet (about 2 acres) per capita, while land-poor Household C had long-term access to only about 24,000 square feet (1/2 acre) per person. A household's reputation for being land-rich or land-poor clearly did not correlate simply with the number of lands its members owned or with its total acreage. Its people/land ratio was the important determinant. Household C, for example, actually had more land holdings than the others and its total acreage was comparable to "average" Household A—but it was the only household to work all its available taro pits and ranked lowest on acreage per capita. Clearly, a simple count of land holdings, detached from supporting information about household membership and use patterns, could not have provided a complete assessment of resource availability.

Furthermore, the fact that most households did not use all the taro pits available to them suggested that labor might be an important constraint on production, affecting not only taro and pulaka root crop cultivation but probably copra production, too. Finally, the survey showed us how closely traditional exchange practices interfaced with and supported household subsistence strategies. As will be described in the next chapter, people in all four households enjoyed adequate and varied diets regardless of per capita differences in access to land. We were beginning to suspect that exchange practices had important effects on household subsistence patterns. If this were true, access to land was just one of the factors that governed resource availability.

ૐ
## COCONUT AND WATER

Another fortuitous conversation with Venu helped us glimpse other connections between cultural expectations and resource use. Venu and his
family lived toward the rear of the Lolua village side along the leeward
shore near the road whose construction Tofe had supervised long ago.
Like other older village houses, Venu's house was small, perched on a
coral-cement platform. Its open sides were framed by vertical poles, and
coconut leaf shutters were tidily tucked up under the eaves of its thatched
roof. Venu's family could look out on the ocean reef with its distant line
of breakers, and they had an equally good view of anyone coming down
the road from the church and the pastor's house. One afternoon as we
walked by, Venu hailed us: "Come and eat some coconut, come drink
some water." We could see that he was just finishing a meal, sitting cross-
legged on a mat alone in his house. We walked over toward him, formu-
lating a polite disclaimer about not being hungry, wondering why we had
escaped the usual island greeting of "Where are you going?" Venu ges-
tured for us to join him and then proceeded to pour us each a mug of tea-
colored water flavored with coconut molasses from the large teapot by
his side. "Have some fish, some taro pudding, too," he invited warmly. We
looked at him and at the food in surprise: a half coconut shell sat empty
beside the plate of food and he was drinking diluted coconut molasses,
not water. Why had he specifically invited us to consume items that he
didn't have on hand?

Amused by our literal mindedness, Venu explained that he had simply offered the traditional greeting that anyone who eats food in the public view should make to people passing by. It is greedy not to share food,
but to call out the particulars of the menu is ostentatious. Only the modest staples of local diet, coconut and water, can be offered by name. In
any case, Venu added, people eat coconut at every meal anyway. It is the
*tapa tolu*, the "third kick," that together with fish and some starch fulfills
the Nanumean ideal of a satisfying meal. Nanumeans are sometimes
teased for being "coconut eaters" by other Tuvaluans, presumably for
needing to eat plain coconut for lack of anything else, but Nanumeans say
that they enjoy the succulent crispness of mature coconut eaten plain.
Here we were being reminded again that, for Nanumeans, the coconut is
the staff of life, equivalent both symbolically and pragmatically to the
bread of Western societies.

In fact, as we were coming to realize, the variety of food produced
by the coconut palm is astounding. Highly nutritious coconut sap can be
made to drip from the tree's bound flower spathes into an empty con-

tainer suspended below. Gathered twice daily, the sap is used fresh in household cooking or boiled into a long-keeping molasses. Because it ferments quickly, fresh "toddy" (*kaleve*) destined for the household cooking pot is usually boiled briefly to stop fermentation until it can be used. Left to sit, toddy ferments to a sour but potent alcoholic drink. Because toddy production involves climbing into the crown of the palm, it is customarily the work of young men, and they often leave extra toddy to ferment in the treetops for their own use. Immature green-skinned drinking coconuts provide a refreshing, slightly effervescent liquid and thin jellylike custard to be scooped out of the shell. The development stages of these immature nuts are named, and local recipes specify which stage to use.

Mature coconuts with dry, brown husks have thick, white, crunchy flesh, which can be eaten in slices or grated for consumption by elders with poor teeth. The grated meat is also squeezed to make coconut cream, used widely in recipes or heated to make oil. Mature coconut can be dried into copra and sold for cash. The spongy interior of nuts allowed to germinate was a particular delicacy for us, tasting like an improbable cross between apples and angel food cake. There is even one palm variety that produces sweet-husked coconuts, whose fresh or baked husks can be chewed like sugar cane. These edible-husk nuts (known as *uto*) are an original cultivar developed by ancestors of today's atoll peoples, and probably found their way south to Nanumea from the drier atolls of Micronesia. The uto variety, Nanumeans estimate, makes up about half the palms on the island, a higher proportion than is common on the other islands of Tuvalu or elsewhere in atoll Polynesia.

Given all these palm products, it is not surprising that Anne's survey of household diet showed that in the 1970s Nanumeans consumed on average about one coconut per person each day, an amount that increased when other types of food were less available. We found that this same "one coconut rule" matched the traditional estimate that had long been used to calculate food reserves needed for times of drought and to plan communal feasts.

Nanumeans are critically aware of the limits that drought places on their environment. In good years, Nanumean rainfall is plentiful and frequent, averaging 113 inches annually over the 45 years from 1947 to 1993, the period for which full data is available from New Zealand meteorological records. Like many averages, however, this figure conceals a huge degree of variability. The highest annual total recorded in this period was 193 inches in 1987, while the lowest was just 46 inches in 1962. Other dry years with less than 78 inches of rain included 1950, 1955, 1956, 1971, 1974, 1975, 1976 and 1989, while rainfall measured over 150 inches in 1953, 1958, 1977, 1982, 1983 and 1992. Dry periods occur at least every decade and sometimes last several years—and it is these that determine the plants that can survive in the long term. Even in times of adequate rainfall, atoll vegetation is affected by a high rate of evapotranspiration due to the hot climate and to the high porosity of coral soil. In fact, specialists assert that atoll soils are so porous that drainage of rainfall down through the ground is "perfect and almost instantaneous." As a result, less than half and perhaps only a fourth of the rain that falls on an atoll is available to plants after evapotranspiration losses are taken into account. Despite what might seem an ample level of rainfall by continental standards, Nanumea suffers recurrent dry periods that can only be considered as "droughts."

What about people's needs for a reliable source of pure water? Nanumea's domestic water supply is currently provided by catchment from three sources: the large metal roofs of public buildings (church, meeting hall, council offices and workshop, medical clinic), metal roofs on houses built after the late 1980s, and small metal-roofed shelters built especially to catch rainwater. Large, half-underground cement cisterns, some dating from early this century, collect community water in the village center and at several other locations. Reasonably well sealed to prevent

*New house with water tank (1984)*

contamination, these are viewed as a community resource and people gather to dip out water from them on a schedule supervised by a local government appointee. Most homes now have at least one ferro-cement tank to store household water for washing and drinking, too. These household tanks (and small catchment roofs to feed them) were initiated by the Save the Children Foundation in 1983–84, touching off a period of intensive communal and village rebuilding work that lasted from 1984 to 1989. Most Nanumean households now own at least one water tank, and even households in distant and "undeveloped" Matagi have built them.

Individual household tanks have proved a mixed blessing, however. Perhaps as many as 20 percent have developed leaks, probably mainly due to faulty construction, and these are usually difficult to fix. Other tanks stand abandoned, marking the former or future house sites of absentee owners. Abandoned and leaky tanks retain at least a puddle of water inside, which makes a perfect breeding places for mosquitoes. Health workers routinely warn people to screen tank openings, but proper screening material is rarely available and few people make the effort. In 1996, Nanumeans commented with some discouragement that their island had become *namoa*, "mosquito-ey." They blamed not only the tanks, but also lax enforcement of the rule against planting bananas in the village area. Where banana leaves join the stalk, a funnel-like area holds water, people said, providing a place for mosquito larvae to flourish. In any case, Nanumea islet, which had been famous throughout Tuvalu for being free of night-flying mosquitoes, now has them in abundance. Like other Tuvaluans, Nanumeans now need to sleep under mosquito nets, a phenomenon unknown just a decade ago.

The increase in mosquitoes has health implications. Fortunately there is no malaria in Tuvalu, but other mosquito-borne diseases are present. Filariasis (once called elephantiasis) is now nearly eradicated after a public health campaign in the 1970s. Dengue fever is endemic throughout the Pacific and breaks out in sometimes fatal epidemics. Children scratch mosquito bites on their arms and legs, creating small sores that easily become infected in the warm, humid climate. Mosquito coils are used by some in Funafuti but are ineffective in open-sided houses on the outer islands. Both coils and mosquito repellents are expensive, and the latter are neither available in the stores nor part of the local cultural repertoire, so mosquito bites are simply endured. This approach works reasonably well against the smaller, day-flying mosquitoes, whose bites itch only for a few minutes, but nets are needed for both comfort and health when night-flying mosquitoes are present.

From the perspective of traditional history, this recent increase in mosquitoes is ironic. The "taro pit wars" several centuries ago involved violent confrontations over whether taro pits should be dug in the main village area. The faction that eventually triumphed vehemently refused to allow the pits because of the mosquito infestation that would result. In the 1950s, too, the community refused to allow the Samoan headmaster to dig taro pits near the school, which was then located in Matagi, creating intense debate at public meetings and many oratorical references to the "taro pit wars" of the past. Unfortunately, the potential connection between water storage in private tanks and infestation by night-flying mosquitoes was not anticipated by local health officials, the aid agency, or even by Nanumeans when the tanks were originally introduced.

On the positive side, public cisterns and more than one hundred smaller household tanks allow the community to "bank" effectively the heavy downpours of water that deluge the island in storms. In traditional times, significant water storage was simply not possible. People might catch a little runoff in storms by tying a strip of palm leaf around the smooth trunk of a coconut tree, positioning the leaf to funnel water into a canoe hull or wooden food preparation vessel, the only large containers available to atoll residents. Such relatively small amounts of water would have been used up quickly and could not have been kept clean for long in any case. Unfortunately, water from thatched roofs is contaminated with dirt and debris, colored as brown as strong tea, and not at all suitable for drinking.

Of course, anyone who digs through the sand to the water table will always find water—but in most locations this will be brackish or even quite salty. As rainwater percolates down through the coral sand, it soon meets the level of seawater that permeates the atoll's porous base. Since rainwater floats on top of the slightly denser salt water within the coral and sand base of the island, a freshwater "lens" results. The depth and quality of this freshwater lens varies greatly from place to place on the atoll, seemingly affected by recent rainfall, underlying rock structure, and weather conditions. During prolonged dry periods, the freshwater lens shrinks to become very shallow. Heavy wave action in storms mixes the water layers together, too. Idiosyncratic aspects of atoll geology result in ground water being palatable in some locations and salty in others. In places where layers of naturally cemented sand or "hardpan" interfere, the water table is inaccessible.

The best way to reach the freshwater lens is to dig down just to the surface of the water table and to use a shallow container to scoop out the slightly brackish water, taking care not to mix up the water too much. Shallow wells like these sustained the community in traditional times. Nanumeans told us that the best water holes became community property in droughts, and families were rationed water from them according to how many members each had. As the drought situation worsened, the best water was saved for young children and the sick. The rest of the community drank saltier water from other wells, mixing in coconut molasses (if available) to mask the taste. Of course, as the water table shrank, so did food production. Root crops and tree fruits became scarce and finally even salt-tolerant coconut palms stopped setting fruit.

Elderly people in the 1970s still remembered the threat posed by serious drought and the cultural strategies that the community used to survive. After several months without rain when coconut production began to diminish, an island meeting would be called to divide everyone into two groups, family by family. This process was known as *vaelua*, "divide [the community] in two." One group would be assigned to use the rich resources of Lakena Islet, moving there for the duration of the drought. The other group would continue to live in the main village, using the produce of the rest of the atoll. Each of the two groups had its own leaders, who were charged with rationing resources equally so that all residents would survive. For the duration of the emergency, family land rights were temporarily suspended and all land was used communally. Clearly, making everyone suffer hunger together was preferable to allowing people with greater land resources to eat while others starved. We were told that everyone stayed in the village areas except during communal food collecting expeditions. Every few days families would be told exactly how many coconuts or other foods could be collected per person. The men fished communally, too, and their catch was shared out. Leaders reportedly sometimes patrolled the outskirts of the villages to prevent unauthorized food collection but, in the close confines of a village with open-sided houses, there would have been little opportunity to eat undetected anyway.

Both missionary and administrative reports document vaelua divisions being used to cope with major droughts in the 1890s, in 1908, and in 1924. The first of these drought periods was perhaps the most terrible. Beginning in the early 1890s and lasting about six years, all the northern Tuvalu islands were affected. Administrators described local people as eating tree roots and mangrove seedpods due to the great scarcity of other food, but their reports make no mention of increased deaths. Nanumeans themselves say that virtually everyone survived, although many were very weak. Children aged four or five were reportedly only able to crawl, never learning to walk until the drought ended.

In 1974, we ourselves saw firsthand the power that drought wields over human life on a "dry" atoll. With no substantial rain falling for five months, the community's cistern water was exhausted despite strict rationing by the Island Council. Shallow wells were dug once again across the lagoon in Matagi, and people painstakingly scooped water into glass fishing floats and cooking pots, transporting it back to the village by canoe. The taste of the well water was brackish and unpleasant, though it was not so salty as to be a health hazard. People masked its taste with store-bought sugar or palm molasses. Fortunately, the drought ended with a downpour before too many more weeks, replenishing empty cisterns and rejuvenating island vegetation. As the rain poured down, people rushed outdoors, gathering under overflowing gutters on the large public buildings to enjoy the fresh flowing water. Drought cycles have been endured by atoll peoples from the time of first settlement and, as this one showed us, even metal-roofed buildings and cisterns add only a limited margin to human survival in these difficult environments. Though "drought" may be a relative term here, these dry periods can have major impacts on human subsistence and survival.

ॐ

## Root Crops and Prestige

Lakena Island, at the northern end of the lagoon, symbolizes another important food to Nanumeans: starchy root crops. Blessed with an unusual fresh-water lake and sandy, easily dug soil, Lakena is the prime location for horticulture on the atoll. Crops including taro and its hardier and much bigger cousin, pulaka (or "atoll taro"), are grown here in composted pits dug down to the water table. A few thatched houses cluster by the edge of the lagoon at the near end of Lakena Islet not far from the gardens. Many of these houses are occupied only occasionally, giving Lakena's small village a relaxed feeling. A few people come to live on Lakena for a several weeks or months at a time, but most commute over, do a day's work, and return to the main islet by nightfall. Lakena has no school, store, or health facilities.

It takes about an hour to sail an outrigger canoe to Lakena when the usual trade wind is blowing. Paddling or poling a laden canoe home can take twice as long, even longer if the wind is strong. In the '70s and '80s (and no doubt for decades or centuries before that), Fridays and the days before feasts saw the dawn departure for Lakena of a flotilla of canoes, many with triangular sails set, laden with sacks of compost. The canoes would return home at dusk heavily loaded with bags of taro and pulaka, bunches of bananas and whole pandanus fruits. Today, the scene has changed. Since the late 1980s, the community has provided regularly scheduled trips to Lakena on its outboard-motor powered catamaran, *Togamalie*. Nanumeans (and visitors) can enjoy a ride down the lagoon for a round-trip fare of 40 cents plus a small charge for each sack of compost leaves, harvested roots, or bicycle. Tickets are sold in advance, since there is strong demand to catch the early run at 5:30 A.M. While the advent of the catamaran is change in itself, we were told that its use has also resulted in greater involvement by women in root-crop cultivation, and a tendency for shorter, more regular trips to Lakena. While some Nanumeans still travel by canoe, the flotilla of sails heading out to Lakena in the dawn is now a distant memory.

A newly dug pulaka pit, the generic name, cuts straight down from three to ten feet to the water table, ending in a barren, white, sandy bottom. After decades (perhaps generations) of careful composting, it will gradually become a marsh with pale brown soil, consistently damp and fertile. Though this rich environment could grow many salt-tolerant plants, Nanumeans focus their horticultural efforts on two root crops: "true taro" (*Colocasia esculenta*) and the larger, coarser type (*Cyrto-sperma chamissonis*), pulaka. Although true taro may have been grown here in precontact times, it has never been as important a food source as the hardier pulaka. Both roots (technically, corms) are grown from cuttings and take from three months to a year to develop, depending on the pit's fertility, sunlight, and water conditions. The quicker-growing taro needs to be harvested at maturity, but pulaka tubers can be left growing for several years.

*Newly dug pulaka pit (1974)*

The horticultural area is nestled into the center of Lakena Islet, protected from prevailing salt-laden winds by an area of broad-leaf forest
trees intermixed with coconut palms. Pits closest to the village end of Lakena are sunny and open, showpieces of atoll horticulture. Taro seedlings
with tender, heart-shaped leaves stand in even rows, each plant in its own
circular depression. Larger, rougher leaves of pulaka are arrowhead-
shaped and lighter green, older plants standing taller than a person. Prize
pulaka intended for future presentations grow in separate woven baskets
and are fed special mulches. Deeper into the bush, ancient pits shaded by
surrounding vegetation produce only pulaka. Leaves here are as large as
umbrellas and tower high over an adult's head, although the roots themselves are often no bigger than those grown in sunnier locations.
Throughout the horticultural area, banana trees have been planted along
the pit margins and sugar cane or sweet potatoes are grown in limited
amounts, too. Though Nanumeans appreciate the variety that these secondary crops bring to their diets, horticultural efforts focus on the traditional root crops.

Neither taro nor pulaka are edible until they are cooked. Both are
"aroids" (in the arum family, which also includes antheriums and philo-
dendrons) and in their raw state contain calcium oxalate crystals that provoke a severe reaction, including constriction of the throat. Nowadays
they are usually boiled, but roots can also be grated or pounded, mixed
with coconut cream, molasses, or toddy, and then baked in an earth oven
for more festive occasions. Such complicated recipes take a full day of
preparation and usually are made only for special meals at weddings,
birth celebrations, community feasts, and Sunday dinners. Baking or boil-
ing large roots whole advertises the cultivator's skill.

For everyday meals, Nanumeans turn to breadfruit, a food source
grown near every house on huge, graceful trees. These starchy fruits
about the size of a small melon weigh a pound or more and need only to
have their rough, green, sappy skin scraped away before they can be fried,
baked, roasted in the coals, or boiled with coconut sap into soup. Some
varieties provide edible chestnutlike seeds and sweeter flesh; others are
nearly spherical, seedless, and quite starchy. Breadfruit is in season twice
a year (peaking around October/November and again in April/May) and is
eaten almost daily at these times. The fruits are harvested individually, cut
down using a sharp knife blade attached to a long pole. Since the trees
can be very tall, it is often necessary to climb high and then cut down
each fruit using the twenty-foot pole—a task usually reserved for agile
teenage boys. Breadfruit trees normally belong to the owner of the land
on which they grow, and households using a shared estate usually assign
family members the right to harvest specific trees. Morning and evening,

the village resounds with an industrious sweeping as the children of each user collect the leaves that their trees continually shed, keeping the village tidy and amassing potential compost.

Other food crops add variety to local meals. Bananas grow throughout the village, both the starchy cooking variety that is boiled green and the sweet tiny "ladyfinger" type relished ripe. The berrylike fruit of a small fig (*felo*) is collected in season from people's bush lands and made into puddings or soup. Extremely fibrous pandanus fruits, larger than a basketball but composed of separable wedge-shaped orange segments, are chewed as a sweet snack but are not plentiful enough to be made into dried fruit paste or flour as in the Micronesian atolls.

White rice, flour, and cabin crackers (hardtack) have become the convenience foods of the island. People buy them as their household budgets (and availability in the store) permit. Households with a resident wage earner, especially those who are not Nanumean and thus lack local land rights, rely heavily on store foods, usually purchasing rice and flour by the sack. Other households use money sent by relatives working in Funafuti or overseas to buy store items, with the level of remittances determining their purchases.

Reliance on store food, especially rice, flour, and cabin crackers, has increased markedly over the last twenty years. These items are now eaten regularly at household meals and are even presented on feast platters. Local tastes seem to be changing, too. In the mid-1980s, parents complained to us that their children disdained taro and pulaka, refusing to eat it even at feasts, demanding store starches instead. This pattern was even more pronounced in 1996. The luxury dishes laboriously made from root crops increasingly hold little appeal for many younger Nanumeans. While everyone wants to eat some store foods, people who have worked on the phosphate islands of Banaba or Nauru also remember how tiring an unrelenting diet of store food becomes and how desirable taro, pulaka, coconut, and breadfruit can be. These memories parallel current reality for Tuvaluans living in the capital, where local food is expensive and difficult to obtain. Outer Islanders always take along sacks of coconuts, baskets of roots, and bottles of coconut molasses when they travel to the capital, to help out their host households.

Growing and harvesting local produce is mainly a male responsibility in Nanumea, though sometimes spouses work together. Inherited family knowledge about composting and magically "feeding" crops is valued, though people also recognize that effort expended determines cultivation success, too. Giving a large root to the pastor at the public presentations each May or providing substantial amounts of root crops for wedding feasts are traditional ways that men prove their cultivation skills. Though pulaka and taro are both prestige crops, reputation as an expert cultivator doesn't confer the same degree of community renown as does the status of fishing expert. Plentiful root crops and the discipline implied in their production, however, symbolize the community's economic security and productive vigor. Local work routines still allocate Fridays to crop cultivation and Saturdays to processing the roots into Sabbath puddings.

ર≥

## Using the Sea

As dusk descended on the village most weekday evenings until the late 1980s, groups of young men would assemble at ocean-going canoes beached along the lagoon shore just above the high-tide line. Crewmembers brought scoop nets, paddles, and a kerosene pressure lantern to lash to a pole in the middle of each canoe. A few decades earlier, braided coconut-frond torches would have been brought to provide illumination. For the next few hours, the canoes would be taken into the open sea, forming a loosely organized flotilla united in pursuit of flying fish, *hahave* (*Exocoetidae*). The canoes would move together along the leeward shore of Nanumea island just outside the breaking waves. Trout-sized flying fish, startled from the waves by light from the moving canoes, were netted in midair. This style of fishing, called *llama*, was hard work, requiring strong paddlers who could sustain a steady pace, skillful net handlers, and an experienced steersman to guide the canoe through the passage and among the ocean swells in the dark. It was also highly productive. Night after night, the fishermen returned to the lagoon laden with fish. The catch divided out to four or five fish per crewmember at worst, with occasional catches as high as three or even four hundred fish per canoe. Households regularly had flying fish to salt and dry in the sun the next day, even after they ate some fresh and shared some with nonfishing relatives and neighbors. Specially prepared raw flying fish, their eyes and fins removed and artistically positioned two or three on a cord, were often given as tokens of appreciation, suspended stealthily in the predawn by a young man from the eaves of his lover's house or given to those helping care for a relative's newborn baby. In 1973 and 1974, our dietary survey found that flying fish were eaten at one quarter of all Nanumean meals. The community relied on them as a staple—abundant, tasty, and regularly available.

In 1984, we were surprised to find that flying fish catches were declining. Young men still fished in the nightly flotillas, but with far less return. We thought at the time that El Niño weather disturbances might somehow be related to the decrease in flying fish. By 1996, Nanumeans were no longer fishing for flying fish at all. A major source of ocean protein

*Siose, Kaino, and Talake with a good night's catch (1974)*

had essentially become a memory from the past. Since El Niño and La Niña fluctuations in weather patterns have continued to come and go, and fishing for flying fish is reportedly still continuing on the other Tuvalu outer islands and in Tokelau, a simple connection to world weather patterns seems unlikely. What had led the community to give up a highly productive and efficient fishing method, well integrated with local activity patterns and eminently suitable to available technology? The answer according to Nanumeans was a plague of dolphins. Fishermen told dramatic stories of schools of dolphins that closely followed the nightly expeditions of fishing canoes, grabbing the light-startled flying fish from the sea or even from the air before they could be netted. With dolphins snatching the catch, fishing for flying fish had become a waste of effort, even dangerous, men claimed, and Nanumeans had to turn to other fishing techniques.

Laina Teuea, an active Nanumean fisherman during our several periods in Nanumea, offered an explanation for the dolphin plague that disrupted flying-fish catches in the 1980s, and in doing so evoked the long-standing link believed to exist between the traditional chieftainship and the bounty of land and sea. The reestablishment of the chieftainship in the 1980s, he hypothesized, and the installation of a reigning high chief after some decades of hiatus had brought a "blessing" to the island in the form of abundant *tafolaa*, dolphins. The decline of flying fish was one result, as the dolphins gathered and then fed on them.

Luckily, nightly netting of flying fish was only one technique in the traditional fishing repertoire. Trolling for larger ocean fish, especially skipjack tuna or bonito (*atu*) was one culturally elaborated method. Carefully made mother-of-pearl shell lures, *paa*, were treasured family heirlooms, their beauty celebrated in poetic descriptions. Attached to long poles with twelve- to fifteen-foot lines, the lures were trailed behind as a canoe was paddled through a school of tuna feeding on a rapidly moving mass of smaller fish. Skillful, lucky fishermen could pull in a hundred tuna or more before the school dissipated and moved on, sometimes completely filling the narrow hull of their canoe with fish. Deeper swimming fish such as yellow-fin tuna (*takuo*) or castor-oil fish (*palu*) were caught by lowering baited hooks several hundred feet below the surface, a fishing strategy best suited to calm conditions. Larger ocean fish could also be noosed or lassoed. *Ulua* (trevally), *haku-laa* (marlin), and *magoo* (shark) were all targeted by specific methods, most of which involved one or two fishermen working from smaller canoes.

*Teoti and Teaikafa hew a two-person canoe (1996)*

Fishermen also used throw nets, made since the 1950s of monofilament line but before that of coconut fiber sennit or wild hibiscus cord, to catch schooling fish such as mullet on the reef flats or in the lagoon shallows. Coral heads in the lagoon are productive places to fish for colorful reef fish, some of which are favored as delicacies. Using hand lines to catch these reef fish requires patience and time rather than paddling strength and can be undertaken by a single fisherman. Nanumeans also eat a wide variety of shellfish, eels, octopus, and other small fish that can be gathered from the reef and sandy beaches.

All the more culturally elaborated fishing techniques depend on canoes, hewn by experts from large hardwood trees. The standard four-person ocean-going canoe, about twenty-eight feet in length, is a sophisticated, sea-worthy vessel, a valuable family possession. Nanumean canoes were usually paddled on ocean fishing expeditions rather than sailed, requiring a crew of energetic paddlers. Though expeditions aimed to stay within sight of land, a fast-moving squall could always blow a canoe far out into the open ocean where the fishermen could become lost. The island's many canoes, beached along the lagoon above the high-tide line, carefully leveled and shaded to prevent damage from the sun, have long demonstrated the community's intensive connection with the sea.

But as table 1 shows, Nanumean fishing practices are changing. In 1974, 218 traditional paddling and sailing canoes were in use on the island, about a quarter of them large, ocean-going fishing canoes. Second only to dwellings in value, these *vaka kaiva* were complex and "expensive" cultural products. Expert canoe makers were often booked up far into the future to supervise their construction, and Nanumean men

Table 1
Decline in Nanumean Canoes/Increase in Small Boats, 1974–1996

| Year | Canoes | | | | | Small Boats |
|---|---|---|---|---|---|---|
| | Large[a] 24 ft. + | Medium 15–24 ft. | Small 15 ft./less | Kiribati[b] style | Total | Total |
| 1974 | 51 | 73 | 60 | 34 | 218 | 6 |
| 1996[c] | 12 | 16 | 55 | 6 | 89 | 11 |
| % of Change | −76% | −78% | −8% | −82% | −59% | +83% |

[a] Of the 51 largest canoes in 1974, 41 were maintained as ocean-going fishing canoes, vaka kaiva. In 1996, only 8 large canoes on the island had this capability. However, many of the unlashed canoe hulls being cared for as family valuables were large canoes.

[b] All light-framed, one person canoes brought home by returning workers.

[c] Of the canoes under construction in July 1996, one was medium-sized and four were small canoes.

shared a complex of knowledge and skills focused on building, maintaining, and fishing from canoes. Somewhere in the village, a new canoe was always under construction, relatives cooperating to feed the master builder and helping with less specialized work. But by 1996, canoe numbers had dropped by almost 60 percent. Only twelve large canoes now existed, and only eight of these were well enough maintained to be taken out to sea. While local investment in large, ocean-going fishing canoes had virtually ceased, the number of small canoes had nearly doubled, and we saw several of these under construction in 1996.

Nanumea's declining use and production of large canoes parallels similar trends elsewhere in the Pacific and provides a barometer of local culture change (see table 1). It is not simply that old maritime technology has been replaced by imported improvements. The abandonment of ocean-going canoes represents such an extensive change in local fishing practices that social expectations, exchange patterns, and the community's subsistence orientation will all have been altered, too. We couldn't help but wonder about the causes and effects involved. With so many younger men away, seeking work in Funafuti or overseas, were there simply too few left to maintain and use the Nanumean canoe fleet? Had the increase in small boats, which had nearly doubled in number over the last two decades, caused the decline in large canoes? Or had the boats become more necessary because interest waned in ocean fishing from canoes? Nanumeans told us that stronger and more reliable outboard engines were becoming available and that rising family incomes permitted investment in this more expensive technology.

Many men in Nanumea are ambivalent about the recent decline in large canoes, though they also appreciate how much easier fishing from motor-powered boats can be. While it is too early to be certain that ocean-going canoe fishing has really become a thing of the past, the many disembodied canoe hulls lying about the village in 1996 suggested this. Some were protected inside houses or even hoisted into attics, others were propped up carefully outdoors and shaded from the sun. Too valuable to abandon, they also represented a traditional focus of men's activities and an avenue to prestige whose loss would fundamentally affect island society.

By contrast with the rich cultural symbolism associated with canoes, motor boats are utilitarian items whose value lies in their ability to accomplish the same task as canoes with less human effort. Workers returning from overseas have been bringing small wooden boats home for several generations, though engine maintenance has always been difficult once the equipment reaches Nanumea. In 1996, reliable 15–25 horsepower Yamaha engines had become the norm, though these cost $3,000 or more each. Sturdy twelve- to sixteen-foot plywood boats could be ordered from a thriving boat-building industry in Funafuti by those with savings from overseas work or a small business loan from the Development Bank of Tuvalu. For all owners, motor boats open up enticing new fishing possibilities. The operator of a powerboat can bring home a substantial catch of tuna on nearly every fishing trip, provided he is reasonably lucky and has some fishing knowledge. He does not have to gather a crew of paddlers or share his catch with them. He and a single companion can range effortlessly over a wide area, moving much more quickly than a canoe crew to locate feeding schools of fish. Circumnavigating the atoll is even possible, an undertaking not usually feasible in a canoe.

These efficiencies do have a downside, however. When Nanumea's fishing depended on canoes, each ocean-going *vaka kaiva* required a four-man crew. Over a hundred skilled and fit young men were involved in regular flying-fish expeditions each night. Motorboats require only a two-person crew and just eleven boats were supplying Nanumea's main fish needs in 1996. Some twenty men were now accomplishing the work that had engaged over a hundred men a decade before. Such a drop in subsistence employment is often ignored in national economic statistics, though this change represents a major decline in productive labor opportunities for Nanumean young men (and since this technological change is countrywide, throughout Tuvalu, too).

Keeping motorboats in working order is a significant challenge in the salty atoll environment. Some men are adept at mechanical tinkering, but the local store stocks very few spare parts for boat engines and major repairs must be done in the capital. Gasoline is in chronically short supply, and the store periodically sells out of gasoline completely. During our 1996 stay, motorboat fishermen were rationed fuel each week, and the available stock of gasoline was nearly depleted when we left. Gasoline is also very expensive, costing $1.15 per liter in 1996 (the equivalent of U.S.$3.50 per gallon) in an economy where average household earnings are usually only a small fraction of what they are in the United States.

Meticulous fishing records kept in 1995–96 by Tie Maheu provide insights into current motorboat economics. Tie's catches were extremely variable, ranging from nothing to several hundred tuna in a single expedition. The bonito tuna he caught varied between four to sixteen pounds, while yellow-fin tuna and the juvenile stage known as *tavatava* ranged from eleven to over fifty pounds per fish. His fishing expeditions lasted between two and four hours, using five to seven gallons of gasoline per trip (which cost U.S.$18–$25 each time). Tie fished first to meet his family needs, often using his catch to meet traditional obligations connected with birth celebrations, weddings, or funerals. He sometimes sold fish to the fish jerky project (see the next chapter), but usually, at least part of his catch was sold to eager local buyers. Tie had successfully captained his own four-man fishing canoe for over two decades, and he was making a reasonable income from his motorboat operation. But as they do for all motorboat fishermen, traditional obligations to share fish within the community created dilemmas in selling the catch. We will consider this topic further in the next chapter.

Expertise in ocean fishing is still a source of prestige, especially for young and middle-aged men who are building reputations for maturity and competence. In the past, an acknowledged fishing expert (*tautai*) would have earned that title by captaining a canoe that caught at least one hundred tuna on a single expedition. By the 1970s, with tuna catches severely reduced through commercial fishing, tautai were the canoe captains who repeatedly had led the community in large fish catches connected with village feasts and celebrations. In the late 1990s, motorboat captains still donate fish catches to community events, but tautai status seems less often discussed and is not usually applied to motorboat operators.

Nanumeans expect sons of fishermen naturally to follow in their fathers' expertise because they will have been able to learn their methods as well as secret family lore about fishing. While magical knowledge has long been condemned by the Tuvalu church, many Nanumeans believe that fishing spells may still be secretly used. Some known varieties of magic are specific to the fish sought; others empower a canoe or net to constant success. Local attitudes to magic are now ambivalent, partly because of Christian influence. Magic is feared to endanger not only the fisherman but also his family. Taboos are numerous and must be followed scrupulously. While several renowned fishermen have come from families long known for their fishing skill, others have developed their own skills by practice and observation, professing to rely neither on inherited knowledge nor family magic. Men's shared fishing culture includes stories about remarkable catches and complicated techniques, which can be guarded or generously shared. In this island community, fishing still provides a focus for men's personal achievement that everyone regards as valuable.

Ocean resources are community property, and anyone resident on the atoll can use them freely. In 1974, most households ate fish on a daily basis (usually locally caught fish or shellfish). Tinned meat or fish was bought only occasionally and chickens and pigs were usually saved for feasts. Though the cooperative store now sells some imported frozen meat, and the local pig population has vastly increased, households in the 1990s still appear to rely on locally caught fish as a key staple of their diets. Nanumeans do not regard marine resources as in scarce supply, though a continuing decline in canoe numbers could result in decreased local access to fish.

At the start of the twenty-first century, Nanumea's economy (and that of Tuvalu as well) stands at a crossroads. Its cash sector continues to grow, bringing new options. Fish, land produce, and human labor can now be sold to make a good living. But the local way of life, since before living memory, has relied on shared resources. As the next chapter describes, people increasingly must make hard choices about who will benefit from their labor. These choices impact not only local living standards but also the cultural values that have long guided Nanumea's atoll adaptation.

ε⋩

## NOTES AND SUGGESTIONS FOR FURTHER READING

### *The Structure of Atolls*

The quotation from Charles Darwin that heads this chapter is from his *Voyage of the Beagle* (1962:458–9). Darwin's theory of atoll formation (coral slowly building atop sinking volcanic peaks) was tested in several expeditions mounted by the Royal Society in 1896–1898 at Funafuti atoll, today Tuvalu's capital. The British scientific team drilled several test bores and eventually reached a depth of 1,114 feet without reaching bedrock. The costly, breakdown-plagued effort is described in a colorful account written by the wife of one of the expedition leaders (David 1899). Sollas (1899) provides a scientific overview of the effort and Rodgers and Cantrell's (1991) recent assessment is useful. Darwin's theory was finally verified in 1951 independently by British and U.S. teams. The British used seismic surveys at Funafuti and Nukufetau to demonstrate that the carbonates (coral remains) had a depth of 1,804–2,493 feet (Rodgers 1991). That same year a U.S. team reached volcanic bedrock at Eniwetok atoll in the Marshall Islands after drilling through nearly a mile of coral (Wiens 1962:85–6; Engel 1962:xviii). Information on atoll structure and ecology is available in the long-running series *Atoll Research Bulletin*, published by the Smithsonian Institution. Two excellent early works in this series are Fosberg and Sachet's (1953) *Handbook for Atoll Research*, and Catala (1957). Other key sources on atoll ecological systems are Wiens (1962) and, for Tuvalu specifically, McLean et al. (1986). Rodgers (1991) provides a good overview and bibliography of Tuvalu natural history. Bailey (1977) describes Christmas Island, the world's largest atoll.

### *Land Area and Population*

Our estimates of Nanumea's land area and population density come from the 1973 and 1991 censuses (Bailey 1975; Tuvalu Government 1991a and 1991b). Historical population data is from Bedford, Macdonald, and Munro (1980) and from specific census reports. Newton (1967), using missionary reports primarily, estimates that the Nanumean population was stable at about 650 people in the early nineteenth century (a population density of 430 persons per square mile). The 1991 census, the most recent for Tuvalu, gives Nanumea's resident population as 824, but another 549 Nanumeans were enumerated elsewhere in Tuvalu at that time (primarily in the capital) with several hundred additional Nanumeans temporarily overseas (primarily studying or working as seamen). For an analysis of local population issues see Anne Chambers (1984).

Tuvalu's population density is extremely high compared to most other Pacific Island nations. In recent years, successive Tuvalu prime ministers have petitioned New Zealand (thus far unsuccessfully) for a more open entry policy, citing both population density relative to local resources and the threat of rising sea levels.

### Cognatic Descent

Cognatic descent, prevalent throughout Oceania, is discussed in Goodenough (1955), Firth (1957, 1963), Davenport (1959), and Keesing (1975). This flexible system of assigning property rights and maintaining connections among a wide network of relatives appears especially well adapted to small, densely settled communities of Polynesia. Noricks (1983) describes descent and land tenure customs for Niutao, a neighboring Tuvalu community, offering an insightful life-cycle analysis of landholding estates.

Huntsman and Hooper's (1996) meticulously crafted "historical ethnography" of the Tokelau Islands describes cognatic descent, land use practices, and the interface between village and family in this group of three atolls located about 500 miles east of Tuvalu. Tuvalu and Tokelau share similar cultural origins and ecological constraints, inviting systematic cultural comparison.

### Land Commission and Cadastral Survey

Our source for the land tenure work of the Kennedy Commission is Kennedy (1953). In the mid-1980s, a Tuvalu-wide cadastral mapping project was carried out through a United Nations sponsored program, producing maps of the land plots on each island (Tuvalu Government 1986). Corresponding ownership data was also collected but as of this writing had not yet been published or collated with the maps. Nanumea's set of thirteen 24" x 36" sheets (plus an index sheet) took a full-time surveyor over a year to produce. Accompanying land resource surveys, produced by geographers from the University of Auckland, provide data on vegetation, landforms, and climate for each Tuvalu island. See McLean et al. (1986) and McLean and Hosking (1991) for examples.

### Atoll Water Situation

The atoll phenomenon in which fresh water floats on the slightly denser saltwater, forming a lens shape within a layer of porous rock and sand is known as the Ghyben-Herzberg principle. This was described as early as 1860 by Charles Darwin (1962:457). Fosberg (1965) compares Pacific Island environments as human habitats. See also Wiens (1962:317–26) or McLean et al. (1986) for discussion of evapotranspiration and related processes in atolls. Annual rainfall data is from Tuvalu Government 1996. Mahaffy (1909) describes drought conditions and community response.

### Fishing

Only a few years before our arrival in Nanumea, braided coconut-frond torches, *lama*, were still used as the light source for nightly flying-fish expeditions. Drawings and descriptions in Koch (1961) depict torches, canoes, lures, nets, and other material culture items similar to those used on Nanumea. Tuvalu fishing is also discussed in Kennedy (1931) and Turbott (1950), and a canoe flotilla illuminated by torches is pictured on the cover of Geddes et al. (1979). Michael Lieber's (1994) analysis of Kapingamarangi fishing practices and their link to the community's social/religious organization suggests the central role that fishing practices and beliefs likely played in precontact Nanumean society as well.

# ৵ 6

# Something for All

It is dawn, but barely. The last moments of sleep are slowly replaced by consciousness of sounds: surf on the distant reef and, closer, the swish and flick of the rising breeze through coconut palm fronds. A cock crows nearby, urging sleepers to stretch and rise. In the distance someone begins to sweep. In moments, several brooms have joined in scratching out the morning serenade. The first person to wake feels the indefinable weight of someone's gaze. A boy has been standing just beyond the open, low wall of the house, patiently waiting for someone to stir. "Your fish," he says, handing an enamel dish. Three silvery flying fish are arranged side by side on a banana leaf. I take the plate and carry the fish to the screened cupboard used to store food away from flies. Returning, I hand back the plate. "I am going," the boy announces, using the standard phrase of leave-taking. "Bye," *tofaa*, is the only response given, or necessary.

Field Journal
May 1974

For those of us raised in Western societies, the economic rationality that lies behind aphorisms such as "everyone for himself" or "get yours while you can" is natural. Many of us have deeply held (and realistic) fears that we might not be able to "get ahead" or "make it," that we'll be left behind in a competitive economic rat race where workers constantly must prove themselves worthy of continuing employment. Our worldview rationalizes the comfortable lifestyles of some and the degrading poverty of others as the deserved results of individual merit. We have even invented a word for it: meritocracy. For most Westerners, "looking out for number one" (with a few exceptions made for close relatives and friends), privileging personal desires, and profiting from other people's mistakes are all seen as reasonable economic behavior. As Daniel Pinkwater commented in a National Public Radio broadcast, the "ancient and vital political principle . . . called 'gimmee' or 'where's mine?'" pervades our thinking.

This view, of course, is not altogether foreign to Nanumeans and other Tuvaluans. Having enough income to save for major purchases such as a concrete-block home, a motorcycle, or a television and video player are increasingly accepted as an important goal. But another version of economic reality, quite different from the bottom-line thinking that drives our decision making in the West, also informs Tuvaluan thinking. In Nanumea, the well-being of all community members traditionally has been set above the needs of any single individual. This is a "sharing economy," a long-term adaptation to the demands of a precarious atoll environment, where collective welfare and survival of the entire community are institutionalized as the bottom line. A web of generalized reciprocity pervades relationships, values, and expectations in every realm of local life. Small gifts of fish and other foods flow among the island's households. Nanumeans working overseas send money back to support relatives working at home. People dig deep into their assets to fund communal projects and to honor requests from relatives. Births, marriages, funerals, and feasts intensify the pooling of resources and their dispersal. If these transactions were counted, they would number in the hundreds each day. As resources are shared, people's lives become connected, too. How better to express *alofa* (compassion, love, concern) than by sharing what you have? How better to be sure that everyone survives difficult times than by institutionalizing generosity so that it becomes a "natural" part of everyday life?

But buying and selling are equally important in contemporary Nanumea. The same people who share fish with neighbors work for wages, pay taxes, buy imported store goods (sometimes local produce, too), and make copra for export. A rational calculation of economic benefits and costs is expected in all these transactions. While a century of Western contact has made Nanumeans familiar with money and market principles, it has also increasingly posed dilemmas. Should community members profit from each others' needs? Can differences in wealth be tolerated? Can people run small businesses and still meet traditional obligations to neighbors and kin? How will the community continue to function when institutionalized generosity has been replaced by family self-interest? These questions arise from the clash of two opposed economic value systems, exemplifying the gulf separating the logic of sharing from the logic of market exchange. Individual by individual, family by family, and at the community level, too, Nanumeans are struggling to find workable compromises to bridge this gulf and appropriate ways to integrate money transactions into local life.

❧

## CATEGORIZING EXCHANGE

How do Nanumeans think about exchange? Do local categories separate transactions of calculated benefit from sharing? As table 2 affirms, these two spheres are indeed served by a very different vocabulary. The category termed *fehuiaki* or *huihui* ("exchange") includes balanced, impersonal transactions focused on obtaining a material good. These can involve buying and selling through monetized market exchange (which Nanumeans term *togi*) or negotiated trade or barter (*taui*) in which equivalent returns are specified. The opposite category of *kai fakatahi* (literally "eating as one") can be translated as "sharing" in English. These transactions highlight sociability and compassion rather than material gain or narrow economic rationality, and include "gifts" (*meaalofa*) given in response to recipient need as well as "requests" (*akai*) made to others for assistance.

Exchange categories are not neutral labels applied dispassionately to economic activities. In all societies, economics and values are tightly interdependent. Exchange is always morally charged, rich with connotations and ethical imperatives, many of which are tacit parts of local worldview and cultural expectations. Steeped as most of us are in the impersonality of the market exchange tradition, it seems reasonable to think of exchange as primarily about the transfer of goods and services. From this perspective, behaving economically implies setting aside personal relationships so that value can be maximized. Wise consumers, we remind ourselves, cannot afford to personalize transactions. Though these assumptions are reasonable in a money-based exchange system, very different assumptions are made when exchange is primarily about maintaining social relationships through "eating as one" from shared resources. Understanding the philosophy and emotional connotations of Nanumean exchange relationships became central to our ethnographic work. But in order to see how exchange defined the contours of social life, we needed to set aside some tacit assumptions of our own.

Our first inkling of dissonance between local exchange assumptions and our own came from problems we had in understanding the Nanumean category of taui, "barter." Taui had been described in other ethno-

Table 2
Nanumean Exchange Categories

| General Terms | fehuiaki or huihui 'exchange' | | kai fakatahi (literally, "eat as one") 'sharing' | |
|---|---|---|---|---|
| Specific Terms | togi 'sale' (market exchange) | taui 'barter' (negotiated trade) | akai 'request' (solicited gift) | meaalofa 'gift' (unsolicited gift) |
| Range of Application | purchase from or sale to a commercial institution | negotiated trade by two parties | recipient asking that an item be given to him for consumption or use | "diffuse sharing" of goods and services on a casual basis at the discretion of the donor |
| | purchase from or sale to an individual | organized exchanges of prescribed items among pairs of group members | | "specified giving" of items and assistance stipulated by role obligations, life crisis ceremonies, and particular circumstances |
| | purchase in connection with auctions and suppers organized by groups | exchanging of complementary food items by children | | "community contributions" made to feasts, group projects and presentations, and any share received from them |

graphic writings about Tuvalu, presented as a common and accepted way to obtain local foods or store goods that were temporarily out of stock. We had used this information in preparing a form that we had intended to use to record data for our planned household survey. We had even duplicated the forms while still in New Zealand and brought copies with us to Nanumea since we would have no way to duplicate them there. When Anne later began to interview households about their economic activities, the form's design proved to be quite useful—with one exception. Nanumeans apparently were not making taui exchanges with each other. The space allotted to taui on the forms either remained blank or was used to record meaalofa gifts, which proved to be more numerous than could be recorded in their allocated space. Nanumeans were not trading but they certainly were sharing with other households. Puzzled by this divergence from a supposedly Tuvalu-wide pattern, and not fully comprehending local economic values, we decided that the category of taui needed more investigation, and we kept a careful eye out for examples of trading.

Meanwhile, our life as honored guests in the Nanumean community went on. We were surrounded, as we had been since our first days on the island, by continuous generosity. Not only had community households fed us staple foods for months on a roster that alternated between the two village sides, but many people also brought us individual gifts of food from time to time. Not long after the taui puzzle had come to our attention, Tagialofa stopped by our cookhouse. We invited her in, and after a few minutes of casual talk as we sat together on our kitchen platform, she carefully took three eggs from the cloth bundle she carried and gave them to us. Anne, receiving the gift, was grateful to her, for eggs were hard to come by. As she voiced her gratitude, she suddenly remembered that just yesterday Tagialofa's daughter had come to ask if we had any extra kerosene, since the store had run out. We had given her a bottleful. The taui mystery reared its head: Were these two events connected perhaps? Could this be an example of taui trade—kerosene for eggs?

Ethnographic curiosity overcoming her politeness, Anne asked whether Tagialofa had brought us eggs because of yesterday's gift of kerosene? "No! Oh no!" she replied, quite shocked. Tagialofa sat quietly for a moment, looking at the eggs still in her hand and then patiently tried to explain. "Alofa [love, compassion] is to be returned with alofa. People are kind to me. I also have compassion for them. Just as with your bottle of kerosene. My daughter came to buy it, but you refused. You would not sell it."

Anne, though embarrassed and aware that her question was making something simple more complicated, pressed on anyway: "So a gift is properly returned with a gift?" "Yes," Tagialofa replied, looking pleased that Anne seemed to have some understanding about the eggs after all.

"Taui trade is 'stingy' (*oge*). When you have things, you should give them to people. *Alofa ke taui mo alofa.* Compassion should be met with compassion." It sounded as though she believed that giving things back to people who gave things to you was fine, but that calculated trading was not. Several motivations seemed to be intertwined in Tagialofa's gift of eggs: compassion for us as *fakaalofa*, "pitiable," strangers in the community; hope that our relationship with her would develop further; recognition that eggs were a scarce and valued food item; and gratitude that we had shared our kerosene with her when none was available to buy. All of these motivations were relevant, but, taken alone, any one of them misrepresented the transaction's cultural meaning.

### SHARING AND COMPASSION

As the record of daily household transactions accumulated in our household survey, we saw that a continuing flow of small gifts, sometimes sent spontaneously by the giver and sometimes prompted by a recipient's request, linked the community's households. Even when two items were "exchanged" within hours of each other, their meaning lay in the wider system of which they formed just a part. Pairing two transactions together and separating them from the rest as if they were a taui trade distorted their meaning. This interpretation crystallized still more clearly one afternoon, while Anne sat with Lepa recording his household's transactions for the household survey:

"We sent over a pot of tea and a plate of rice," Lepa said. "The old woman over there has been sick, you know." Then he paused. Apparently his household had not given any other gifts that day.

"What about gifts other people gave you?" Anne prompted. "Did you receive anything yourselves yesterday?"

"Yes," Lepa replied, used to such inquiries after several weeks of interviewing. "Our neighbors over there gave us some fish. Four flying fish, salted. And a dish of breadfruit soup." Anne wrote quickly as he spoke, and then asked: "So then, with these neighbors, you made a trade. You gave them tea and rice for the sick woman, and then they reciprocated by giving you what they had."

"No," Lepa insisted. "It wasn't a trade. We each just sent over a gift, as we often do."

"But it looks like a trade to me," Anne persisted, intent on understanding why taui was not involved. "Why wasn't it?"

"We weren't trading. We were giving gifts," Lepa asserted firmly. "We felt pity for the old woman and gave her tea. They care about us, so they gave us fish. You might look at your paper and think: 'this is a trade.' It might look like a trade to you. But no, for us who gave them, these things are gifts. Separate gifts that both happened yesterday."

Conversations such as these helped us understand that negotiating a direct trade was repugnant to the Nanumean ethos. Explicitly calculating one's own interest and bringing balance to a transaction was stigmatized as greedy and selfish. Only two stereotypical taui situations, mentioned approvingly many times by many people, escape this condemnation. A social group, perhaps a woman's club, might agree to exchange equivalent plates of food at a meeting or to swap dresses prior to Christmas. In this situation, taui promotes group solidarity, since assigned partners provision each other with whatever the group deems necessary. The second hypothetical example follows this same model. Two hungry children playing together might decide to run to their respective homes and each bring back a different food item. Each gives the other part of what has been obtained, and they both eat together.

Nanumeans object to classifying other gift giving as taui because so much more is involved. While the goods transferred are undeniably important, Nanumeans insist that gift giving and receiving have a more transcendent value: the creation of the community's social fabric. As relatives, neighbors, and community members, people should give and receive, request and assent, not simply because they need things but as expressions of caring and solidarity. The Nanumean ideal is that those with a surplus will voluntarily share with those in need, making meaalofa gifts that take account of people's different resources and meeting any akai requests that others make. While people wholeheartedly love some of the people with whom they share, their relationship with others is often simply conventional sociability. Recipients must be careful not to take unfair advantage of others' generosity. Requests should be made only of people with whom close, supportive relationships are maintained, since the existence of mutual alofa (love, compassion, empathy) in these relationships is the basis on which the request is justified. Someone who makes requests outside the customary circle of neighbors and kin, or who refuses to work to support him- or herself, is ridiculed through shaming gossip and eventually meets with refusals.

The importance of generosity is impressed on Nanumeans from childhood, as an incident involving our three-year-old daughter, Claire, showed us. While her sister Lorien was in school, Claire often spent mornings playing with Una. These two little girls enjoyed each other and got along well most of the time, but one day Claire came home for lunch upset and angry. Una, she said, had said a bad word to her, and she did not deserve it. As Claire related the story, the two little girls had been playing house when Una asked Claire to give her the cup she was using. Claire refused to hand it over, at least not right away, prompting Una to call "Oge! (stingy), oge!" in angry frustration. As even three-year-olds knew, oge is truly a "bad word." Labeling someone as "stingy" calls into question his or her personal character, implying that the person is more attached to material possessions than to other people, faults that will hold the person aloof from normal social relationships.

In the Nanumean view, there is a natural connection between material generosity and alofa. The strength of feeling that relatives (even neighbors and fellow community members) have for each other is not gauged through words but through sharing food, giving away material goods as they are needed by others, lending tools, and providing help. Since caring about people implies these behaviors to Nanumeans, generosity offers only limited status rewards. People who have resources and are generous with them are thought well of, sometimes even praised publicly as role models, but they do not build up a network of indebtedness that serves as economic capital. Instead, other people's needs provide an opportunity for givers to demonstrate that they are good people: that they care about others as anyone of integrity should. The social relationships created through this system of generalized reciprocity are as important as the transfers of material goods.

☙

## Sharing in Practice

Do these lofty sentiments translate into behavior? Our intensive survey of nineteen households over an eight-week period in 1973–75 showed that sharing was pervasive indeed. Households on average each participated in about thirteen gift-giving or receiving transactions per week. Most of these were donor-initiated gifts, with only 13 percent being responses to akai requests. Within the sample, exchange activities were determined by the needs and situations of people within the household, so there was great variation in what was given and received. Transactions were often unbalanced in the short term, with a household being mainly a donor or a recipient for a few weeks, or even a few months. But in a longer time frame, interhousehold flows usually evened out so that households were donors and recipients with fairly equal frequency. Perhaps because of this, we found, recipients did not feel an obligation to "repay" the specific gifts they were given. Instead, they felt connected to the donor and expected to be helpful in the future. Givers did not expect explicit repayments either, though they knew that kin and neighbors would be well disposed to their requests should a future need arise.

*Readying the wedding feast (1974)*

Most food gifts consist of small amounts of common items. Fish play a large role, accounting for more than a third of all the recorded transactions. Typically a few small reef or flying fish, a single larger fish, or just a piece of a large tuna is given. Amounts depend on the size of the catch and the needs of the recipient. Large catches are shared more widely and in larger amounts than smaller ones; large families receive bigger portions. Cooked foods, which households usually prepare once a day in quantity, are also often distributed. A plate of breadfruit soup or a few doughnuts can easily be carried next door. Sometimes delicacies are shared, too: a few roasted noddy terns; a plate of crabs, cooked octopus, or eels; a loaf of yeast bread or coconut bread if someone bakes. Raw food items are given occasionally. Food gifts often respond to specific obligations related to birth, marriage, or funeral feasts or tempt the appetite of someone who is ill. For all households, receiving food from neighbors and relatives adds a welcome variety to the daily menu, which usually features a single starchy dish in ample quantity, supplemented with fish and coconut.

Fish sharing in particular is supported by specific customary rules. Fishermen are expected to offer some of their catch to any adults they meet while they are carrying fish home or unloading it from a canoe, especially if these passersby are women or older men. If the person designated to receive the *pakupaku* gift by the owner of an ocean-going canoe does not take part in the expedition, a share of the fish catch is given to him by the crew. A good catch should also be shared with the pastor. The remainder is divided among crew members. Once the catch is brought to the fisherman's own household, it should be further distributed to any neighbors and relatives who might need fish. The general priority is first to neighbors (a contradiction of Nanumea's cultural prioritizing of kinship); next to close relatives, especially those living nearby; and then to distant kin. Even women who are cooking or cleaning fish reserved for the household should offer some to anyone who stops to chat. A special custom specifies that turtle, a rare delicacy, should be shared even further: a basket containing the full variety of edible parts must be given to any woman pregnant for the first time.

The diversity of relationships involved in these obligations is striking. Even more striking is how regularly fish-sharing obligations are put into practice. In our consumption survey, households without an active fisherman actually ate fish slightly more often than did those with an active fisherman. While fish is highly perishable and few households have refrigerators, Nanumeans could bake or salt their surplus fish for future use. Instead, they frequently choose to share their surplus with relatives and neighbors, as local norms prescribe.

Strategies inform people's generosity, of course. Individuals must decide how best to distribute their scarce resources, which relationships to nurture with gifts, and when sharing expectations must give way to the household's own needs. These strategies are seldom openly discussed, but the survey showed that cultural expectations for sharing were so numerous and extensive that people sometimes were forced by economic reality to make hard decisions. Fishermen using throw nets along the leeward reef, for example, sometimes decide simply to avoid situations that might test their generosity too severely. We were told that when household needs for fish were high, a reef fisherman might stash his catch in the bush and then walk home empty-handed. Later, a boy with a bicycle could be sent to retrieve the fish, wrapped inconspicuously in a sack. Precautions like these are the exceptions that prove the rule. If being labeled "stingy" were not a significant stigma with real power to harm personal and family reputations, no one would need to be so careful in deciding when not to share.

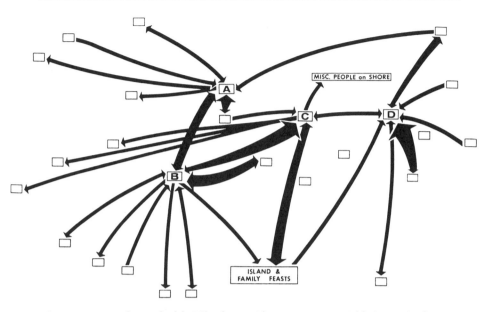

**Figure 5    Interhousehold Gift Flows.** The narrowest width is equivalent to 1 gift transaction, the largest to 5. The spatial positioning of the houses is relative to each other in general distance.

The constant flow of gifts through the community links households together in what Niko Besnier has called "an economy of affect," a description that aptly evokes the intertwined economic and social importance of gift giving in Tuvalu. In figure 5, the connections among four sample households during the week of July 16–22, 1974, are illustrated by the flow of gifts between them. All the households gave and received gifts from several others, but their specific connections (and their motivations) were determined by each one's particular socioeconomic situation. For example, Household B was making special presentations associated with first pregnancy to Household C, since their recently married daughter now lived there. The head of Household D was elderly and ill, prompting relatives such as a son living nearby to send food over to him. Households C and D are very distantly related, so it is not surprising that few gifts flowed between them, especially since both also have active fishermen. If they lived further apart, these households probably would not share much at all since carrying gifts of food across the village without an explicit reason seems ostentatious.

Diffuse sharing obligations distribute resources through a community as effectively as commercial exchange (and certainly more equitably). Our survey showed that food gifts received by the four households in figure 5 provided 20 to 25 percent of all the food their members consumed. In 1973–75, the amount of food transferred within the community by sharing was about equal to the amount households purchased at the store. Maintaining this network of food gifts has "insurance value" for households' economic security. While the store will dispense goods only to those who have money to pay for them, a generous family can count on help from relatives and neighbors should difficulties arise. Better still, they will find a wide base of support when they interact in wider village activities.

૨૭

## THE LOCAL COOPERATIVE STORE

Nanumea's single cooperative store is the focus for most of the island's monetized exchange. It is one store in a system of island cooperatives developed in the 1930s throughout Tuvalu and Kiribati by the colonial government. At first, Nanumea's two village sides each ran separate stores, with small stocks of irregularly received merchandise. In 1946, they combined into a single, better-supplied community store whose decisions were overseen by a local committee assisted by a national "parent cooperative." This same organization continues successfully in Tuvalu today, with outer island stores linked to central management and warehouse facilities that provide economies of scale in ordering goods and organize shipment to outer islands. The cooperative's original goal of promoting economic development and reducing exploitation by outsiders seems to have been well met. In Tuvalu, the store's profit-sharing orientation fits with the community's emphasis on cooperation, and its existence has undoubtedly protected Islanders from more exploitative forms of commercial exchange.

But though the store "belongs" to its shareholders, in Nanumea it is seen as a government institution rather than a community one. Any resident can purchase a membership share, costing $14 in 1974. About three hundred shares are currently in existence, about half of them used regularly. Members receive a yearly cash bonus on the value of all their transactions with the store, not only on their purchases but also on any sales of copra or local produce they make. Transactions are recorded in a ledger along with the customer's membership number, and customers receive a small receipt. Members with fully paid-up shares receive their bonuses in cash (and usually spend them immediately on store goods). For shares not fully paid up, or where no one comes to collect the bonus, it is added to the share value. Bonus rates, set annually by the cooperative administration, have ranged up to 6 percent of the value of transactions in good years. At present, the cooperative store plays a conservative role in island society, discouraging through its own success the development of individually owned businesses, which are, in any case, culturally problematic.

On our first visit to the store in June 1973, we found a line of some thirty eager customers filling the doorway and stretching down the path outside. Most of the waiting customers were women, but there were a few older men, too. A crowd of children played nearby. Those waiting in line carried metal basins, pots, or plastic tubs. A sense of expectation and excitement lent an air of festivity to the occasion, for the monthly ship had recently unloaded its cargo and buyers were eager to see what was available. As the line moved slowly forward, people chatted and joked, watching eagerly as each new customer emerged from the dim recesses of the store, their heavy basins of rice, flour, or cabin crackers dotted with a selection of small tins and packets. Many purchasers needed help to carry home whole tins of cabin crackers or entire sacks of rice or flour.

We learned the next day that in this one afternoon the store had sold out its entire newly arrived stock of cabin crackers (fifty large tins) and that only ten sacks of rice remained. Flour and sugar also had come into short supply. Apparently the store had been completely out of all these foods during most of the previous month, and the cargo our ship had brought was only a disappointingly small portion of the manager's order. The island's kerosene supply was also running out and would have to be rationed.[1] With the next ship's visit at least a month away, and its cargo unpredictable, Nanumeans with money were eager to buy store goods while they could.

Only later did we realize how unusual this scene of eager buying was. On most days, the doorway of the store was empty of waiting customers. Those who did trickle in purchased only small amounts for their household's immediate use. On outer islands like Nanumea, money is in limited supply and people must maintain a restrained balance between

---

[1]Shortages of any staple cause economic disruption to the Nanumean community. But in this society, where most adult men and 30–40 percent of women smoke tobacco, any break in tobacco supply is felt with special intensity. Such a nicotine drought (*oge baka*) was in progress during our visit in 1996. Young and older adults alike joked about raking around under mats in their houses and in the gravel outside to look for old cigarette stubs, made locally from pandanus leaves and chopped tobacco. When cake and stick tobacco finally became available again, tobacco (jokingly referred to as *te ola o Tuvalu*, "the life/sustenance of Tuvalu") was strictly rationed. Tuvalu's high level of tobacco use undoubtedly undermines local health. The United Nations Development Programme's *Report 1999* urges smaller Pacific countries like Tuvalu to make antismoking campaigns a central feature of all future health improvement efforts.

their desires for imported goods and their ability to afford them. The island's century-long connection to the world market economy has brought it only limited control over external aspects of its economic system and inflows of cash and goods. Nanumeans understand that local crops and fish are more predictable subsistence sources than store goods—which are sometimes plentiful, occasionally nonexistent, but always expensive for local household budgets. In the 1970s, many people were concerned about becoming too dependent on the store. But by the 1990s, these concerns had dissolved into a memory, for the most part, and basic store foods had become accepted staples in local diet.

Nanumea's cooperative store is housed in a modest cement-block building with a metal roof, built on an outcrop jutting out into the lagoon near the middle of the village. When the store is open, sticks prop up its heavy board shutters, letting some light into the dim interior. There is a waist-high counter not far from the door, bare except for a large register book in which purchases are recorded. Behind the counter, shelves of cans, bottles, and small store goods line the back and side walls except where another small door enters the storeroom behind. This is where the unopened sacks and boxes of merchandise are kept. Kerosene and drums of gasoline are stored in a detached shed some distance away, where they are hand pumped from drums directly into customers' bottles or fuel cans.

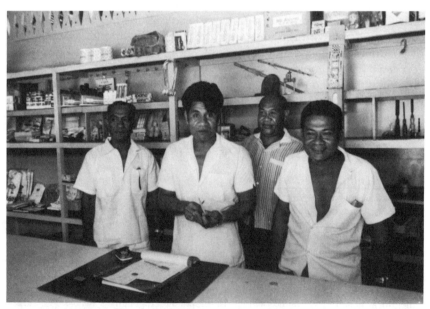

*Nanumea's Cooperative Store and employees: Alesana, Sosemea, Tuia, and Tefono (1974)*

The store buys handicrafts and local produce (such as dried fish, toddy molasses, coconut oil, handicrafts, even occasionally live pigs) for resale to visitors and local residents. Copra is stored in a separate building nearby. Copra sales have long been a key source of income for most households, but the amount of copra produced fluctuates due to a variety of factors that will be discussed later.

In addition to basic staples, the store also stocks a wide variety of goods, ordered several cases at a time as the store manager deems appropriate. Corn flakes, cookies and crackers, chewing gum, packets of hard candies. Canned fruit, sweet cordials to mix with water, custard powder, instant coffee, powdered milk, tea. Canned corned beef, mackerel, sardines, Vienna sausage. Bolts of cloth, thread, needles, school notebooks, pens, pencils. Mantles for pressure lamps, a few spare parts for bicycles and bicycle tire repair. Talcum powder, cologne. The goods available vary continuously and customers can never be entirely sure that the item they hope to purchase will be available. Sometimes there are surprises—perhaps tiny bottles of lemon extract, deodorant, baby lotion, or vacuum-sealed cans of rolled oats. The store does not sell alcoholic spirits, but beer is sometimes available, depending on current local ordinance. Most often, Nanumea is a "dry" community, except for sour toddy.

Because the cooperative store is the focus of buying and selling in the community, its annual sales volume provides a useful gauge of local income levels, including both local wages and remittances sent home by relatives working overseas. Most recently, from 1993–1996, store transactions have totaled about A$350,000 per year. About A$20,000 of this consists of local produce purchased by the store but the rest is sales of imported merchandise. This purchasing level averages out to nearly A$400 per resident annually. Twenty years ago, in the mid-1970s, Nanumean store transactions totaled only about A$55,000 each year (an average of A$55 per person). In the early 1980s, sales volumes of about A$135,000 were typical. Nanumeans as a community clearly have more access to money today than in the past, a trend that holds true nationwide. As will be discussed toward the end of this chapter, their relative buying power has also increased.

An isolated store like Nanumea's requires astute management from its manager and store committee, who must decide credit policy and ensure that everyone pays for what she or he gets. These responsibilities can be difficult ones in a small, kinship-based community where money is in chronically short supply. The store manager must also have a good sense of what community members want to buy and must time orders to fit with the schedule of the single ship that serves all of Tuvalu. Bagged foods such as rice and flour are perishable in an equatorial climate, making purchasing decisions even more difficult. Supply problems in the main warehouse in Funafuti and cargo limitations on the inter-island ship often result in orders for bulky items (rice, flour, sugar, bicycles) or highly flammable gasoline going unfilled.

૨ક

## DILEMMAS FACING ENTREPRENEURS

When the 1974 water shortage finally ended, Nanumeans found themselves with an abundance of coconuts, and income from copra production soared. People felt optimistic and prosperous, and many told us of ideas they had for starting small businesses. Restaurants or bakeries were often mentioned as possibilities, as were raising extra chickens or even some root crops for sale. None of these enterprises had materialized by the time we returned to the community a decade later, even though many Nanumeans had shopped in privately owned stores in the capital, and the national government (in cooperation with overseas aid agencies) had been offering loans and small business advice in the hope of promoting outer island economic development. By 1996, though, private businesses were beginning to appear in Nanumea. Some motorboat fishermen were regularly selling their catches. A few small stores and one informal bakery operated from village houses. Some women regularly sold local cigarettes made of chopped tobacco (called Irish Cake) rolled in prepared pandanus leaves. One man had obtained a small business loan to import a pool table and another family had invested in a freezer and generator, selling ice, Popsicles, and cold water. Most Nanumeans, however, were still ambivalent about personal profits derived directly from the needs of their relatives and neighbors.

Entrepreneurial activity is an issue with which Nanumeans have been struggling for a long time. Doing business appears enticingly profitable but is fraught with cultural dilemmas. Following a pattern common throughout the Pacific, most small businesses do not last very long. In a typical instance, two brothers set up a small store on Nanumea in the mid-1960s using $400 in savings. They sold imported foods, locally baked goods, hard candies, and soap, ordering their stock directly from Fiji by telegram and timing their orders to coincide with the voyages of government ships. They accepted either money or coconuts in payment. By the end of their venture, they were making an excellent profit of about $90 per month, in addition to the store items their households consumed directly. The brothers paid several employees to make copra from the traded coconuts and to bake bread. But after about nine months, the men said, they began to "lose interest" in the enterprise and closed up shop soon afterward. Even though they had made a practice of sharing food with many relatives who dropped by at mealtimes, they felt that their relationships with other community members were strained by envy. By contrast, a small business founded about the same time by one of the women's groups was a resounding success. The women sold fishhooks, soap, and perfume for over a decade without incurring hostility or envy. The difference, apparently, was whether the profits benefited the wider community or only a few people.

An older entrepreneur with economic ambitions encouraged by years of overseas employment also faced cultural pressure. He invested nearly $2,000 in a generator and a movie projector, ordered films directly from Fiji, and ran shows on Nanumea as often as three times a week. He charged ten to twenty cents for admission but allowed elderly people and young children (as well as some people from what he termed "poor families") free admission. He reportedly made a good profit in spite of mechanical breakdowns and shipping delays until he finally lost his projector in a boat mishap in the Nanumea passage while trying to relocate his business to the capital. This entrepreneur said he had been surprised by the harassment he received from some younger men who lacked the price of admission. His decision to allow elders free admittance "out of respect," he soon realized, also provided moral support that permitted his business to continue. Entrepreneurs had to be clever, he said, in order to overcome the antagonism that wanting an item, but not having the money to pay for it, often created among community members.

These cases illustrate a key dilemma confounding local entrepreneurial efforts. Small businesses that run in accord with impersonal market principles contradict the central principle of Nanumean culture— relatives and neighbors need to turn to each other for help in solving the problems of daily life. People who share a supportive relationship ought to be able to request what they need, whether goods or assistance, from someone who seems able to help. Assistance might take the form of labor on a building project, aid in an emergency, sharing fish with a household lacking an active fisherman, offering plates of food to tempt the appetite of the sick, offering the use of a needed item, helping make food for a wedding, and so on. People who purport to care about each other must show that they do by helping out if they can. They should look for ways to make a tangible statement of their caring. Not doing so raises questions about the depth of a person's commitment and sincerity. Allowing relatives and neighbors to pay for goods you are selling, or to make loans that require repayment, contradicts these cultural values.

While most Nanumeans still maintain that it *is* better to share fish, chickens, and even scarce store items through normal social networks, many people will purchase what others offer to sell provided they have money. These buyers might complain that the price of a bottle of toddy molasses was higher than expected or the scale used to weigh fish seemed erratic, but they have come to accept monetary exchange as a possibility that offers economic opportunities even as it raises moral dilemmas. The people most enthusiastic about commercial selling tend to be those who have sizable, regular cash incomes from a career government job or who have returned home with savings from overseas employment. The diffuse obligations of reciprocity tend to drain the resources and monthly paychecks of such people. Traditionally, having more has meant an expectation to give more—and to receive less, at least for a while. By following customary sharing expectations, everyone can come out with enough in the end, but seldom more than enough, and certainly not with a nest egg or with more than others have.

For these reasons, commercial exchange between community members is an emotional topic in Nanumea. Some people simply refuse to buy

*Weighing pulaka and taro gifts to the pastor (1973)*

and sell. In the 1970s, Lilo was one of these, an elderly man prominent in church affairs who lived with his wife in a small household, supported mainly by gifts of money sent by children employed overseas. "People who seek to trade are stingy," he asserted one afternoon, as he braided coconut cord while the village drowsed around him in the afternoon heat. "If you have more than you need, you should give it to people." This was standard advice that we had already heard many times before. But we wanted to get beyond ideology to understand how people actually put this value into practice.

"Is trading really no different from selling then?" Anne asked him.

"No," Lilo replied, looking up. "Trading or selling, in both you give something equivalent. It is bad to sell things to people. You should give them." He paused meditatively. Thoughts of his reputation flashed through Anne's mind. A respected village leader, a deacon in the church, a member of the Land Court. Truly a pillar of the community. "My son on Banaba sent me two bags of sugar once," he continued. "The sugar came about Christmas time, when the store had none. People came to me, asking to buy some of it. But I said to them, 'No. I don't sell things. I only help people as they need it.' So I gave away one whole bag. A little bit to everyone who asked," he finished, smiling, clearly still pleased by the memory of his generosity.

Most Nanumeans who start up small businesses have spent years as wage earners, often overseas, participating in market exchange activities. They have had some practice in limiting the help they give to relatives and the contributions they make to community projects, and tend to allocate more of their resources for the needs of immediate family members. They provide the community contributions that are stipulated, but they have individualized economic goals, too. Their overseas experiences have led many of them to rethink their approach to economic decision making and their commitment to traditional sharing obligations. Nanumean society has, of course, been impacted by the Western monetized economy since earliest contact over a century ago. In the last two decades, however, market exchange has increasingly come to offer a possible new answer to the age-old question of how best to lead a good life, both economically and socially. But it is only a tentative answer, one that may ultimately undermine traditional social expectations and weaken community solidarity.

ॐ

## GROUP SELLING

Commercial activities sponsored by a group avoid the moral dilemmas and practical problems that plague individual profit-making ventures. Choirs, women's clubs, and even the two village sides periodically hold

*A women's group makes thatch for sale (1973)*

auctions or "suppers," often combined with a dance, as fund raisers for their activities. Some women's groups also make thatch or mats on special order. While all of this involves buying and selling, Nanumeans see these groups as working for the well-being of the community, so this type of commerce is not censured. In fact, group business activities are valued by Nanumeans. They provide needed funds for community projects, create enjoyable public festivities, and help equalize access to money across the island. Families with money can purchase what they need and want, while those who would otherwise be hard pressed to meet the required donation have a way to earn it.

Clubs and groups usually raise funds by assigning a standard contribution (ranging from $5 to $100) to each member, payable by a specified time. Holding an auction or supper is a popular way of raising the required sum. At an auction, people may offer such items as bottles of scented coconut oil, rolls of thin pandanus leaves to use as cigarette paper, head wreaths, hard boiled eggs, salted fish, plates of cooked taro, breadfruit, papayas, bananas, raw taro, or coconut molasses candy. Small imported goods such as tobacco or rolled smokes, matches, or embroidery thread can also be sold. Suppers typically feature complete meals, enough to feed a couple of people, in freshly woven coconut frond platters or baskets. In a community without restaurants or fast food outlets, these go quickly.

Transactions at auctions and suppers, however, are not governed solely by supply and demand. Prices tend to be determined by social considerations instead. Identical items sold at the same auction may fetch radically different prices and there is really nothing like a "going rate" for anything. One reason for this is that those who are known to have regular access to money are expected to pay more than others. These are, after all, community fund-raising events. People who recently have received money from an overseas relative should also be generous. Another factor that skews prices is that some bidders are interested in bidding only on items offered by a particular individual, usually a relative, intending to help that person raise his or her specified contribution. Members sometimes bid on their own items, too, in order to attain the price they desire if other bids are lacking. The item's price at least will be credited toward their required donation. If the item is not perishable, it can be offered again at the next auction when public demand may be greater.

People are encouraged to spend money at auctions and at "island night" dances by their festive atmosphere. Young people especially value these diversions as a break from everyday routine. Since group money-raising activities are very labor intensive, those directly involved in the fund drive (and their households) work almost full time for the event. The scale of many group efforts is massive. In the late 1980s, the community renovated the island's Protestant Church, calling home a Nanumean who lived in Australia to be the project engineer and contractor. The church was renewed from the cement foundation up, with an elaborate stained glass window and a new bell tower added. Total cost of the project, accomplished entirely with volunteer labor, was about A$500,000, raised by contributions from Nanumeans at home and off the island through innumerable fund-raising events. More recently, fund-raising has focused on a new pastor's house and compound. This project began to be discussed as early as the 1960s, but it languished until the early 1990s when Nanumeans suddenly raised over A$25,000 in less than a year. At the same time, Nanumeans in the capital contributed to the huge campaign to build a new church for the Fakkaifou neighborhood. This was completed in 1998, at an estimated cost of nearly half a million dollars.

Money-raising efforts such as these tap into Tuvalu-wide and international networks. Fund-raising coordinators write letters to all overseas Nanumeans, wherever they live, pulling in contributions from far beyond the local community. Assessments are levied on each family (often on each worker and each service club member, too), and heavy social pressure is applied, making contributions more a requirement for community membership than a voluntary donation. Those living from wages overseas or in the capital can find the levies economically devastating. But even in periods without a major fund-raising effort, Nanumeans spend a considerable portion of household earnings on gifts and contributions. In 1973–74, a period without any building projects, Nanumean households were giving about 20 percent of their very slim monetary incomes as gifts and contributions, the remaining 80 percent being spent on store purchases or locally produced items. The proportion of income going to donations would be much higher during a major fund-raising drive.

ટ●

## HOUSEHOLD STRATEGIES FOR MAKING MONEY

Beyond purchasing store goods, Nanumeans also need money to equip schoolchildren with basic supplies and provide a simple uniform of a blue shift or shorts. Each adult between the ages of eighteen and fifty-four must pay an annual personal tax of $4, and there are also license fees for bicycles, motorcycles, handcarts, small businesses, and dogs. Land taxes are also required. Taxes are used to maintain government buildings and purchase equipment like a tractor or catamaran, which benefits the community as a whole. A household of moderate size and assets would need several hundred dollars per year to pay taxes and fees. Altogether, locally resident Nanumeans paid a total of $3,000 in local taxes in 1995. Most households also contribute to the routine expenses and special projects of the Tuvalu church: the pastor's salary, maintenance of church buildings, various annual drives, and competitively organized fund-raisers. People of other religions need to support their worship activities as well. In view of all these monetary obligations, Nanumeans' keen interest in obtaining a cash income is not surprising.

Four possibilities for obtaining money are available on Nanumea. A household can gather coconuts, extract and dry the flesh, and sell it to the cooperative store as copra. Second, household members can sell local produce and handicraft items either to private buyers or to the cooperative store (and since 1995, to the fish cooperative). Third, a few government jobs such as teacher, nurse, policeman, telephone operator, or island clerk are available. And finally, households or individuals may receive gifts of money from relatives working elsewhere in Tuvalu or overseas, sent back through a system of telegraphic orders and faxes to the central Tuvalu bank in Funafuti and then on to the island. Some of these possibilities are more lucrative than others, but all have inherent limitations of some sort. Because of this, most households rely on multiple money-making strategies. The possibilities that are pursued at any point in time depend on the skills and energies of household members, as well as on their land resources and the external economic situation.

## Copra

Copra production, introduced to Tuvalu well over a century ago by traders and missionaries, involves hard work. First of all, the nuts must be laboriously collected from among the brush, creeping vines, and fallen palm leaves that form the understory on bush lands. Then either husked or unhusked (when they are twice as heavy and bulky), they must be transported back to the village for processing. The most distant land parcels are usually the least used, so it is from these out-of-the-way land holdings that extra coconuts can be collected to make copra. Until the community purchased its tractor and trailer, coconuts were carried home in small bundles by bicycle, on a handcart, or loaded onto the platform of an outrigger canoe. These methods all require considerable effort and cooperation among household members. Now that the tractor and its Island Council driver is available for hire (for four cents per minute in 1996), several hun-

*Lilo's copra dries in the sun (1974)*

dred nuts can be transported home at once, though labor is still needed to collect and load them. Once the nuts are brought home, they are split open and the firm white meat is cut out of the shell in segments. These segments must then be sun dried for several days, protected from hungry animals and also from sudden rains and night-time dampness, lest they mold.

Earnings from copra are limited by households' land resources and by their subsistence need for coconuts. Families must plan ahead to be sure they will also have nuts to eat and feed to their pigs, taking account of the constant possibility of drought and the inevitable loss of some immature coconuts to rats. Since copra income depends on surplus coconuts, households with a lot of productive bush land or a low resident/land ratio are best able to use this income source. But in years of reasonable coconut production, most village households usually make some copra for sale.

After World War II, Nanumea produced an average of about twenty-seven metric tons of copra annually through the 1980s, though production falls to nothing in drought years and has occasionally soared for short periods. The price paid to local producers is set by the Tuvalu Copra Board based on demand for copra on the notoriously fickle world market. Copra prices fluctuated between two cents and six cents per pound in the 1970s and 1980s but have recently attained more attractive levels, rising to fourteen cents per pound by 1993, increasing again to twenty cents per pound in 1997, and to thirty-six cents per pound in 1999. Board policy tries to stabilize copra prices by setting aside a portion of copra revenues from good years to support prices in bad years. Greater price stability (and higher prices, too) makes copra a more attractive and reliable source of household income.

Coconut is the only local crop with current export potential, and it makes an important contribution to Tuvalu's balance of payments. Agriculture department employees have long conducted research aimed at increasing copra exports, including trials for optimal palm spacing and nut selection as well as rat eradication programs. When the copra market entered a long-term depression in the late 1980s, this single-minded focus on maximizing copra exports became too limited. The Tuvalu Coconut Traders Cooperative (TCTC), newly formed to market Tuvalu's coconut crop overseas, began searching for ways to diversify coconut exports in forms other than copra. A trial container of unhusked coconuts was sent to New Zealand in 1995, and there is some hope that New Zealand's increasing number of Polynesian migrants might provide a market for regular exports of fresh coconuts. Satisfying New Zealand's strict quarantine regulations for plant imports, however, may be a difficult hurdle to overcome. At about the same time, the TCTC began producing coconut oil on a relatively large scale, using a commercial expelling operation in Funafuti.

Meanwhile, back on Nanumea, people found another way to use their surplus coconuts when the copra market collapsed in the late 1980s. Since coconuts are the main item in local pig diets, having extra coconuts available allowed pig production to soar. Not only are pigs useful for local feasts, but the cooperative store also added a freezer so that pork could be exported to the capital. In 1974, village households on Nanumea raised an average of only four pigs each (though the few households located outside the village averaged more). The 1991 census found that the island average had skyrocketed to twenty pigs per household. This enthusiasm for pig raising, we saw, was continuing unabated in 1996. Many households maintained several separate feeding stations in the bush areas of Nanumea Islet, including the Matagi area. The pigs were allowed to root freely in the bush but were fed a daily ration of household slops and chopped coconut to keep them relatively tame and accessible. Their foraging was denuding ground level vegetation throughout much of the main Nanumea Islet, a change not perceived locally as problematic. With copra marketable again, it will be interesting to see whether households return to using their surplus coconuts for copra or use them primarily for feeding pigs. Regardless of the choice made, the island will certainly continue its export of unhusked nuts to the capital, where they find a ready market among wage earners and for oil production.

### Local Sales

Both the cooperative store and the women's handicraft center purchase locally made items such as coconut molasses, salted fish, scented oil, dancing skirts, woven mats, canoe models, and shell necklaces. Some of these items are sold to occasional visitors on the island but most are sent on to the capital for marketing. These items are also made for their own use by most households, and the low prices offered by handicraft-buying organizations limit people's interest in production for sale. For example, the durable *papa* mats that are used as floor coverings in every household take at least two days of effort to weave, not counting the time-consuming gathering and preparation of materials. In 1974, these mats brought producers just $.71 each. Though the 1996 price had risen to $5.50 to $9.00 (depending on quality), this was still regarded as a poor return on the labor expended to make them.

Fish sales provide more attractive levels of household income. People understand that motorboat fishermen need to purchase gasoline and spare parts and that they, unlike canoe fishermen, cannot fish for free. Selling some of the catch allows the owner to continue to provide tuna and other large, deep-sea fish, which community members enjoy eating. In 1974, fish caught from powerboats sold for about $.25 per kilo live weight (normally $3 to $5 per fish). In 1996, the price had risen to $1 per kilo, an increase that approximates the inflation rate during the interven-ing period. Demand for these desirable fish typically exceeds supply, so only buyers first on the scene are successful in purchasing them.

From 1995 to 1998, powerboat fishermen had an additional outlet for their fish catches. A fish market initiated as an Australian aid project bought yellow-fin and bonito tuna for salting and processing into tuna jerky. The market was owned by the community and run by the Island Council, which hired several workers to process the fish and do the book-keeping. The dried fish produced was shipped out to the capital intended for export, but marketing was difficult and the business had not yet made a profit by our visit in mid-1996. Nonetheless, this fish market provided a more impersonal way for powerboat operators to sell their fish. In 1996, there was some local discussion about developing this enterprise into a profit-sharing cooperative for the fishermen and processing workers. By 1999, however, overseas marketing efforts had not been successful and the market was suspended.

Though selling fish is now a common occurrence in Nanumea, expectations rooted in the community's sharing-based economy still make these commercial transactions problematic. People know that every sale of fish, even when justified as covering fuel expenses, erodes tradi-tional obligations to share fish widely with relatives, neighbors, and peo-ple like the Tuvalu church pastor, for whom the community as a whole takes responsibility. Fish always finds willing buyers—but a subtle discon-tent is often apparent in comments some community members later make. "That fellow would sell fish to his brother!" someone might remark disparagingly when a fisherman's name comes up in conversation.

These issues are not new. Tuupau's debt a century ago, as well as similar cases in other Tuvalu islands (chapter 4), demonstrate the clash between local values and Western economics. For fishermen, profit-ori-ented business practices often vie with traditional obligations, creating personal dilemmas. In 1975, for example, two brothers returned from a night's canoe fishing outside the reef with a spectacular catch: about one hundred rainbow runner (*Elagatis bipinnulatus*) weighing three to five pounds each. With far more fish than their household could use, the brothers detoured to Lakena Islet to give fish to the households scattered along the shore. They arrived home with only about sixty fish. Deciding that fifteen of the largest would meet their own needs, they debated about what to do with the remainder. Finally, one of the household's young women was sent to sell them in the village. She was told to charge only $.10 per kilo, a fraction of the going price, and within twenty min-utes the catch was sold. This low price reflected the men's doubts about whether the fish should be sold at all. They lacked the usual excuse of gasoline expenses to justify the sale, but they had shared with neighbors and kin, met their household's needs, and still had a surplus. They believed it was better to share fish than to sell, but their catch had been more a matter of luck than design. Lacking other income sources, they needed the money the sale would bring in. Their solution to the dilemma was to meet sharing obligations first, then set a low price and send a child to do the selling.

Today, Nanumea's transition from a sharing economy to a commercial one continues. As a result, powerboat operators must make some hard decisions in their fish sales. Which relatives, if any, should be given gifts of fish? What about neighbors? The pastor? Some people coming to buy will be kin: Should their money be accepted? Should sales on credit be allowed, and, if so, how aggressively should debts by those promising to pay "tomorrow" be pursued? Should some debts be pursued but not others?

Each fisherman must devise his own answers and compromises. Some will remind themselves that giving away fish is now sometimes ridiculed as a lost opportunity. Those who have borrowed to purchase a boat and motor need to consider their loan repayment obligations. Continuing the traditional practice of inviting bathers in the vicinity of their boat's docking place to eat raw fish, a delicacy appreciated by everyone, may salve the conscience of some. Others may decide to divide their catch, allocating a portion to sales and a portion to sharing—and perhaps decide never to chase up the debts that drag on unpaid. Some relatives who come to buy fish may be given it instead, at least occasionally. None of these strategies is entirely satisfying, either for the boat owners or the wider community. Partly in response to these dilemmas, the dozen or so active motorboat fishermen founded a Nanumean fisherman's association in mid-1996, intending to formulate a policy regarding credit sales to relatives and neighbors.

Similar dilemmas are involved in akai requests, too. Traditionally, people have felt able to ask close relatives or neighbors for help or for use of items they need. Distant relatives can also be asked for assistance though this involves greater social risk, since being turned down can be shameful even when the refusal is plausibly explained. Recipients, on the other hand, often feel both aggrieved and shamed if they sense that the donor has complied unwillingly. Because of these considerations, most people are careful to make akai requests only of those who are likely to compassionately accept them.

As local sales have increased, the distinction between requests and purchases has become fuzzy. Requests can be made more widely than in the past, provided that one offers to purchase the item requested. An impersonal buyer/seller relationship becomes a fallback, cushioning differences in the commitment people feel for each other. This strategy has become especially familiar to people raising large numbers of chickens and pigs. Should an animal be needed for a family feast, community members know where to ask to buy one. The difficult decision of whether to sell the animal or to make a gift of it, if that is more appropriate, is left to the owner. As local sales become an accepted possibility in Tuvaluan life, people must find ways to reconcile traditional expectations that relatives and neighbors should help and share with each other, with small business opportunities.

Traditional healers and canoe builders should receive something in recognition for their help, but items given to these specialists are thought of as gifts (meaalofa) rather than as payment for services. Canoe builders are customarily supplied with food on the days they work since construction keeps them from their household's normal subsistence tasks. Traditional medical practitioners are usually given gifts such as cloth, clothing, or amounts of substantial food only for lengthy curing ceremonies. A plate of food to carry home, a meal shared with the patient's family, or some tobacco is usually sufficient reward for minor massage or herbal therapies. People turn first to their close relatives for healing skills anyway, so this help is easily incorporated into wider sharing networks.

### Wages and Employment

Wage employment opportunities have long been scarce in outer island communities like Nanumea. In 1973–74, only 12 (8 percent) of Nanumea's 145 households relied primarily on local salaries to meet their subsistence and cash needs. An additional 15 to 20 households (10 to 15 percent of the community) received some supplementary income from wages. The 1991 census showed a continuation of this same pattern, with only 11 percent of Nanumea's economically active population having paying jobs. Employment opportunities are limited in the capital, too, with only about half the adults classed as economically active there actually employed. Networks of generalized reciprocity extend the benefits of employment income widely, but the fact remains that wages and employment provide the primary subsistence base for only a limited number of households.

Salaried positions such as teacher, nurse, store manager, radio/telephone operator, government administrator, and meteorological observer are relatively well paid, but all require years of overseas education. Community-financed jobs, including police orderlies, health aides, office clerks, and store assistants, usually paid no more than a dollar per hour in 1996, and many of these are part time. (In the 1970s and 1980s, the prevailing wage was one dollar per day.) Casual work occasionally becomes available in connection with government projects but seldom lasts long. Local public officials such as Island Council members, Magistrates, or Land Court members receive a few dollars' compensation for the long meetings they attend, but these token amounts are more like pocket money than salary. If either of the island's two members of parliament are appointed to a cabinet post in the government, they are paid substantial salaries of several hundred dollars per month. Opposition MP's receive a salary only when Parliament is in session. As elected officials representing the community, all members of parliament are expected to be generous, especially when they return home. These expectations easily can deplete members' resources.

Salary earners regularly purchase store goods such as sugar and starchy foods (flour, rice, cabin crackers) as well as canned goods, condiments, and drinks (coffee, tea, cordial, milk powder). Since everyone on Nanumea can use ocean resources, all households eat local fish whether they buy it from powerboat fishermen, receive it as gifts from relatives, or catch it themselves. Workers who are not Nanumean lack access to land and thus to coconuts and root crops unless they become connected to a local family. Some households activate relationships with close or distant kin; others develop new adoptive relationships with a coworker. In either case, resources flow both ways. This may explain why the 1991 census found that half of all Nanumean households had access to a wage income though only 10 percent of economically active adults held jobs.

### Remittances

Nanumeans working overseas have brought (and sent back) goods and cash to relatives at home since the earliest contact period. By middle age, most men have spent some time working overseas, most often in the phosphate mines of Banaba and Nauru, in the administrative centers of Tarawa or Funafuti, or on ships. In the 1970s, over six hundred Nanumeans were living overseas or on other islands in Tuvalu, a number that has grown to more than a thousand today. Many of these people are away on short-term employment contracts and will soon return, but some have moved semi-permanently to the capital or overseas in connection with work (as well as education, medical services, or the bustle of this urban environment).

Nanumeans appreciate overseas work both for the income it provides and the travel opportunities it offers, and people overseas are still assumed to be connected to the community. While they are away, absentees write letters home and (most importantly) send gifts of money to their relatives. They are also expected to contribute toward community fund drives. These remittances sent home by relatives are currently the most important source of income throughout Tuvalu. During 1973 and 1974, remittances brought in about $25,000 annually to the Nanumean community, increasing to $42,000 in 1980–83. By 1995, remittance levels had quadrupled to $160,000 yearly. As will be discussed in the next section, this represents a significant increase in real income. The largest and most regular remittance sums have always been sent by workers on the phosphate islands and on ships, all of whom receive room-and-board allowances in addition to wages. Urban workers must provision their own households and cope with much higher costs of living and usually send less home.

Every household would like to be able to rely on regular remittances sent home by a relative overseas. In 1973–74, about a third of Nanumean households actually achieved this goal, a proportion that the 1991 census shows continuing in the 1990s. Sending money home has been made quite easy. Workers usually arrange that a designated sum be deducted from their pay each month and forwarded to specific relatives. They can also send additional sums via telegraphic money order (*telemo*) in order to help relatives cover expenses for Christmas, the annual May gift to the pastor, weddings, or funerals. Overseas workers usually set up savings accounts themselves, too. They dip into these to provide the large sums that are needed for major projects such as building a concrete-block house or purchasing a motorboat.

Once remittance income reaches Nanumea, it tends to be spent on food or small purchases at the cooperative store and enters household sharing networks. The names of telemo recipients used to be posted outside the radio office, and though this is no longer done, social expectations that remittances and other money gifts will be shared remains strong. Because overseas contracts usually last only one to three years at a time, workers stay connected to their families. Most households find that remittance income waxes and wanes.

When overseas workers return home, they usually bring their savings plus a wide range of consumer goods intended for their own use and to share with relatives. On the first evening home, their female relatives traditionally bring new floor mats (*kapau* and *papa*) and are invited to join in a feast of imported food: corned beef, rice, and cabin crackers. In the next few days, the worker and his family share out food, cloth, clothing, and small household items. Sewing machines, bicycles, outboard motors, and aluminum boats are rarely given away outright, but relatives will expect to use them as needed in the months to come. A week or ten days later, a public feast in the community hall honors the returned worker. A final contribution to the community fund is expected at this feast, often accompanied by tobacco, matches, and chewing gum to be distributed to all present. The amount of money given is announced during speeches following the feast, and a generous donation confirms the social standing of the worker and his family.

ià

## Changes in Cash Income

Nanumea is directly connected with the global economy. Changes in the levels and sources of the community's cash income have profound effects on local economic life. Table 3 presents our best estimate of recent economic trends, using data drawn from telemo receipts, copra export records, and household survey data. These figures, as well as the level of local store

Table 3
Nanumean Income Levels and Sources, 1970s–1990s

|  | 1970s (1973) | 1980s (1980–83) | 1990s (1995–96) |
|---|---|---|---|
| Resident Population of Nanumea | 978 | 906 | 824 |
| **Copra** |  |  |  |
| Annual Production, metric tons | 23.60 | 26.60 | .28 |
| Income to Copra Producers | $1,571 | $5,124 | insignificant[a] |
| **Annual Per Capita Income from Copra** | **$1.61** | **$5.86** | insignificant |
| (% of total income) | 4% | 6% | 0% |
| **Remittances** |  |  |  |
| Annual Remittance Income | $25,030[b] | $42,096[c] | $159,893[d] |
| **Annual Per Capital Income from Remittances** | **$25.59** | **$46.46** | **$194.04** |
| (% of total income) | 58% | 51% | 74% |
| **Wages** |  |  |  |
| Estimated Income from Wages and Official Payments | no data | $35,191 | ca. $55,000 |
| **Estimated Annual Per Capita Income from Wages** | **$16.85** | **$38.84** | **$66.75** |
| (% of total income) | 38% | 43% | 26% |
| **Estimated Annual Per Capita Income from _All_ Sources** | **$44.05** | **$91.16** | **$260.79** |

Sources: 1973, Anne Chambers (1984); 1980–83, authors' field research, Tuvalu Government (1984), and various government reports; 1995–96, authors' field research, and Tuvalu Government (1991a).
[a]Copra production in 1994–96 was low throughout Tuvalu due to depressed world prices. In 1997, prices rose and production has resumed since that time.
[b]mean, 1973–1974
[c]1983
[d]1995

sales discussed earlier, show that annual per capita income has increased markedly over the last twenty-five years, rising from an estimated $44 in 1973 and $91 in the early 1980s, to $261 per person in the mid-1990s.

Do these increases represent an actual rise in Nanumean income levels? Or have these increases simply allowed local income levels to keep pace with inflation? Using the government's estimate of a domestic inflation rate of approximately 10 percent from 1978 through 1983 and estimating half that rate for the 1974–77 period, Nanumean annual per capita income levels appear to have been stable from the early 1970s to about 1983. Tuvalu inflation rates parallel (and are largely determined by) Australian inflation patterns, and the late 1970s and early 1980s were a time of economic difficulties and high inflation in Australia. Thus, Nanumea's average annual per capita income of $44 in 1973 would have had an inflation-adjusted purchasing power of $92 in 1983, nearly identical to the community's annual per capita income of $91 calculated for that period. Although precise inflation data is not available for the period of the mid-1980s to mid-1990s, Tuvalu's current development plan says that inflation rates were "low" during that time and mentions a trend inflation rate of 3.4 percent as "predicted to continue." Based on this trend inflation rate, an income of $91 in 1984 would have had purchasing power of $136 twelve years later. As table 3 shows, Nanumean income estimates had risen much higher than this level— to $261 in the mid-1990s, almost double the predicted inflation increase.

While the income estimates in table 3 are necessarily rough, having been compiled from statistics relating variously to several years, we believe that they accurately depict two important trends in Nanumea's economic situation over the last quarter century. First, real cash income is increasing in the community as a whole. While local produce was still plentiful in both 1984 and 1996, and Nanumeans were continuing to fish and cultivate taro and pulaka, reliance on store foods was clearly increasing. Owning a tape recorder, camera, refrigerator, electronic keyboard, or motorbike has become common, too. Most families now use solar-powered lights or pressure lanterns daily. The tiny, homemade kerosene bottle lamps on which many families depended in the 1970s have disappeared. Our fieldwork impression in 1996 was of steadily increasing affluence and access to imported material goods.

A second important trend involves a shift in local income sources. In the 1970s and 1980s, gifts of money from overseas workers provided about half the cash income available to Nanumeans. By the 1990s, remittance income provided 75 percent of all income. Copra, once the community's routine source of cash for paying land taxes and school fees, had totally evaporated for nearly a decade, making remittance income even more essential.

Tuvalu's national economy is equally vulnerable to external changes and constraints. Since independence in 1978, Tuvalu has coped with unexpected declines in philatelic revenues and copra exports. Since the mid '90s, however, leases of fishing rights in Tuvalu's Exclusive Economic Zone have brought in substantial sums, augmented today by the high-tech opportunities described in chapter 4. As a result, the national economy has been able to rely less heavily on overseas aid donations. The national trust fund established in 1987 to support government programs had a balance nearing A$70,000,000 at the end of 1998, with most of these funds invested overseas. In that same year, interest from the fund totaling A$11,000,000 was fed into government coffers for use at home. While the fund is vulnerable to recessions in Australia and New Zealand, where most investments are made, Tuvalu appears now to have a stable economic base with a diverse array of income sources, all of which support its growing trust fund reserves.

Despite per capita income levels that are very low by world standards, Nanumeans (and all Tuvaluans) live increasingly comfortable, even prosperous, lives. Both Tuvaluans and official development planners alike recognize the crucial roles played by traditional values and a sharing-based economy in sustaining the enviably high quality of local life. Contemporary planning documents specify that development efforts should "build on the strengths of existing social structures and customs rather than attempting to replace them." But "restructuring the economy toward export oriented business investment" is also a high priority development goal, one that will require increased local savings and market orientation. Can Tuvalu's increasing integration into the global economy continue to support traditional social, political, and cultural institutions? An answer to this question can be framed only through understanding the complex interplay linking family goals with community ones and individual decision making with collective responsibilities.

಄

## NOTES AND SUGGESTIONS FOR FURTHER READING

### Currency and Exchange Value
Tuvalu's official currency is the Australian dollar, though some distinctive Tuvalu coins have been produced for local use. The value of the Australian dollar (relative to the United States dollar) has varied over the last three decades, ranging from U.S.$1.40 per A$1.00 (in the early 1970s) to about U.S.$.60 per A$1.00 in 2000. The Australian consumer price index is used to gauge inflation in Tuvalu.

### Sharing and Generalized Reciprocity

Marcel Mauss's (1967 [1934]) *The Gift* is a classic analysis of social connections created through gift exchange. *Stone Age Economics* by Marshall Sahlins (1972) emphasizes the interplay between domestic economics and wider social, ritual, and political institutions, describing a continuum of reciprocal exchange types that parallel different styles of social relationship. For a wry description of the difficulties outsiders can have in understanding generalized reciprocity, see David Counts' (2000) description of his family's exchange experiences in a small village in Melanesian New Britain. Niko Besnier discusses the Tuvaluan "economy of affect" in his book *Literacy, Emotion and Authority: Reading and Writing on a Polynesian Atoll,* describing how letter writing helps maintain an essential flow of gifts and remittances to outer island communities (1995:99). See Anne Chambers (1983) for more information on sharing in Nanumea. Daniel Pinkwater's remarks were part of his NPR commentary on "All Things Considered," August 13, 1999. They can be heard (in "Real Audio") in the NPR archives at: www.npr.org/programs/atc/.

### Substantivist/Formalist Controversy

For half a century, anthropologists have debated whether economic generalizations derived from Western economic models can be applied to small-scale, nonmonetary traditional economies, a debate often referred to as the Substantivist/Formalist controversy. Substantivists maintain that differences in peoples' motivations and cultural values are so fundamental that using Western economic concepts to analyze traditional systems distorts them. Formalists contend that basic similarities underlie all economic systems and that cultural differences are superficial enough to allow cross-cultural economic generalizations to be developed. Wilk (1996:24–41) provides a readable overview of this issue.

### Tuvaluan Commerce

A history of the trade in coconut oil and copra is recounted in Maude and Leeson (1968). Maude (1949) describes the goals and organization of the colony's early cooperative network. A baseline ethnographic description with information on the social context of exchange (focusing on southern Tuvalu) is Ivan Brady (1972). Recent compilations of national economic data are available in the 1991 census analysis (Tuvalu Government 1991b), the National Development Plan, *Kakeega* (Tuvalu Government 1995), and the government's Tuvalu national accounts 1996–1998 (Tuvalu Government 1999).

*Entrepreneurial Strategies and Development*
*Contemporary Pacific Societies: Studies in Development and Change*
edited by Lockwood, Harding, and Wallace (1993) offers case studies
assessing the economic situation in the Pacific Islands today. Articles in this
collection show how migration, remittances, and copra production relate
to various sociocultural and economic constraints. Glenn Petersen's
(1993) account of the way that small businesses are used to create social
capital in Pohnpei, and the different reckoning of business success that this
engenders, may be of particular interest. Western-trained economists typically recommend private sector development as a key part of national economic planning (see papers from the Pacific Islands Development Program
series, such as Halapua [1993] or Pollard and Qalo [1993]). Pollard (1988)
provides a review of changing development approaches to Pacific atoll
economies. Also see our note on economic development at the end of
chapter 9. The United Nations Development Programme's *Pacific Human
Development Report 1999* offers a perceptive comparison of life situations
in societies throughout the Pacific. Our data on tobacco use in Tuvalu
comes from pp. 62–65 in this source, as well as from personal observation.

Inflation rate information comes from Tuvalu Government (1984:5–7
and 1995:34). Our quotation regarding "building on the strengths of existing social structures and customs" is from Tuvalu Government (1995:24);
"restructuring the economy towards export oriented business investment"
is from p. iii.

# ॐ 7

# Family Matters

"I just delivered my mats to my relative's house," Sunema announced one morning as she arrived to work with us. She went on to explain that her fourth cousin was getting married in a few days and all his *tuagane*, even fourth cousins like herself, were contributing them so that the wedding guests could sit in a house completely spread with new mats. Tuagane related through the groom's mother would give one pandanus *papa* mat plus a *kapau* undermat woven from brown coconut leaves. Those related through the groom's father should provide five mats of each type.

After explaining all this, Sunema added reflectively that some of her own second cousins, though related to the groom in the same way she was, were not making any contributions. "Why not?" we asked with some surprise. A complicated story unfolded. A relative of Sunema's second cousin had a long-standing affair with one of the bridegroom's aunts. Several children had resulted and her cousin's branch of the family could no longer think of themselves as relatives of the groom's family. Sunema insisted that having children together made being related an impossibility.

Field Journal
April 1974

161

Nanumeans think of their community as divided into two utterly different categories of people. Some are *kano* or *kaaiga*, "relatives" and "family," people to be trusted and cared for. These are the ones who work to put on weddings, mourn at funerals, sit together at public festivities, gossip at the cistern, and support each other politically, socially, and economically. The rest of the community are nonrelatives: people to gossip about, to compete against, to marry. The common identity that relatives share through land rights, descent, and family reputation also leads them to care a great deal about each other's behavior. If someone is lazy, stingy, or bad tempered, relatives who interact with him or her everyday, year after year, will suffer. Perhaps even worse, the whole family may be stereotyped as being that way, too.

At a personal level, kinship creates wide networks of support for individuals. Spread throughout the wider community, these relationships also create a hidden web of overlapping loyalties, a network of related-ness that crosscuts the structured groupings that dominate public life. The village sides, women's clubs, choirs, feast-related groups, chiefly groups, and other groups all rely on competition to inspire their members' participation. Without the influence of supportive obligations between relatives, intergroup rivalries easily could degenerate into factional conflict and threaten community unity.

☙

## NETWORKS OF KIN

The Nanumean ideal is to have many relatives. People connect themselves to both their mother's and father's families, tracing ties to cousins of their grandparents—and beyond. Personal kinship networks of several hundred people are common. While relationships among past generations partly determine the extent of kin ties today, contemporary residence choices, disputes, and romantic liaisons are also important in strengthening some potential ties and weakening others. Most people see themselves as related to a large proportion of the community. When they use the word kaaiga, "family," Nanumeans primarily mean the wide networks of kinship that include close and distant relatives alike.

Fourth or fifth cousins are definite "relatives" even though these people are usually not seen as "close kin." Because this is true in every generation, the cohesion of a kinship network depends especially on relationships among its elderly members. Grandparents of one's own fourth or fifth cousins are themselves second or third cousins. The great-grandparents of one's fourth cousins are first cousins. As long as some of these elderly relatives remain alive, they will expect their descendants to behave as close relatives should. Typically, they will find it impossible to think happily of their own grandchildren marrying the descendent of a relative whom they themselves have helped and cared about their whole lives. In the Nanumean view of kinship, no definite boundaries exist for relatedness. Relatives are potentially everyone to whom a genealogical or adoptive connection can be traced, a vast network of diffuse and specific relationships.

Only the sober realities of daily living pare this ideal down to a manageable group of kin. Maintaining supportive relationships over generations can be difficult. Personal dislikes or unresolved arguments can weaken relatives' involvement with each other. Land disputes, especially, can make it awkward to interact. On the other hand, many specific obligations (some of which will be described later) encourage relatives to defer to the ideology of kin solidarity, putting aside any negative feelings they might have. Ultimately, the basic rule governing Nanumean family life is clear and simple: To *be* a relative, one must act like one. Weddings, funerals, squabbles, and daily village life itself all provide situations that test relatedness. Everyone knows that a relative who refuses akai requests, who does not contribute mats and root crops to a wedding, or who gives public support to the other side in a dispute is tangibly demonstrating where his or her loyalties lie. Relatives should enact the value they place on relatedness through caring behavior.

Knowing this, people judge the extent of their relatives' reciprocal feelings by their actions. This reciprocal attachment between kin is called *fia kano*, literally, "wanting to be related." Love, compassion, and sympathy, the complex of positive emotions that Nanumeans term alofa, prompt gifts and assistance, proving that a desire for relatedness is really there. But a sad fact remains. Only some of a person's many potential kin relationships can ever be fully recognized. Against the background of Nanumea's boundless universe of kinship, fia kano presents an elusive ideal that will escape some relationships. Interaction by interaction, some distant kin are defined as relatives—and some are shown to be no longer kin at all.

ह•

## CLUES ABOUT FAMILY RELATIONSHIPS

In every society, the words used to name relatives provide clues about kin relationships. Which relatives are basically similar? Which relationships are distinctive and likely to be marked by special responsibilities or behavior? Patterns in the terms that are used reveal the cultural expectations of relationships. As figure 6 shows, the kinship terms used by Nanumeans are based on a "generational" or "classificatory" logic. The same term is typically applied to relatives across a particular generation, effectively classifying them as "the same" even though their genealogical links to the given focus of the kin group (usually termed ego) may be different. Thus, a granduncle or grandaunt is referred to by the same term as one's grandmother or grandfather. The terms for siblings embrace cousins equally, just as the words for one's own children or grandchildren are applied to

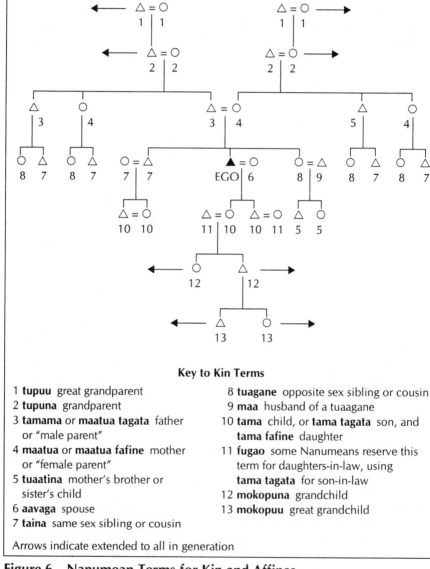

**Key to Kin Terms**

1 **tupuu** great grandparent
2 **tupuna** grandparent
3 **tamama** or **maatua tagata** father or "male parent"
4 **maatua** or **maatua fafine** mother or "female parent"
5 **tuaatina** mother's brother or sister's child
6 **aavaga** spouse
7 **taina** same sex sibling or cousin

8 **tuagane** opposite sex sibling or cousin
9 **maa** husband of a tuaagane
10 **tama** child, or **tama tagata** son, and **tama fafine** daughter
11 **fugao** some Nanumeans reserve this term for daughters-in-law, using **tama tagata** for son-in-law
12 **mokopuna** grandchild
13 **mokopuu** great grandchild

Arrows indicate extended to all in generation

Figure 6    Nanumean Terms for Kin and Affines.

the children or grandchildren of one's cousins or siblings, too. Within these generational groupings, gender differences (not genealogical distance) provide the only basis for regular distinctions. Fathers are differentiated from mothers. Siblings and cousins of the same sex are referred to differently from those of the opposite sex. Relative age (older/younger) is not differentiated in Nanumean (or Tuvaluan) kinship terminology. The numbering of kin terms in figure 6 is designed to show the patterns through which generation and gender define Nanumean kin relationships.

A classificatory kinship system like this emphasizes the social equivalency of whole generations of people and masks differences in their biological relationships. English kinship terminology systematically distinguishes nuclear family relationships from more distant ones. By contrast, Nanumean kin terms supporting a wide circle of relatedness do just the opposite. They create a structure obliterating differences based on distance. Of course, being able to distinguish biologically closer relatives from more distant ones is sometimes important. People need the ability to refer to a sibling as different from a cousin, for instance, or to differentiate their mother from their aunt. They do this by adding *tonu*

*Funeral wake for Make (1974)*

("real," "true") to the classificatory term. Many times at weddings or funerals when we were clarifying who was related to whom, we would be told that an older relative was a *tupuna*, a term denoting a kinperson in the generation above father or mother. Since this term could refer either to a man or a woman, and could be an actual grandmother or grandfather as well as one of their brothers, sisters, or distant cousins, we quickly learned to inquire further, using the qualifier tonu. "Is it her tupuna tonu ("real tupuna"), or her *faka* tupuna ("classificatory tupuna")?" The relationship would then be explained: We would be told, "My mother's mother was her sister" or some other specification.

Exceptions to this classificatory pattern point like neon signs to special relationships and distinctive obligations. The *tuaatina* bond between a mother's brother and sister's child (term number 5 in fig. 6) has this exceptional quality. Singled out from all the other "parent" and "child" relationships, tuaatina owe each other great respect and commitment. They are expected to help each other as needed or requested, regardless of the hardship or danger involved. An older tuaatina, for example, might be asked to supply the costly gold ring a groom needs to wed, or to provide refuge should his nephew or niece quarrel with other family members. Traditionally, tuaatina fought for each other if arguments escalated to a fight, and gave support for marriages that went against parental plans. In one celebrated example from 1970, just a few years before our first stay in Nanumea, two despairing lovers made the ultimate protest against their families' refusals to allow them to marry. They stole a canoe and put out to sea. The young man's tuaatina accompanied them on this voyage to almost-certain death. In Nanumea, tuaatina relationships are privileged like no others.

We couldn't help but wonder what social pressures encouraged the tuaatina relationship to develop as an institutionalized part of Nanumean culture. Does this relationship solve some structural problem in the local kinship system? We puzzled over possible answers to this question. In traditional times, could close links with mother's male relatives have counterbalanced the patrilineal emphasis of the kopiti system? Would help from men of another kopiti provide an extra buffer of safety in an emergency? Might violent confrontations between kopiti have been defused by crosscutting tuaatina obligations among their members? By connecting people closely to their mother's family, did tuaatina relationships allow the cognatic ideal of Nanumean kinship to be realized despite the patrilateral slant provided by other aspects of island kinship? Answers to questions like these are tantalizing—though functional explanations can never be proven definitively true. But an institution receiving as much cultural emphasis as tuaatina must serve some social function, we thought.

British anthropologist A. R. Radcliffe-Brown's classic analysis of the structural logic behind the mother's brother institution proposed one answer. Drawing on cultural information from several African societies as well as from Fiji and Tonga in the Pacific, he suggested that institutionalizing a relationship with maternal relatives (especially where these relatives' nurturing role was stressed) would complement the influence of powerful patrilateral groupings, reinforcing the bilateral structure important in kinship-based societies. But this explanation assumed that a complementary linkage with the father's sister would be needed to balance the institutionalized relationship with the mother's brother. Though formal respect relationships with the father's sister are indeed found in some other western Polynesian societies (notably the high islands of Samoa and Tonga), such a relationship is not distinguished in Nanumea. Here a person's father's sister is classed as a "mother," no different from any of the other women in the generation above oneself. But Nanumean kinship does demarcate a special relationship with one particular type of very distant "father's sister," the *matua ofo*. This special relationship involves a complementary balance between matrilateral and patrilateral kin relationships that is exactly what Radcliffe-Brown's analysis would expect.

The maatua ofo or "volunteer mother" bond connects a woman with the child of one of her distant male cousins, giving a close tie to people who otherwise would be only distant kin and intensifying economic relationships among relatives who are connected patrilaterally. (This kinship term does not appear on figure 6 because the relationship is much more distant than the diagram includes.) Nanumeans say that the maatua ofo relationship is unique even within Tuvalu, and that the customs associated with it contribute to their distinctive cultural identity. Just as its name implies, a woman voluntarily initiates the maatua ofo relationship herself by bringing gifts to the newborn, customarily a bottle of kerosene to a baby's birth to heat the newborn's first bath water. Often another small gift such as a towel, some diapers, baby soap or oil is given, too. Young unmarried women are most suited to take on the volunteer mother role because they are responsible and knowledgeable caretakers but have not yet become preoccupied with their own children or running a household. Older women and even school girls may offer their services as well.

If the infant is a much-awaited first child, several women may gather at the birth in implicit competition for this role. Island regulations limit maatua ofo to just one, but when two or three women eagerly show up at the birth to volunteer, the baby's relatives will sometimes decide to let all the "mothers" share the role, each taking a week in turn, so that no offer will have to be refused. Even if no maatua ofo rush with kerosene to

*A maatua ofo carries her "child" home from the birth clinic. The mother is second from right (1974)*

attend the birth, the relationship is so important in later life that someone will offer her services eventually, even if her connection to the child differs from the ideal. An unusual case, in which the infant's birth severely embarrassed its father's relatives, illustrates how important Nanumeans feel it is for each child to have a maatua ofo. When the nurse attending the birth realized that no relatives of the child's father were going to come to volunteer, she declared that her own daughter would be the maatua ofo. Although no one present could trace the exact genealogical connection, the nurse knew herself to be a distantly related "mother" to the child's father. Her own daughter was thus a distant cousin of the baby's father and therefore eligible—but since she was only three years old, the nurse herself performed the daily duties involved in the role. The nurse told us that pity for the newborn prompted her offer, which was gratefully accepted. Had she not volunteered, someone else probably would have done so eventually since leaving a child without maatua ofo support for life is unthinkable.

Maatua ofo relationships create economic links among distant patrilateral kin. In contrast to the diffuse expectations of help-as-needed among most relatives, volunteer mothers and their children's families have specific and balanced exchange connections. The maatua ofo role can thus offer economic benefits to the "mother"—though there are costs to her, too. The economic value of the maatua ofo role becomes apparent in the eager attention paid to creating these ties with children born overseas. On our return to Nanumea in 1984, before we could even set foot on shore, our daughters were swooped up by "volunteer mothers" as soon as the ship's boat neared the beach. They were taken home by them for a meal and presented with sleeping mats. This is the usual reception for the returning children of overseas workers. Since establishing a link with these resource-rich families can result in economic spin-offs, competition for the maatua ofo role can be intense, even to the point where contenders argue among themselves about who is most suited to take on the relationship.

Especially during the first year of an infant's life, exchanges of food and labor create a dense web of reciprocity. The volunteer mother visits the baby once or twice a day, helping with its care and washing its soiled clothing. The baby's father, assisted by other men in his household, devotes extra effort to fishing so that the maatua ofo can be given daily gifts of fish. Eventually the maatua ofo carries the baby out for its first church service. As it gets older, she takes it visiting to her own household each afternoon, taking with her a large bowl of starchy food prepared by the baby's father's relatives, ostensibly to feed the baby. Specific food gifts also pass between the volunteer mother and her "child" at family feasts marking the child's birth, its first tooth, either person's wedding, and on Children's Day each October. By the time they reach middle age, most women have taken on half a dozen maatua ofo relationships.

Few can easily specify the exact kinship connections with their volunteer children, since these involve distant genealogical ties. However, the regular interaction that volunteer mothers have with the child's family strengthens relationships among all these relatives, making the patrilateral kin group less susceptible to the inroads of marriage. Marriage into the family of a "volunteer child" seems incongruous even though these distant relationships might otherwise offer a reasonable marriage possibility. Of course, given the realities of daily life in a small community, contradictions sometimes do develop between marriage and maatua ofo responsibilities. If a maatua ofo or her close relative marries into her volunteer child's family, she will delegate her role to a classificatory sister whose relationship is not at odds with the marriage. Nanumea's classificatory kinship system makes "sisters" natural substitutes for each other in role obligations and life crisis festivities anyway, so this is not a problem.

૨ર્

## BALANCING RESPECT AND CARING

As is common in families around the world, children owe respect, obedience, and assistance to their elder-generation relatives. Care is usually focused on the parents and grandparents with whom a person lives, but formal respect is hard to maintain with these people, given constant household interaction. Alone together, siblings may joke about a parent's mistakes or complain about annoying habits, something they would never do in public. The more distant a relationship is, the more important obedience and respectful behavior become. We saw this principle clearly at one of the weddings we attended. After the noontime feast and speeches, a string band began to play and an afternoon of dancing started. Sitting with her entourage on the mound of newly plaited *epa* fine mats at one end of the house, the bride watched the dancing. In an aside, her father directed her to invite an older male relative to dance. She sat still, ignoring him. Her grandmother repeated the command but still the bride made no response. When her father's distant cousin made the request again a few minutes later, she acquiesced immediately and was soon dancing. This relative's instruction could not be ignored.

Balance between caring and respect is especially evident in sibling relationships, which are pivotal in Nanumean (and Tuvaluan) life, as they are in Polynesia generally. While sibling terms in English are determined by the gender of the individual referred to (e.g., "brother" or "sister"), Nanumean terms depend on the gender "equation" between the individuals involved (similar or different). Siblings or cousins of the same sex as oneself (the specified "ego"), whether male or female, are *taina*. Those of the opposite sex are *tuagane*.

Relationships between same sex siblings and cousins should be warm and supportive. These people work closely together, relax in each other's company, and joke casually. Taina can discuss any topic. They are expected to help each other meet obligations and overcome difficulties. An especially notable taina role is to provide formal support at funerals. People in the core family of the deceased (for example, on a man's death, his wife and children) will receive a taina supporter to serve as a companion during the mourning period. A same sex cousin for each bereaved family member comes forward, offering whatever comfort and help he or she can provide. This involves staying with the mourner during the first few weeks of grief, usually until the placement of the gravestone in the cemetery ends the formal mourning period. Attending taina sit with the mourners at the wake, assist with changes of clothing, visit and help decorate the grave, sleeping and eating with the bereaved to provide ongoing comfort and

support. Taina support in times of great stress such as this underscores the
key position that taina play in Nanumean society. Taina should be, and generally are, *there* for each other throughout life.

By contrast, opposite sex siblings and cousins, tuagane, must be
polite and reserved toward each other, taking special care to avoid any
topic or action with a sexual connotation. Caring and respect even
beyond that owed to parents and grandparents, Nanumeans say, is obligatory between siblings and cousins of the opposite sex. But relationships
between opposite sex siblings or cousins also involve inherent tensions
because of contradictory values: love and compassion, on one hand, and
respect and avoidance on the other.

Opposite sex siblings who share kin ties and rights to land often
grow up together in the same household and are expected to be caring
and protective of each other. On the other hand, they must also be respectful to the point of deference. People say that "tuagane are more venerated
than siblings of the same sex." They must not be provoked or embarrassed
since "it is forbidden to spill the tears of a tuagane." In particular, sexual
connotations must be avoided in interactions with opposite sex siblings.
Menstruation, love affairs, and bodily functions must be dealt with discretely so as not to cause embarrassment. On account of such precautions,
opposite sex siblings and cousins normally are reserved, protective, and
extremely careful toward each other. They try to show *aava*, "respect."

Special care is required for more distant (i.e., fourth or fifth) cousins. People say that if distantly related tuagane see each other approach-
ing on a path, one should change course to avoid their meeting. In
gossiping and joking, people must also be careful not to relate critical,
embarrassing, or sexually orientated accounts of someone's behavior in
the presence of his or her tuagane. Hearing such things of a tuagane
causes both embarrassment and anger and is regarded as an affront. The
ambiguous boundary between relatedness and marriage is the issue here.
Though distant tuagane are regarded as kin, they are also potential marriage partners, though their kinship relationship would necessarily be
severed should they marry. These conflicting possibilities make distant
tuagane relationships problematic. Attraction is tempered with reticence
and the threat of incest.

Because they are regarded as the "pillars" of the family, men are also
expected to protect the honor of their sisters. If their brother is present,
women will avoid any contact with a potential suitor out of pity for the
brother's potential embarrassment. Brothers thus constitute effective
chaperones, and younger brothers are often sent along with a daughter
who must go on an errand after dark. Women say that the potential anger
of their older brothers (especially if they are locally resident) is something

they explicitly consider when deciding whether to have an affair. As one young woman commented to us, "I have four older brothers, I have to take care!"

The utter seriousness of these respect rules became clear during our first village census when we realized that the presence of a tuagane could cause people purposely to misrepresent (or avoid mentioning) socially awkward facts. As we walked home one morning after visiting a helpful and gracious household, Sunema reminded us to be sure to correct the name given for the mother of one of the household's children. Another woman, she said, was really the child's mother. The presence of his tuagane had apparently prompted the father to name his current wife as the child's mother, even though all present (except us) knew this was not the case. In other households, too, we found that women would often choose not to mention their own out-of-marriage children if a brother or male cousin was present. Talking about children born outside marriage raises connotations of sexuality that violate the respect and avoidance required between tuagane.

Given these respect rules, we began to wonder, how can opposite sex siblings ever manage to share the same household? How do tuagane participate in the chores of daily life without infringing on these obligations? Maintaining a properly circumspect relationship between sibling tuagane actually turns out to be less of a problem than it might seem. After all, subsistence chores are generally sex-segregated. Men and boys fish, climb for coconuts, and take the main responsibility for cultivating root crops. Women and girls cook, weave mats, and care for children. People socialize in these same work groups, too. Furthermore, as in relationships with other relatives, respect is expected to increase with kinship distance. Sibling tuagane must take care not to embarrass or provoke each other as they share household life—but distant tuagane must be so much more careful that avoidance becomes the best strategy.

Given the Nanumean emphasis on widespread kinship, perhaps it is not surprising that Nanumeans do not regard people connected through marriage (in-laws or affines) as relatives. Spouses and their in-laws may develop close, supportive relationships, but these people have been brought together by marriage, and loyalty to their respective kin groups remains most important. Since relatives cannot marry by definition, in-laws must be classified as "not kin." Nanumeans say that in-laws need to be careful in their interactions, since without explicit kinship support to fall back on, there are endless possibilities for conflict. In this context, the lack of terms for affinal relationships makes cultural sense. Parents can refer to their child's spouse (a son- or daughter-in-law to an English speaker) as *fugao* (see term number 11 in fig. 6). There is no reciprocal term for parents-in-law, so people in this relationship simply use first names.

But a close look at the kin terms in figure 6 reveals a mystery that seems to contradict all the rules of Nanumean kin terminology. Notice that the term applied to a woman married to a man's brother is the same one he uses for his own brothers and same sex cousins. Why would an in-law married to your same sex sibling or cousin (your *taina*) also be referred to as a taina? Don't Nanumeans feel that relationships with in-laws are problematic? The lack of terms for most other affines shows the distance at which people in these relationships are kept. While your own taina are vitally important, why should someone married to one of them be singled out with a special term? What about people married to your tuagane? How are they referred to? And most puzzling of all: If kin terms symbolically group relatives together as similar, how could an affine ever be even remotely like a taina? Taina, we were told so many times, are just like each other. The same generation, the same gender. The person married to your taina would have to be the opposite gender from yourself. How *could* such an affine be like a taina?

The answer to this mystery, we gradually realized, probably lies back in time, in the family dynamics of the kopiti era. As Raymond Firth has pointed out, a kin term pattern like this implies that "spouses are sociologically one person." In Nanumea, identity between spouses makes perfect sense from the viewpoint of kopiti relatives. Imagine how a new wife would be received by her husband's siblings. She would enter the family "on the body of her husband," as Nanumeans say, her relationship to kopiti members having no basis other than through being his wife. To the rest of the kopiti, she is identified with her husband to the point that her gender difference becomes insignificant by comparison. Referring to the new spouse as a taina emphasizes the willingness of kopiti members to include the new bride in the family's easy, supportive interaction, providing acceptance that is essential if people are to cooperate in daily household tasks. In the same way, sisters married into different kopiti still need to visit and rely on each other. Being able to relate familiarly to each other's husbands as taina would allow them to interact easily in each other's households, too.

This explanation receives additional support from the term used for the spouse of a man's opposite sex siblings or cousins (that is, his tuagane). These in-laws are referred to as *maa*, a term that combines connotations of shyness, embarrassment, and shame (see term number 9 in fig. 6). Relationships with maa require even greater restraint and avoidance than do those with tuagane. Since women typically go to live with their husband's family at marriage, there would have been very limited contact with maa in the precontact era when people lived in kopiti groups. The affines who normally would have interacted most closely would have been the in-marrying wives of the family's sons, the women termed taina by their husband's brothers and cousins. Their relating together warmly, it seems likely, would have contributed to family cohesiveness.

Widely extended taina relationships serve as a cohesive force throughout the community. Sunema, we found, had many taina throughout the village, some first cousins and a host of others more distant. Because Sunema considered herself Anne's "sister," Sunema's own taina should relate as taina to Keith as well, able to joke with him in a relaxed and carefree way. Early in our first stay on Nanumea, when we did not yet fully understand the great extent to which personal interactions are determined by kinship, we assumed that women enjoyed teasing Keith to test his developing language ability. One evening some of this joking turned toward explicit sexual repartee. Worried that Anne might not understand that the joking was culturally acceptable, even prescribed, Sunema's father, Rongorongo, reassured Anne: "You must not be offended, Ane. This is our custom, for your taina relatives to joke with Kiti." But at the times when Sunema's brothers were present, all joking among taina stopped.

With people's interaction so heavily determined by kinship ties, it is polite to avoid groups where one's presence will inhibit others. One afternoon, Anne was visiting with a newly married couple and some brothers of the groom, all of whom were taina to each other. Sunema needed Anne to clarify something and had been looking through the village for her. As Sunema approached the wedding house, the new bride politely called out to invite Sunema to join the group. Sunema ignored the first invitation and responded to successive ones with excuses: she had to talk to someone next door, she had already eaten, and so forth. Sunema later told us that it would have been most inappropriate for her, as a tuagane (opposite sex cousin) of the groom, to sit with the group. Had she done so, all casual talk and joking would have stopped immediately.

Given the cultural gulf between relatives and nonrelatives, enfolding outsiders within the web of kinship can be useful when other kin support is lacking. Take, for example, the situation of a family working away from Nanumea. Relatives are few but people still think of kinship as the proper basis for caring and support. Two coworkers might become friendly or the children in two nearby families might come to like each other and become constant playmates. The caring relationships that develop between such people are like those that would normally link relatives. By formally acknowledging this, people can be spared the dilemma of treating nonrelatives with the care and concern due to kin. Perhaps because sibling relationships entail specific behavioral rules, these are most often used to formalize relationships with non-kin. Two male friends may decide to become taina "brothers," themselves—or they may proclaim their sons to be "brothers," becoming brothers, too, as an extension of their sons' relationship. Women friends can similarly unite (or two girls can be united by their families) as taina. The relatives of each become involved in the appropriate kinship categories too. Creating kinship extensions like this is described as *hai taina* ("tying same sex siblings [together]"). Family feasts involving exchanges of food and clothing mark these new relationships as serious undertakings. Some of these "tied sibling" relationships endure for generations while others may wither as situations change.

An even more powerful kin bond can be forged by linking opposite sex tuagane. We watched an instance of this developing in Nanumea between the families of two civil servants. One of the wives had gone to another island to give birth among relatives, and her husband had been misbehaving in her absence, visiting girls at night, sending love letters, and getting drunk. Meeting the husband in passing one day, his wife's friend gently remonstrated with him. She told us that she talked "politely, like he was related to me" (he was not) because she felt compassion for his wife and for their coming baby. The next day, the man came to his wife's friend's house to speak to her husband, proposing that he and she become tuagane. After asking his wife, who then checked with her own father, the linkage was formalized by a small feast. When the man's wife returned to Nanumea several months later with the baby, this new tuagane of its father brought a mat to welcome the child just as his other sisters and cousins.

ૐ

## TO MARRY OR NOT TO MARRY

In all societies, marriage arrangements fit with wider social structures. In Western societies, as popular romantic fiction reminds us, individuals themselves bear the heavy responsibility of finding true love. The idea of having a spouse "arranged" by others is strongly resisted by many young people. But where the well-being of wider groupings of relatives is paramount, marriages provide a way to create supportive alliances with other family groups. Marriages may be entered into to gain resources, create politically useful ties, or build support networks beyond a single descent group. In these societies, affinal relationships are seen as valuable extensions of kinship ties. In Nanumea, however, it is useful to think of marriage in another way. Here, it serves to narrow extended families by paring away distant kin from the category of relatives. Marriage splits family chunks off the perimeter of extended families because Nanumeans conceptualize marriage and kinship as opposites. One cannot marry kin, however distant. By this definition, even remote relatives are not appropriate marriage choices. But can this be feasible in a society of just a thousand residents? Isn't the pool of marriageable partners so small that sometimes distant kin must marry? Precisely! The indefinite boundaries of the Nanumean kinship network allow revisions to be made as they are needed. When very distantly related families agree to marriage between their children, they sever their kinship link, too. Dozens of people then rearrange their thinking and behavior toward each other, and those who consider themselves related to both families now maintain their relatedness to only one of them.

Marriage is thus the dynamic element in Nanumean kinship, realigning social obligations and substituting specified affinal roles for the diffuse ones of distant kin. Marriage also narrows kinship responsibilities down through the generations. Families who intermarry replenish the category of nonrelatives as some of their members forego their distant genealogical connections. Since people remain related as long as they *act* related, weddings and other "life stage" festivities involving cooperation among large numbers of relatives provide watersheds that define kinship. At these events, kin ties are enacted (or conspicuously not enacted) publicly. As Sunema's explanation (see the vignette that starts this chapter) made clear to us when she contributed a mat to her tuagane's wedding though some similarly related kin did not, behavior that is not tolerable among relatives breaks kinship bonds. The relationships that were adjusted in this particular case are diagrammed in figure 7.

Tuvalu law is interpreted to allow marriage between third cousins but not between closer kin.[1] Nanumeans, however, continue to feel that it is preferable to marry more distantly than fourth cousins. Beyond a certain point, which varies among families and personal situations, very dis-

---

[1] In the most recent Laws of Tuvalu (revised 1978, Tuvalu Government [1979], Section 29–11), marriage, for women, is specifically prohibited with persons in the following relationships: father, son, father's father, mother's father, son's son, daughter's son, brother, husband's father, husband's son, mother's husband, daughter's husband, father's mother's husband, mother's mother's husband, husband's father's father, husband's mother's father, husband's son's son, husband's daughter's son, son's daughter's husband, daughter's daughter's husband, father's brother, mother's brother, brother's son, and sister's son. The reciprocals of these relationships are prohibited to men.

The particular relationships singled out as prohibited, especially the large number of affines of very different generations, puzzles us. For example, it is not clear whether terms such as "brother" in the above list are used in a classificatory sense (the laws are written in English). If they are, then marrying any cousin still considered a tuagane would be considered incestuous. If the term applies only to the English meaning of brother (male sibling of whole or half blood), then even first cousins would be allowed to marry. We would like to investigate this issue further and clarify the exact definitions for the prohibited relationships.

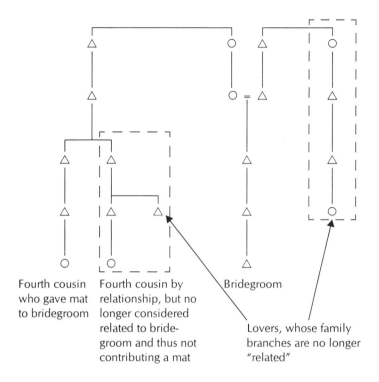

Fourth cousin who gave mat to bridegroom

Fourth cousin by relationship, but no longer considered related to bridegroom and thus not contributing a mat

Bridegroom

Lovers, whose family branches are no longer "related"

Figure 7    Distant Kin Become Nonrelatives.

tant kin make tempting marriage choices. Parents often feel that a distant kin connection makes the relationship with in-laws seem safer and more predictable. They are less the unknown "other." Young people, of course, have a different perspective. Often they can hardly name their genealogical connections to sixth or even fifth cousins. They may not even be aware that connections exist. The people who really care about maintaining distant kin ties are the very old, who may fondly remember their life-long cooperation with their third cousins. Thus the most polite way to decline a marriage proposal is always that of *fia kano* ("desire [to be] kin"): The family prefers to continue being related and therefore must decline the marriage offer. Fia kano is also sometimes invoked to preserve a created kin tie, such as a taina relationship between coworkers.

Although young people are encouraged to state their preferences, most first marriages are arranged by the families concerned. The groom's family usually decides that the time has come for the young man to marry. His relatives hear his choices and evaluate these in relation to other possibilities (always a limited number), considering the women's reputations, their work habits and their temperaments, as well as the social and economic positions of their families. Though young men and women are attracted by personality and looks, they can usually comprehend how important these other considerations are. Possible partners for a first marriage in Nanumea are especially limited since "relatives," nonrelatives who have already been married, and the mothers (but not the fathers) of children born outside marriage are usually ruled out. Once a marriage does occur between former distant kin, the realignment of relationships makes it easy for other marriages and liaisons to follow.

A newly married couple usually comes to live in the groom's parents' household, following a pattern dating back to the kopiti era. This move is understandably difficult for the new bride. Perhaps in recognition of this, one of her close cousins serves as her *uosili*, attendant, staying at her side during the week-long wedding celebrations to ease her transition into her husband's family. The groom's relatives treat the new bride with great respect and politeness, too, and only gradually does she begin to participate in household chores alongside the groom's sisters and other women of the household. Despite their best intentions, though, these women may find it hard to see the bride as anyone but an outsider who now has access to private aspects of their family life. They might worry, for example, that when she visits her relatives, she will gossip about what family meals are like, how much money is spent for what, or reveal current domestic stresses. Because the village is densely populated and many houses are open-sided, people normally try to limit others' knowledge about them. The new bride might potentially deliver up to public scrutiny, purposely or accidentally, domestic secrets that could fuel the mills of gossip and possibly damage the family's reputation. Despite such worries about the loyalty of the new bride, she provides valuable labor power to her husband's household. From the bride's point of view, joining the extended family of her in-laws allows her to get to know her husband gradually. In any case, the extended family orientation of Nanumean society makes it inconceivable for the new couple to set up a separate household of their own. After years of marriage and the birth of children stabilize a couple's relationship, they have greater freedom to move in with the bride's family, if resources are greater there, or establish a separate household of their own.

Most Nanumean men are in their mid-twenties when they marry, with women slightly younger. Before marriage, families take care to chaperone their daughters and explicitly protect them from the overtures of young men. Sons, however, are allowed considerable freedom for sexual "play," so long as they pursue affairs discretely. This double standard for sexual behavior is very similar to the gender dichotomy traditional in Western society. Divorce is seen as both religiously and socially acceptable—but it is a last resort used only if mediation by relatives and the pastor cannot reconcile the couple's differences. Estranged couples usually separate and live with their own kin for some months before seeking an official divorce. Afterward, remarriage is common, especially for men.

Women who are still unmarried by their late twenties commonly decide to have a child. Women say that they need a *tausi* ("caregiver"), a child who can look after them in their declining years. Adopting a child from a sibling or close cousin is a more proper thing to do but this alternative is not always possible. Marriage chances decrease for women after a love-child is born, since marriage to a man not previously married will usually be impossible. Her reputation (and that of her family) may be somewhat tarnished, too.

Since young men are expected to be sexually adventurous before marriage, fathering an extramarital child does not reflect badly on a man's character. However, Nanumean law requires that all children must have an officially recognized father so that they can inherit his land. Should no man claim a child as his own, the Land Court will hear evidence and make a binding paternity decision. The patrilateral bias in local family structure gives the father's family the right to claim the child and to raise it. As a result, despite her hopes, an unmarried mother may not be able to raise her tausi herself. In deciding who should have guardianship of a child in the rare event of a dispute, the court is bound to maximize "the child's best interests," a stricture that allows wide interpretation.

Although marriage is the career traditionally expected for women, there has been a scarcity of marriageable men in Nanumea for decades. Men leave home to work more often than women do and some of them marry overseas or while visiting other Tuvalu islands. Men are also older when they marry, and thus able to choose spouses from a larger pool of women. When relatives do not agree to the marriage plans of sweethearts, or a lover's promises are not supported by his family, women usually are the more vulnerable ones. However, Nanumean women usually do not romanticize marriage. Some single women value being able to remain securely within their own birth families. Many married women look nostalgically back to their youth, remembering that they worked hard as young women but enjoyed cooperating with their own relatives. Single women, those who never married as well as those who have divorced, are the most active participants in women's club activities. Many club members contrast their current "freedom" with the restrictions they would face as wives and assert that they are happy not to be married.

## Children as a Blessing

For Nanumean parents and relatives, children are important beyond the largely personal significance they have come to have in Western industrial societies. They ensure a family's social and economic well-being and its influence in community affairs. Since children represent both labor power and the family's continuation through time, family size and composition are matters about which most people hold strong opinions. If a topic as complex and personal as ideal family size can be simplified into a single number, the "magic number" in Nanumea is most often four: two boys and two girls. This frequently mentioned ideal hinges on two main considerations. First, people are concerned that their children not exceed the family resources available for their care. This leads most couples to consider limiting their natural fertility. Secondly, Nanumeans want to have children of each sex. This consideration is so important that ideal family size ultimately becomes not so much "four children" as it is "two children of each sex."

There are several reasons for wanting both boys and girls. Men need sisters and women need brothers, that is, each child needs an opposite sex sibling (tuagane). Both men and women also need a sibling of the same sex, a taina, just as each parent needs a "replacement" (*hui*) to take over gender-appropriate subsistence chores. Given the importance of money income to family well-being and men's greater employment opportunities, one son is needed to work overseas and send home remittances and the other is needed to stay home to fish, garden, and provide help locally.

Having an opposite sex sibling is particularly important for women because men are the foundation of the family, providing for subsistence goods as well as family leadership. A woman without a brother lacks a secure social and economic basis from which to function in the community. One woman told us that "the problem about not having a tuagane is that there is no one to rely on once your parents are dead. No one to act for your family." Since married women usually use their husband's family's resources rather than their own, and their children will usually inherit mainly from this source, too, a mother's lack of a tuagane has no economic disadvantage for married women in the short term. However, should her marriage fail or difficulties develop with in-laws, a woman will have no strong base of moral support or household to return to. One widowed woman with two daughters explained that she had felt compelled to conceive a subsequent child outside of marriage for exactly this reason:

I wanted to give my girls a tuagane. They have no father [he is deceased] and even I myself wasn't raised with my father. I wanted them to have a place to live always, someone to look after them and to provide men's things like coconut sap and fish.

With a brother, women have "someone to help them in life." Sons take over subsistence and leadership roles from their father, and a woman's children should look to her brother (their tuaatina) to help them in strife or an emergency. Even though the male cousins of their mother will help out, too, her actual brothers are most important as tuaatina. Lack of a sister has fewer economic effects for men. They might sometimes lack mats or other woven objects, but they can get these things without too much difficulty from their classificatory "sisters."

Both men and women also need a same sex sibling since taina are the persons to whom one first turns for help and support. Usually there is no need to seek further. One woman told us:

real taina have compassion (alofa) for each other. First cousins may have compassion or they may not. When their parents grow old and die, in their taina children will have someone they know is willing to help them.

Another woman aptly described the characteristic relationship between taina as "reciprocated love" (*alofa feaalofani*). Nanumeans especially want their taina to help with large work projects where cooperation from many relatives is needed. Since sibling taina share identical genealogical relationships, they have the same role obligations and can substitute for each other in life crisis events. Men have fishing and taro cultivating companions in their taina, and women have partners in cooking and mat weaving. Not only is the responsibility and labor of each individual lessened, but work also goes much more pleasantly when taina share it.

Parents rely on their children to look after them in old age though the help children give their parents begins well before this. Daughters assist their mothers with child care and household chores, at least until they marry and "go to care for their husband's families." But even after marriage, daughters should show alofa to their parents by paying attention to their parents' needs. Having sons or daughters as economic "replacements" for themselves, older people can turn their attention away from family subsistence and focus more energy on community affairs. But, as one woman said about her only son, "One is not enough. If he goes away to work, there is no one to look after me here. If he stays and cares for me, no one earns any money overseas." Another woman described how wise her husband had been to insist that they needed more children than just a single replacement for each of them:

> My husband said no, we need more children than that. He said that if
> we had many children, we might have a smart one who could go on
> to school and get good work. He will be our "road to money." It isn't
> as though we can only raise a limited number of children. Our liveli-
> hood comes from our hands. If we are hardworking we can easily get
> more fish, breadfruit and coconuts to feed more children.

Accepting this argument, his wife went on to have several children. In retrospect, she was glad she did. Most Nanumeans would agree that this
strategy increases family options.

But other parents are concerned that their resources will not be
adequate to meet their children's needs. The island environment is limited and there is little hope for agricultural development or diversifica-
tion. Especially if the many Nanumeans who live away from the atoll are
considered, population pressure could rise to extreme heights in the
future. One woman with eight living children commented that her children would be lucky to get a single piece of land each if the family estate
were divided among them all. Another woman (herself an only child)
described how her husband, coming from a land-poor family, was pleased
that their marriage would allow their children access to her family's land.
(Her husband's own parents carefully explained to us, however, that such
calculations did not always work out in the long term and that it was better to choose marriage partners on a noneconomic basis.) Nonetheless,
concern about the long-term availability of local resources is widespread
in Nanumea. One family with three sons told us that they would try to
arrange a separate niche for each son, one overseas, one on another
Tuvalu island, and one on Nanumea so that their descendants would not
have to compete for the family's scarce local lands.

In this situation, the flexibility inherent in cognatic descent moder-
ates the influence of patrilocal residence after marriage. Children of
daughters are typically "gone" (*galo*) from their mother's family, but they
can use their father's land. They may gain access to some share of their
mother's family estate eventually, if they need it, depending on the needs
of other descendents. Daughters' children will be primary members of
their father's land corporation. Though all children normally "eat from
the lands of their father," it will be sons who normally pass primary rights
in this estate on to their children. In the short term, however, access to
local produce rather than actual title is emphasized for everyone.

People always mention the industriousness of a family's members as
the key to its well-being. Parents who are *maalosi* ("strong," i.e., hardworking) can provide for more children (and do this more adequately)
than those who are *paiee* ("lazy"). As one woman phrased it, "If you are

hardworking, your life will be good. If you are lazy, it will be bad." From this point of view, families with limited land resources simply have to work harder to develop skills that will effectively enlarge their resource base. These can include fishing and cultivation prowess, educational success, and diligence in paid employment. A family reputation for being hardworking will attract desirable marriage proposals, too.

Most people believe that large families are also inherently stronger families. Many children ensure that there will always be people to help with family projects such as house building or preparation for life-crisis feasts. Individuals can rely on their taina and tuagane for support, and parents can be sure of having adequate help without imposing heavily on any one child. "If each child gives just one fish," explained one mother, "the parents will have a lot." People are also explicitly aware that large families have greater possibilities for developing a range of skills among their members. At least one of the children, people say, is likely to be successful in landing a long-term job overseas, and at least one will do well at school. Large families can play vigorous roles in local affairs, too, both because of their labor and voting power and because of the support siblings give each other.

Not all couples approach parenthood with firm goals in mind, and many develop opinions about the most advantageous number of children only after many have been born. In general, however, fertility decision making is optimistic. While people recognize that land resources impose basic limits, they also believe that diligence, resourcefulness, and effort by those who are "strong" (maalosi) can effectively counter these limitations. In addition, because extended families are the basic social unit, a couple's children are neither solely their responsibility nor solely their delight.

Western methods of contraception have been widely available in Tuvalu since the mid-1960s and the nation currently has one of the lowest population growth rates in the Pacific region. Birth control pills, Depo Provera injections, and condoms are currently given out by nurses in the village dispensary. IUDs were heavily promoted in the first decade of the family planning program but are used infrequently today because of their high rates of complications. National family planning efforts emphasize child spacing, using the effective metaphor of well-spaced coconut seedlings. Most couples have used contraception to space some births but further reductions in population growth rates to the level envisioned by current policy will require a more intensive commitment. Specifically, the 1995 development plan seeks to reduce further annual population growth rates from 1.7 percent to below 1 percent by the year 2004 and to reduce the total fertility rate from 3.6 (1991) to below 3.0 in 2004. These fertility reductions are to be achieved by continued promotion of voluntary fertility regulation methods, encouraged by further decreases in infant mortality, by support for education, housing equity, and status improvements for women.

Ironically, until missionaries and administrators banned the practice as barbaric, Tuvaluans enforced strict limits on family size. Nanumean couples were reportedly allowed to have only two children (accounts differ on whether the limit was simply two children or one child of each sex). Additional infants were reportedly suffocated by a relative at birth. Though the severe droughts that periodically threatened the survival of the community would seem to be enough of a rationale for these restrictions, Nanumeans insist instead that the limits were politically motivated. By equalizing the size of families, no group could easily gain a dominant political position. People say that in traditional times before missionary and government influence put an end to "the days of darkness," interfamily feuding continually threatened personal security and community stability. Though the chiefly lineages drew support from a wide power base, strong warriors sometimes played violent roles. Remember how the taro pit wars erupted over a difference of opinion about the location of root crops and how Kalihi was set adrift in a leaky canoe. Large families could wield power and influence denied to small or less cohesive families. Family rivalry must have always been a concern, perhaps especially when years of low rainfall or storm devastation reduced food supplies and the community hovered on the brink of declaring a vaelua division, splitting the community into two parts to conserve resources.

Because traditional limitations on family size were enacted through infanticide, missionaries and administrators unanimously tried to halt the custom. Traditional population control practices, though reasonable at the time, are now seen as benighted and shameful—although the values on which they were based (e.g., community unity and survival, and equality between families) continue to be admired. While people realize the personal advantage of having a large family, most also recognize that their decisions have wider impacts. Maintaining the community's well-being has now become a matter of personal responsibility rather than cultural mandate, like so many other dimensions of life in a democratic society. Decisions supporting family well-being, too, no longer have the fixed reference point of a discrete extended family whose members live as a named kopiti and jointly use the family lands. Families clearly matter on Nanumea. But what forms do family groups now take? In what domestic groupings do people enact the obligations of relatives and make the countless small decisions that shape life today?

𝕾

# HOUSEHOLD DYNAMICS

The Nanumean term *fale* means both the family dwelling and the relatives who jointly inhabit it. With large kopiti groupings now a memory from the past, the relatives who live together in a household form the basic socioeconomic units of local life. Sometimes Nanumeans refer to households as *matakaaiga*, "core family," a focused group of relatives who "eat together" not only in the sense of sharing meals but also in joint use of family lands. Within the intimacy of households, through days of work and days of festivity, people demonstrate (and test) their reciprocal commitment to each other as kin.

Nanumeans typically talk about households as though they had an enduring social reality. Households are identified with particular family estates, especially with the land parcel on which the house is built. The stout forked posts that support the roofs of many houses have been used by the same family for generations, even as new foundations have come and gone. Households are referred to by the name of the oldest member, evoking the personal and family history connected to the life span of that person. It is difficult to leave a family house standing empty. When a worker and his family leave for overseas, usually relatives are asked to occupy their house, even if this diminishes an existing extended family household. In fact, as discussed further below, caretaking for absentees is probably the main reason why household numbers have steadily increased in Nanumea over the last thirty years despite the declining resident population.

Most households experience a constant (and often short-term) turnover in their membership—a continual coming and going of people. During an eight-week survey period in 1973–74, for example, 70 percent of households underwent some change in membership. About half of these changes involved the loss or addition of only one or two persons, but more substantial changes occurred for 30 percent of the households: movements of family groups of six or more persons, reoccupation of an empty house, or abandonment of an occupied one.

These frequent movements between households made our first efforts at a community census difficult. In the early days when we knew only a few people personally, we sometimes enumerated the same people in different places. With the initial census taking many months to complete, moving slowly down one side of the village and up the other, we needed to find ways to maintain the accuracy of our count. We solved this problem by asking Sunema to inquire about the "usual" residents of each household when she arranged appointments for our census visits. Using this information, we could focus our inquiries on the household's core residents, but taking note of the temporary visitors who made their usual homes elsewhere and being careful to count them at their usual homes eventually. This technique resulted in an overly static view of household composition. We corrected for this by recording movements in and out of our sample village households and departures and returns to the island. We checked the accuracy of our censuses by conducting quick recounts of households and their members both in 1974 and 1984. Gradually, we were able to develop a more realistic understanding of household dynamics.

The motives that lead Nanumeans to move between households epitomize the obligations among kin. Funerals, births, and weddings all call for cooperation among relatives, many of whom move in for the duration of the event. This is partly because the work is very intense. People often work long days and far into the night for several weeks weaving mats and preparing food. Socializing becomes an important part of this work. Older children, unmarried people, and elderly women are typically most free to come and care for a sick person, work on a special handicraft project, or cooperate in intensive gardening or fishing. Being able to move to another household also serves as a vital safety valve for personal relationships. Living elsewhere for a while can help people avoid major arguments and give disputes time to blow over. Live-in visits provide variety in domestic routine, too.

Composite figures like average household size are useful for comparative purposes but they mask the great range of variation in local household composition. In 1973–74, approximately 60 percent of households were composed of extended families. Their memberships ranged from three to twenty people and included as many as four generations. Another 30 percent had a nuclear composition, including only people who were actual or classificatory parents and children. The size of these nuclear households showed a large range, too—from three to twelve members. The remaining 10 percent were "fragments"—single adults or idiosyncratic groupings of distantly related individuals.

This variation notwithstanding, census and head count data document a steady decline in average household size over the last three decades. As table 4 shows, Nanumea had ten more households in 1991 than in 1973—even though 153 fewer people lived on the atoll. In 1996, our count found 175 occupied houses, suggesting that household proliferation is continuing. With local population decreasing, average household size has dropped, too. While island households averaged 7.5 persons each in 1968, the average size had dropped to only 5.3 persons in 1991.

Insofar as households are now the community's basic social and economic units, substantial changes in residence patterns must have

Table 4
Nanumean Residential Population and Households, 1931–1996

| Year | Resident Population | Households | Mean Household Size |
|------|---------------------|------------|---------------------|
| 1931 | 770 | 103 | 7.48 |
| 1947 | 746 | 131 | 5.69 |
| 1963 | 1051 | 135 | 7.79 |
| 1968 | 1076 | 143 | 7.52 |
| 1973 | 977 | 145 | 6.74 |
| 1984 | 929 | 146 | 6.36 |
| 1991 | 824 | 155 | 5.32 |
| 1996 | no accurate data | 175 | no accurate data |

Sources: 1931 Government census (Maude 1932); 1947 Government census (Pusinelli 1947); 1963 Government census (McArthur and McCaig 1964); 1968 Government census (Zwart and Groenewegen 1970); 1973 Government census (Bailey 1975); 1991 Government census (Tuvalu Government 1991a, 1991b); 1973, 1984, 1996: authors' fieldwork data

repercussions on the organization of island society. Values and goals will be subtly colored in response to this altered social fabric, too. The 1991 census confirmed that a quarter of Nanumean households had only three residents or less. How can these tiny households contribute the goods and labor specified for community events? When a third of all local households are of the "nuclear" or "fragment" types, does the extended family ideal begin to have a hollow ring? Even though kinship loyalty may demand that people leave an extended family household to caretake a house for absent relatives, don't these smaller living units inevitably narrow kinship horizons? What changes are occurring in the overlapping responsibilities that people feel to distant relatives and to close ones, to family and community, to Nanumea and to wider Tuvalu? In the next chapter, we take a closer look at community organization and the juxtaposition of community and family loyalties.

ã€‰

NOTES AND SUGGESTIONS FOR FURTHER READING

*Notions of Selfhood*

In every society, ideas regarding the nature of the self provide an implicit foundation for personal relationships. Since selfhood is culturally constructed and normally a tacit dimension of culture, most people cannot easily specify or describe it. Cross-cultural analysis has shown that the autonomous, individuated notion of self characteristic of Western society is not universal (see Shweder and Bourne 1984; Spiro 1993). A more sociocentric, context-dependent, and relational type of self is typical throughout Polynesia, including Tuvalu. Anne Becker's (1995) *Body, Self and Society* provides an overview of cross-cultural differences in self-concept as well as an analysis from Fiji. Helen Morton in *Becoming Tongan* (1996) shows how self-concepts underlie child-rearing practices.

### Kin Terms

Raymond Firth's comment that spouses are "sociologically one person" is from Firth (1970:285). His interpretation stresses the links that would be created between a man and his wife's sister(s). The patrilateral emphasis of Nanumean society has led us to focus instead on the connection between a man's wife and his brother(s). These perspectives are complementary, of course. Sibling terms in most Polynesian societies mark differences in relative age as well as in gender. Firth's (1970) comparative analysis shows that a simpler pattern without relative age terms, such as Nanumeans use, is characteristic of societies that are remote and small (in both geographical and numerical senses). He suggests that the more complex pattern of terminology is not needed where the social universe is small and face-to-face relationships predominate. The classic essay by British anthropologist A. R. Radcliffe-Brown (1965, originally 1924) analyzed the structural importance of a special emphasis on the mother's brother/sister's son dyad in patrilaterally focused societies. Rogers (1977) discusses the father's sister relationship found in the Polynesian society of Tonga. Marck (1996) compares kinship terms in a great range of Polynesian languages.

### Traditional Population Restrictions

These limitations are a well-remembered local tradition. They are also mentioned in accounts by early visitors to Tuvalu. Hedley (1896:54) reported that in Funafuti it had been "obligatory to destroy each alternate child" and that women might give birth in the lagoon so that the child would drown immediately. He also quotes early missionary sources (i.e., Gill 1885:27; Newell 1895:609) that described customs from the communities of Niutao where only two children were reportedly allowed to be reared, though the life of an additional child "might be redeemed," and Nukufetau where only one or possibly two children were permitted to live. Missionary George Turner (1884:292) judged that "foeticide and infanticide were common to keep down the population" in Nanumea, with doomed infants "usually delivered in the sea." See also Kennedy (1931:264) and more recently Bedford, Macdonald, and Munro (1980).

## Demographic Trends

The analytical volume of the 1991 census (Tuvalu Government 1991b:35) assesses recent changes in household size, as has each previous census. Fertility trends and their economic importance are also discussed in the most recent development plan (Tuvalu Government 1995:73–75). *Pacific Human Development Report 1999* (UNDP 1999) compares current demographic and health-related statistics for the Pacific region. See also an earlier comparison of five Pacific Island populations by Norma McArthur (1967). Nanumean customs regarding marriage, fertility, and birth are described in Anne Chambers (1986).

# ৯ 8

# Community

A most embarrassing mistake today! We were over visiting next door and conversation turned to the use of imported building materials like cement and roofing iron in place of local timber and thatch. I couldn't help but remember how hot it had felt when we spent the afternoon on another island in its refurbished, metal-roofed meeting house. That building offered a perfect example of the drawbacks of using imported materials instead of local ones, I thought.

Before I had even finished describing this problem, one of the young women interrupted angrily. She reminded me that she was from that community and objected to hearing anything derogatory said about it. I was aghast! I had never thought of her as an outsider on Nanumea and I had certainly never intended to criticize her home island. I was just meaning to praise the comfort and elegant beauty of the open sides, coral gravel floors and pandanus thatched roofs of traditional building styles. We apologized profusely.

Field Journal
October 1974

This incident reminded us how passionately devoted Tuvaluans are to their home communities. This devotion dwarfs the arguments and the petty jealousies that interrupt village life from time to time, encouraging community members to think of themselves as forming a single community, *te fenua*. Conventionally translated as "island," but having the emotional connotations of "homeland" as well, the term *fenua* evokes both an atoll's physical dimensions and its human residents. Attachment to fenua nurtures a sense of pride in community history, achievements, and culture. It encourages a collective determination to excel: to build the most impressive church, to send many children on to education overseas, to maintain the village beautifully. Island loyalty also provides a sound basis for cooperation among community members away from home, as evidenced by the achievements of Nanufuti, the community of Nanumeans living in the capital.

What is it about island life that prompts this depth of loyalty? What values encourage community members to make the behavior choices that bring their ideals of community cohesion into being? What groupings and institutional structures support the island's unity? Clearly there are no simple answers to questions such as these. Nanumea contends, as all societies must, with a tension between cultural ideals and practical realities, between decisions that support collective well-being and those that maximize benefit to individuals and family groups. Nonetheless, island life honors community to an extent found in few other societies. What sociocultural qualities facilitate this? Our analysis points to four interdependent features: the community's overlapping organization; communal interaction based on a single church and meeting house; service expectations for leaders; and values that stress getting along together, both tacitly and explicitly.

ॐ

## COMMUNITY ORGANIZATION

In 1907, according to mission and government records, Nanumeans began to construct the first of their "new" villages. People moved from their old kopiti residential groups to a defined area centered around the church, community hall, and playing field. As we described in chapter 3, the houses built at that time were identical, small by today's standards, and arranged in a closely spaced grid that allowed little privacy. An imaginary line running from ocean to lagoon shore passed through the middle of the church and community hall, demarcating two village "sides" (feitu) which were named Lolua and Haumaefa. Placement of a family's house determined the side to which its members belonged. All households except the pastor's and, in recent years, non-Nanumean government employees, were affiliated with a village side. Gradually, the village sides became the focus of most island-wide activities, serving as moieties, units of complementary opposition.

As competitive halves of the village whole, the "sides" efficiently mobilized labor for village-wide projects, organized community festivities, hosted government visitors, and conducted a range of other activities involving the community as a whole. Ordinarily manifested as friendly competition, rivalry colored all village side interactions and added interest to daily affairs. In the 1970s and 1980s we saw the Island Council ratify its list of communal work projects at an island-wide meeting each year, and then the projects would be divided equally between the two sides. On each appointed workday, the able-bodied members of each village side would turn out in festive uniforms: clothing of a specified color accented with dancing skirts and scented wreaths. With some teasing and laughter thrown in for good measure, each side would then compete to out-build the other as members carried coral gravel for a foundation, helped thatch a building, or built a cistern. Similarly, at the "Big Days" festivities of the New Year, the sides competed at traditional ball games (ano) in a period of feasting and play that lasted several weeks in some years, several months in others.

Longstanding relationships usually link households with one particular village side. Changes can occur if household members have a falling out with side leaders or disagree with decisions about communal projects,

*Worker and family are feasted by the community on their return from overseas (1984)*

but this happens infrequently. Though the households affiliated with a particular side have conventionally been located in its half of the residential area, changes in affiliation do not require a physical move to the other village side. As in so many other areas of island life, rules about side membership are flexible. People who move to another household to help out temporarily do not change their affiliation either. They simply pitch in to help their relatives meet whatever required contribution of labor or goods is needed and resume their normal affiliation when they return home.

As people come and go from the island, the relative balance between the village sides can fluctuate markedly. In 1973–74, our community census showed that Haumaefa side had fourteen fewer households and ninety-eight fewer members than Lolua (see table 5). A decade later, Haumaefa had come to have a majority by four households and fourteen members. This change was due mainly to the large number of overseas workers who had returned recently to Haumaefa, but a few Lolua households had shifted their affiliation due to dissatisfaction with building project decisions, too. Some differences in side memberships are inevitable, but the sides galvanize community energy most effectively when they are in approximate balance.

For the sides' organization to work at all, their constant rivalry must be tempered by goodwill so that slights and irritations do not lead to factionalism. For nearly ninety years, Nanumea seems to have managed this fairly well. In fact, by the 1970s and 1980s, the sides were such an effective structure for village activities that we found it hard to imagine the island functioning without them. In 1994, however, two complicated disputes split the community and effectively crippled the village side organization.

**Table 5**
**Affiliation with Village Sides, 1973 and 1984**

| | Affiliation with Village Sides (*Feitu*) | 1973 | | 1984 | |
|---|---|---|---|---|---|
| | | Number | Percent | Number | Percent |
| Households | Affiliated with Lolua | 78 | 54% | 70 | 48% |
| | Affiliated with Haumaefa | 64 | 44% | 74 | 51% |
| | Not Affiliated | 3 | 2% | 2 | 1% |
| | Total | 145 | 100% | 146 | 100% |
| People | Generally Affiliated with Lolua | 530 | 54% | 448 | 48% |
| | Generally Affiliated with Haumaefa | 432 | 44% | 462 | 50% |
| | Not Affiliated | 14 | 2% | 19 | 2% |
| | Total | 976 | 100% | 929 | 100% |

The original point of contention concerned a "new" religion's right to proselytize. Freedom of religion is guaranteed in Tuvalu's constitution, but the arrival of a Seventh Day Adventist missionary in Nanumea raised community tensions. Some people felt he should be allowed to stay and share his message publicly—but others objected. Nanumea's high chief "settled" the issue by offering the missionary his hospitality, activating a traditional chiefly prerogative to extend support to a stranger caught in a destitute situation, in evocative Nanumean terms to *kopi tana fakaalofa*, "carry the needy one."

The situation soon ramified out to involve other aspects of community governance. The authority of the newly reinstated chieftainship was challenged by the disaffected faction, and then called into question again by a second incident involving the chief's regulation of money-raising activities by the village sides. Alleging favoritism, enough people withheld participation from side activities that community life was almost paralyzed. In 1996, we saw that attendance at community events was poor, and people seemed discouraged that they had not been able to resolve the dispute. Though covert, angry feelings remained strong. People told us resignedly about the failure of mediation efforts by an official government-church-community delegation from Funafuti the previous year. As the dispute dragged on, unsettled for several years, the community struggled to carry on using its existing organization.

Periods of intense community solidarity such as we witnessed during our earlier visits must be part of a longer cycle that includes less cohesive times, too. Disaffection and harmony have probably always alternated in community life. Did similar contention mar solidarity in the late nineteenth century when a small traditionalist faction refused to convert to Christianity? What about the debate that flared in the 1950s over the digging of a taro pit in Matagi? The community's ability to bring its vision of island unity into being has probably always waxed and waned.

Only time can reveal whether the recent dispute will lead to new forms of social organization. It is possible that the village sides have outlived their usefulness and will be replaced by new forms that are somehow better adapted to community needs. But it is also possible that the village sides will weather the current dispute and endure intact. Perhaps the recent factionalism will strengthen Nanumean commitment to "unity of heart," at least for a while. Regardless of the dispute's ultimate effects, a formal reconciliation in May 1999 allowed the village to undertake successful cooperative work projects again, though full healing will inevitably take more time. In February 2000, we heard that Nanumeans had rebuilt one of the church outbuildings as a communal project, though, as Tagisia Kilei put it, "memories of the past four to five years' events are still hanging in the air, fading out slowly."

The tensions precipitating this recent controversy clearly derive in part from forces of modernization and social change important throughout Tuvalu. Personal choice in religion is increasingly emphasized, and younger men (and some women) are taking more active leadership roles in their communities, too. But the current stresses are also fundamentally "traditional" in that they embody a basic tension between authority and egalitarianism that is characteristic of Polynesian culture. Nanumean social life is intensively organized, structured by a vast array of groupings with overlapping memberships. As will become evident, the village sides are just one type of group. The dense social fabric of island life is complemented by a pervasive egalitarianism, especially in political domains. This is a society where high chiefs embody the community good, rather than their own merits, and where individual ambition traditionally has found appropriate expression in collective activity. From this perspective, the dispute's consistent focus on whether competing groups received equal treatment by figures of authority illustrates the inherent difficulty of balancing authority and equality. The community's persistent efforts to find a resolution demonstrate how committed Nanumeans are to the ideal of *lotofenua*, "community heartedness."

One of the enduring strengths of the village side organization is its integration with the local economic system through groups called *fakaua*. Usually composed of several related (but not necessarily neighboring) households, fakaua cooperate to provide whatever specified food contributions are needed for community-organized events. Until recently, each fakaua was linked to one village side or the other. Side leaders would notify fakaua before each event about the type and amount of food each must contribute. Since the reinstatement of Nanumea's chiefly government in the mid-1980s, the reigning chief and his supporting council of elders have taken responsibility for directing fakaua contributions, bypassing the village sides. This system seemed to work well until recently. Each fakaua, regardless of its number of members or resources, is responsible for supplying whatever contribution of food and/or labor is specified. Most larger households can meet the requirement without undue difficulty, but smaller households usually join forces with relatives. In 1996, fifty-one fakaua contributed actively to community events. An additional forty-seven fakaua were listed in the records kept by the secretary of the chiefly council but were not active, typically because some or all of their members were overseas. A few of these latter households were withholding participation because of the recent factional disputes.

Nanumean groups commonly use structured competition as a way to motivate and organize their activities. This was apparent to us almost as soon as we began taking part in community events, because people showed such obvious disappointment if we did not balance our involvement with each group. But the extent to which the community consciously values structured competition as an organizing strategy became even clearer to us during meetings to discuss the planned closing of Nanumea's Catholic school in 1974. An education department officer from the central government had come to Nanumea in order to explain the Catholic school's closure and to reassure the community that its pupils would be accommodated in the government school. By that time, the Catholic school had been operating for about a decade. It had developed a reputation for academic rigor, mainly because one or two staff members initially had been members of religious orders sent down from Tarawa in the Gilbert Islands by Catholic mission headquarters. The sole Catholic family on Nanumea had donated land for the school, but children's attendance was not based on their family's religious commitment. Since pupils from this school could attend the Catholic high school on Tarawa, the community's access to secondary education had doubled. The school had become an integral part of community organization. At the meeting, the education officer heard unanimous protests against the school's closure. One speaker argued eloquently:

> We must have competition. That is why it would be bad to join the two schools together. Now we have the government school and the Catholic school. When it comes time for examinations, everyone concentrates. Each school wants to do best in the exams, to send more students on to secondary school [off the island]. If we had only one school, why would they try? We must have two schools. In everything we need two sides, two groups to join together and compete, to strengthen each other.

The competition praised so fervently by Nanumeans (and other Tuvaluans) has an orientation quite different from the individualistic meanings that this word usually evokes for English speakers. In Tuvalu, paired community groups marshal their energies and resources to outdo their rivals, but the opposing units are emphatically social groups. Individual members' identities and contributions must be submerged within those of the group as a whole. Uniforms, processions through the village, collective work efforts—all declare the shared identity of participants. Structured competition is always yoked explicitly to larger community goals, rather than to the personal ambition of participants.

Structured competition throughout all levels of village organization makes it difficult for any single group to dominate or for any single opposition to develop into enduring factions despite the deep emotional involvement people have with some groups. Two households might be members of different village sides, but some of their members will also be related and others will share membership in some of the same women's groups, service groups, or church-focused work groups. Since none of these groups are hierarchically organized, their crosscutting memberships create a dense web of connections in the community.

The increasing desire of many Nanumeans to live on their own land may pose some threat to community solidarity too. For most people, this means moving outside the village area and building a larger dwelling using imported materials, increasing household autonomy and privacy. People say that living outside the village makes it possible to get ahead economically. Away from the intense interaction demanded by village life, family members can spend more time and energy on projects benefiting their own household, such as raising pigs or chickens to sell. However, all the island's amenities and services are still located in the central village area. As the community's canoe fleet declines, households must increasingly rely on land transport to get about. Where formerly work canoes crossed the lagoon many times a day carrying people to the village or to their lands on the far side, the main transportation today is wheeled vehicles, which have increased markedly on the island since the 1970s. While only 5 percent of Nanumean households owned a motorbike in 1973–74, 13 percent did by 1991. Similarly, bicycle ownership increased from half of the island's households in 1973–74 to three-quarters in 1991. Since households were becoming smaller and more numerous during this period, these percentage increases mean that significantly more bicycles and motor scooters now travel the island pathways. Indeed, in 1996 the Island Council expected to collect taxes on 39 motorbikes and 120 bicycles. Public enthusiasm was strong for building a causeway between Motu Foliki and Matagi so that the islet could be accessed overland and thus be available for house sites. While the increase in bicycle and motor scooter use illustrates the community's greater access to remittance income, it also highlights the abandonment of canoe-based transport.

The desire to live on family land so resonates with kinship expectations that Nanumeans have voiced little concern thus far about the disintegration of their tightly bounded traditional village. Whereas "the village" in 1973–74 meant the areas of Lolua and Haumaefa immediately adjacent to the church and meeting hall, this term refers today to the entire village peninsula—not only the old village area but also the government station at Mataluafatu and even households near the medical clinic at Hauma (see fig. 3 in chapter 2). Place names like Mataluafatu or Hauma are still used to pinpoint a household's location, but they no longer are conceptual contrasts with *fakkai*, "village." By contrast, households across the lagoon in Matagi or along the shore toward Tefaga are said to be located outside, in the *vao* or "bush." The recent conceptual expansion of village boundaries has allowed the proportion of households technically outside the village to hold steady over the last two decades (see table 6). The village continues to be the center of community life, both ideologically and practically.

Table 6
Location of Nanumean Households in 1973, 1984, and 1996

| Household | 1973 | | 1984 | | 1996 | |
| Location | Number | Percent | Number | Percent | Number | Percent |
|---|---|---|---|---|---|---|
| Within Village | | | | | | |
| Area | 121 | 83% | 132 | 90% | 151 | 86% |
| Lakena | 11 | 8% | 3 | 2% | 4 | 2% |
| Other Location | | | | | | |
| Outside Village | 13 | 9% | 11 | 8% | 20 | 11% |
| Total | 145 | 100% | 146 | 100% | 175 | 99%* |

*due to rounding

ଓ

## HEART OF THE COMMUNITY

Two other institutions bind Nanumeans together. Both have spiritual qualities, one overt, the other less obvious. Located at the heart of the main village, both symbolize the community feeling that Nanumeans call lotofenua. The Protestant Church is one of these unifying institutions, and the community hall is the other.

### The Church

The whitewashed cement church with its red-roofed bell tower stands as a landmark on the island, its five stories visible from far out to sea. It is also tangible testimony to a century of religious unity. The church is Congregational Protestant, now a branch of the Church of Tuvalu, a product of nineteenth century endeavors by the London Missionary Society. Membership in this church has long been a requirement for full social acceptance. In 1991, 96 percent of the community considered themselves its members, a proportion that has held steady for decades. The remaining 4 percent adhere to "new religions," as they are termed locally, which include Bahai, Seventh Day Adventist, Jehovah's Witness, and Catholic (listed in decreasing order of membership). Since the capitulation to Christianity in 1922 by the last Nanumean traditionalists, rejection of the community's dominant religion has been interpreted as a rejection of the community itself. People

*Nanumea's newly renovated church (1996)*

who join a "new" religion are regarded with suspicion by other villagers and find it difficult to be active in social and political affairs, though this choice now carries much less stigma than in the past. Tuvalu Church leaders are increasingly advocating an ecumenical tolerance for other Christian religions. In the capital at least, religion is coming to be seen as a matter of personal conscience and "new religion" adherents can remain actively involved in community activities. This change in attitude has been helped along by the growth of "new religions" there: The 1991 census indicated that 13 percent of Funafuti residents belonged to religions other than the Tuvalu Church. Outer-island Nanumeans, however, continue to value their community's religious unity. In fact, the decision to limit proselytizing by a "new religion" was a precipitating cause of the recent dispute.

The organization of the Tuvalu Church is pyramidal. Each congregation is headed by the pastor, who has been a Tuvaluan since the 1960s (previously usually a Samoan), though seldom a native of the island on which he serves. The pastor is supported by his wife, a group of deacons (largely male but with an occasional female member), male lay preachers, and a "Women's Committee." Membership in these three groups carries substantial prestige and includes the most influential people in the community. Association with the church is expected to be a lifetime affair, beginning when infants are baptized and continuing on with Sunday school attendance, membership in youth activities, and, finally, membership in the adult church body (the Ekalesia). Ekalesia members also sing in the choir and teach Sunday school classes.

The pastor's position is unique on the island. As a spokesman for an often-stern, moral point of view, he may comment obliquely from the pulpit on current events and issues, subtly linking these to Biblical themes and admonishing his congregation. On Nanumea, the pastor's elevated status and the expectation that he model decorum and moral rectitude limit his ability to socialize informally with the community. However, he plays a key role in most island festivities and officiates at weddings and funerals. The pastor is increasingly expected to remain apart from island politics, a contrast to his activities in the past.

Individual rights to freedom of religion, guaranteed in Tuvalu's constitution, are at odds with the value placed on group welfare and its expression in shared religious activities and beliefs. In the precontact era, religious practice was characterized by worship of island-wide gods and by the veneration of family deities, often the spirits of long-departed ancestors. In that period, so far as we know, there were few or no religious dissenters and competition between religious ideas was probably extremely rare. Though "troublemakers" did sometimes disrupt island tranquillity, their contention probably had a sociopolitical focus rather than a religious one. Today, competition between religious doctrines can create tension between expectations of community solidarity and individual human rights. Most Tuvaluans, indeed, support the right to chose a religion that fits personal beliefs and needs. On the other hand, people are also wary of promoting religious factionalism, which is so common in other parts of the world. They worry that religious proselytizing, in the name of religious freedom, could undercut the solidarity that a dominant religion has long provided throughout Tuvalu.

*Sunday service with Pastor Penitusi, Nanumea (1996)*

## The Meeting Hall

Nanumea's other force for solidarity, the ancient institution known as the aahiga, is embraced by all community members. The second largest building on Nanumea, the community hall stands in the village center adjacent to an open field, the village *malae* (see fig. 3 in chapter 2). Its name, "Nameana," is an archaic poetic version of the word "Nanumea." Nanumeans living in the capital have built a similar hall, named Seimeana, a name evocative of home because it combines the poetic name for Lakena Islet (Seilona) with that of Nanumea (Nameana).

Formerly an immense thatched-roof structure with low open sides surrounding a coral-gravel floor, today's aahiga has a silvery aluminum roof that glitters brightly in the equatorial sun, a cement floor, and low open walls. The Nanumean building measures 60 by 107 feet, its roof supported by cement pillars spaced at 12-foot intervals inset from the edge of the building (see fig. 8). The meeting hall in the capital is similar in size and construction. At any given time, a few drooping ceiling panels might need replacing and some of the canvas covers that protect against penetrating wind and rain might need repair. To outsiders, the buildings appear empty, even a little neglected, for there are no furnishings, no internal walls, no chairs or benches, no stage, no podium. They are essentially roofs over raised cement foundations. But the physical simplicity of the aahiga belies its importance to the community.

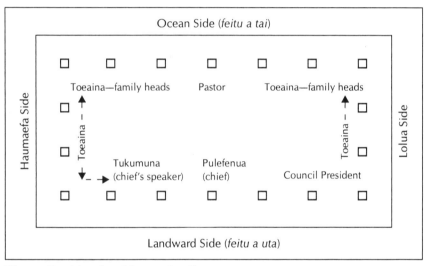

**Figure 8 Meeting House Seating.**

Whenever Nanumeans meet for an event that involves the whole community, the fenua, they gather in this building. It is the venue for feasts on important occasions and for holiday festivities in December and January. Island meetings take place there, visiting dignitaries are feted there, people gather there for choir competitions, dances, and innumerable other social events "of the island." The aahiga is the gathering place, the eating place, the speech-making place, and the playing place for Nanumeans in their interaction as a secular community. During events that are "of the island," traditional rules determine seating patterns and behavior. All events held there gain significance from the ancient meaning and sacred dignity of the hall.

On public occasions, the hall is thought of as having three zones. The center-most area within the building's internal pillars is restricted, and no one normally sits or walks there. A speaker might venture a few feet into this area in the midst of a speech if he becomes excited and has "caught the wind" (*poko te matagi*), as people say. Generally, however, only activities involving the whole community (such as dances, choir competitions, or other festivities) are located there. Small children or wandering dogs that enter the central area, especially during formal speech making, are quickly removed.

A second zone, the "front" seating and speaking area, is reserved for male elders, the chiefs, members of the Island Council, government officials, the pastor, and any visitors who are accorded dignitary status. Elders sit cross-legged in front of the central pillars (or in the intervals between them), in places customarily assigned to their families. Everyone faces inward toward the center of the building. Except for visitors, front seating is reserved for family heads considered old enough (generally over sixty) to fill public roles—the community's rightful leaders and public speakers.

Finally, the "back" of the building comprises the area just inside the low outer wall surrounding the hall. This "off-stage" area is where families sit, where baskets of food are stored before and after a meal, and where younger children entertain themselves quietly. It is the domain of women and younger men. People can move freely within this area and even walk from one end of the hall to the other along the outer perimeter.

Just as the village is divided into two halves, the aahiga also encloses two moieties. Haumaefa elders sit at posts toward the southeastern end, Lolua elders at the opposite end of the hall, with their respective families behind them. Each village side uses a small thatched building attached to its end of the aahiga as a work area to prepare food for community functions. In the days of great solidarity we observed in the 1970s and 1980s, feasts began with impressive lines of gaily costumed young women, all wearing dresses of the same color, streaming simultaneously in from the Lolua and Haumaefa work areas with trays of food to feed the elders and visitors on their side.

Referring to the aahiga as the "house of men" evokes the speeches that are made there and the hall's importance to the political life of the community. Women do use the building, sometimes taking it over for festive occasions of their own, and they are involved in community-wide events. However, women seldom sit at the posts or the "seats" of the house, and they are rarely speech makers themselves except at all-women gatherings. Rather, the elder men who head family groups are conceived as the supports, the strength, of the aahiga. These male elders are described as the "pillars of the house," its *pou*, fittingly occupying the seating positions at those pillars. Thus, when orators repeatedly invoke the "dignity and honor of the house and its pillars and its positions" in their speeches, they refer to the male-focused social structure implied in the community hall as a social institution. They also refer to the extended family corporations that, backed up by the chiefly descent groups, have long articulated political decisions. Traditionally, a family's oldest competent man represents the interests of its women, younger men, and children.

The metaphors used to describe Nanumea's aahiga illustrate the male-centered orientation of traditional society. But as the secular focus for community life, meeting house protocol has undergone some changes to accommodate new political institutions. When the aahiga is used for activities "of the government," traditional seating and speaking patterns give way to a democratic style of interaction. People are free to sit wherever they enter at meetings led by members of parliament or touring government officials. Younger men join in debates and all present usually vote to decide the issues.

Regular public meetings where matters are debated at length in the presence of a good part of the adult community are intrinsic to Nanumean unity. The function of such discussion is to clarify issues and crystallize the main opposing viewpoints. Discussion is often prolonged, allowing people to weigh pros and cons and to reach as enlightened a decision as possible, given the information available. This process gives participants time to reach consensus, building enough public support for a decision that it will later be adhered to. Sometimes a more speedy resolution is needed and a vote may be called before a clear consensus has emerged. If the decision does not have public support, the issue will probably arise again for discussion at a future meeting and may even be voted on again. A prolonged process of consensus building about issues affecting the whole community has long unified Nanumea, as it has other islands of Tuvalu and small communities the world over.

à&

## SERVICE-ORIENTED LEADERSHIP

Nanumea's political system today is a complex, dynamic, and somewhat contested blend of democratic and traditional institutions. Nanumeans elect many office holders, casting votes for island representatives to the national parliament, for members of the newly instituted *Falekaupule*, "Council,"[1] and for leaders of religious, social, and public service groups.

---

[1]Tuvalu's transition in 1978 from colonial status to independence has encouraged "decompression" of political leadership, resulting in a gradual blending of democratic and traditional forms of leadership. The reinstitution of the traditional chieftainship on each island in the 1970s and 1980s was one instance of this process. Another is the passage by Tuvalu's parliament of the "Falekaupule Bill" in 1997, designed to revitalize local island governments and give them more budgetary and decision-making authority. This ambitious project also sought to meld traditional governance by the (usually male) elders and chiefs who traditionally met in each island's meeting house with the elected Island Council system instituted under British rule in 1965. We will discuss this change more fully later in the chapter.

In these contexts, the person with the most votes wins the right to fill the position. Nanumeans also acknowledge the legitimacy of other means of filling public office, including consensus-based appointments for "traditional" chiefly positions.

Elders in the 1970s and 1980s, many of whom had themselves held chiefly roles, described traditional leadership to us as rotating between (or shared out among) a handful of chiefly descent groups whose obligation was to the well-being of the entire community. Using public office overtly to consolidate personal power and status is culturally unacceptable. Leaders, like everyone else, are expected to behave humbly, control their tempers, and cooperate with others. They attract a following through their active contribution to community affairs.

Virtually any man or woman with time and energy available can find some group to lead—at one time or another. (Though most leadership roles are filled by older men, Nanumean women have served on the Land Court, the Island Council, and in the national parliament from time to time.) In most people's thinking, power is a temporary attribute and leadership a temporary role. Nanumeans say their community is one composed of equals, with leadership an obligation that everyone must assume at some time, in whatever way they are best suited. Those who do a particularly competent job tend to serve longer terms, but they, too, are eventually relieved of their duties. Especially with positions such as a member of parliament, which have a handsome salary, government housing, and elite urban lifestyle attached, Nanumean voters seldom retain an individual in office for successive terms. Traditional leadership roles were also characterized by similar turnover since high chiefs were expected to abdicate when conditions became adverse. Nanumeans expect their leaders to be fairly well in control of things and, if they are not, to step down and let someone else try. In keeping with the community's egalitarian orientation, people tend to be critical of those in power and place little value on experience gained by length of service.

To be someone of influence in Nanumea, ideally one should work hard, participate actively in community affairs, be morally upright, and be associated with a reputable family. In this way, gradually over a lifetime, it is possible to build a solid reputation and some political influence. Emphasizing close links to the community's founder also helps. People strive to present themselves as "true descendants of Tefolaha," thereby claiming insider status in a social system that is egalitarian yet also oriented by a descent-based hierarchy. To be descended from the founder is to be indigenous to Nanumea, from the land instead of "from the sea," having an ancient heritage instead of only a recent connection and, at least in former times, allied with the unseen powers of the universe. The chiefly lineages not only claim descent from Tefolaha but also the right to fill the special duties, *pologa*, associated with each lineage. The "facts" of one's ancestry are always subject to debate, of course, as is the structure of "traditional" society itself. A person's claims may be subtly challenged by others.

In the past, individuals' connection to the community could be dramatized (and legitimated) by "feeding" the entire island, contributing so vast a quantity of subsistence foods that everyone could feast together in the meeting house. Nanumea's master fishermen regularly did this. Those who were able to donate an entire canoe catch of large ocean-going fish on several occasions won prestige and fame for themselves, they were "talked-about" (*takutakua*) and acclaimed. Such a person could speak with authority in the aahiga.

Produce of the land can also be given to the community in a similar gesture, as is memorialized in a famous incident that happened a century ago. At the beginning of the severe 1890s drought, the island had begun to suffer as food resources were depleted. Many families had scarcely enough to eat, let alone extra food to give to others. An elder named Matakea, however, decided to "feed" the community in a magnificent display of generosity. He and his relatives collected a vast number of coconuts from their lands and donated them to provide a feast in the meeting house. In doing this, Matakea was said to *lafo tona kaafaga*, "donate his tree-climbing loop" (a fiber loop that ties the ankles together and makes it possible to more easily climb a coconut tree and then stand high up on the trunk to harvest nuts) to the community. People told us that Matakea's sons and grandsons have subsequently derived some authority in island affairs from their ancestor's memorable act of generosity. Coming together for this feast must have given the community a welcome prelude to the process of vaelua division which soon followed. A commemorative song, a *mako*, is still sung today commemorating Matakea's deed.

As we saw in chapter 2, Nanumeans separate local politics into two conceptual spheres, what they term "affairs of the island" (*faifaiga o te fenua*), based on customary roles and institutions specific to Nanumea, and "affairs of the government" (*faifaiga o te maaloo*), based on the political system imposed by the colonial administration and continued in the national government of Tuvalu. "Affairs of the island" include the wide array of "traditional" social groupings, from family estate groups to fakaua units, which structure Nanumean social life. Also important are political groupings such as the seven "branches of chiefs" *maga o aliki*, which have a traditional right to lead the community. The chiefly groups trace their descent directly from Tefolaha. They are organized into seven named lineages, each of which has a specific role to play in island governance, ranging from serving as ruling chief to various protective and productive specialties.

Through the 1970s, all family elders had personal knowledge about how the traditional chieftainship functioned, and there seemed to be general consensus about its structure. Most of these elders have now passed away. In addition, the thirty-year suspension of chiefly leadership roles, lasting from the mid-1950s to the mid-1980s, resulted in contested interpretations of some aspects of the chieftainship. The chiefly system reinstituted in 1986 differs somewhat from the structure previously described to us. Opinion is divided today over whether Nanumea's reigning chief must be chosen from only two of the seven chiefly lineages or whether he can be drawn from any of them. The length of his term and the duties of the other chiefly families also engender debate. Uncertainties about these aspects of the chieftainship lessen its effectiveness and weaken chiefly authority, as the recent factional dispute has illustrated.

The "cultural constitution" currently in preparation by Nanumean elders at the request of the Nanumean community in Funafuti is expected to clarify ambiguous aspects of traditional political roles and establish the chieftainship on a solid foundation for the future. The current form of the Nanumean chieftainship has three main components: a Chiefly Council (*Tokofitu*) composed of elders who represent the seven chiefly lineages, plus a reigning chief or *Pulefenua*, and a "speaker" or *Tukumuna*, both chosen from these same seven lineages. A younger man is also selected as "secretary" to keep records of meetings and decisions. When a ruling chief must be replaced, the Chiefly Council asks the chiefly lineages to propose one of their number to serve in the position. This person's name is forwarded to leaders of the Tuumau lineage, who scrutinize the candidate's character and history and decide whether that man will make an acceptable high chief for Nanumea. If not, the nominating lineage is asked to reconsider and nominate another person. If acceptable, the candidate is installed with the requisite ritual in the meeting hall and becomes Nanumea's Pulefenua, "island leader." Because of his high status and his role as an embodiment of the community, the Pulefenua restricts his activities. The chief's well-being is linked with the good of the community as a whole, so if harm or an accident were to befall the reigning chief, the island could suffer. In particular, the chief should take care not to fall down or to capsize his canoe. Inappropriate personal behavior by a reigning chief is believed to cause bad weather (long droughts or excessively stormy conditions) or declines in fish catches, all of which could endanger the community.

Today's reconstituted chiefly system also includes the role of Tukumuna, "speaker." This person is selected by the Council of Chiefs after the reigning chief is appointed. His role is to articulate the chief's decisions on public occasions and to serve as link between the chief, the Chiefly Council, and the island's elected local government. The speaker also ensures that the Pulefenua's decisions are carried out.

"Affairs of the Island," in which the chiefs and family elders play primary roles, contrast with "affairs of Government," which are dominated by local government groups, the national Parliament, government ministries and employees, and the court system. In December 1997, the previous system of Island Council governance throughout Tuvalu was replaced by a system based on elected *Kaupule* ("council of leaders"). On each island, six members are elected at large to four-year terms by all residents eighteen years of age or older. They receive a small sum each month as reimbursement for their meeting time but are viewed as filling community service positions. Kaupule decide changes in local regulations; plan local development projects; and oversee the annual budget derived from taxes, na-tional government subsidies, and the Falekaupule Trust Fund (established in 1999). They also host visiting officials. Monthly meetings are followed a few days later by island-wide meetings so the Kaupule can explain their decisions and seek community ratification for them.

Nanumea also elects two representatives to the Tuvalu Parliament, which meets in the capital, Funafuti. Both representatives are elected at large to four-year terms. They are expected to consult with constituents and serve as the island's spokespersons in all national government affairs. A representative's influence is increased if she or he is chosen as prime minister or elevated to a cabinet post. The Tuvalu Westminster parliamentary system, with a single house modeled on Great Britain's House of Commons, involves a continual jockeying for power by government and opposition factions.

A constable from the Tuvalu Police Force is also stationed in Nanumea to enforce Tuvalu law and serve as prosecutor in court proceedings. Disputes and criminal charges are heard either in a general court or a Land Court, depending on the nature of the case. A chief magistrate and two assistant magistrates, all Nanumeans, serve as a general court, assisted by the police constable as prosecutor and the council clerk as court recorder. This court has jurisdiction over all minor civil and criminal offenses. Justice is normally swiftly dispensed, with convictions usually resulting in fines. A special Land Court is composed of five respected elders noted for their knowledge of local tradition, their good memories, and their familiarity with local land holdings. The Land Court meets as needed to hear disputes concerning land boundaries, estate division, or paternity. All court decisions can be appealed to the national magistrate, who makes periodic tours to the outer islands to hear appeals. Serious criminal cases, which are extremely rare, are heard in the capital in the High Court presided over by an expatriate chief justice. The High Court usually sits twice a year. Offenders convicted of serious crimes are sent to the country's only prison, in the capital, located conveniently within sight of the High Court.

❧

## Getting Along Together

Individuality is not a highly valued trait in Nanumea (or elsewhere in Tuvalu). People are expected to fulfill their personal goals through cooperation with relatives and fellow community members. The label *fakaatea*, "different," is usually applied negatively to behaviors such as unsociability, erratic behavior, extreme shyness, or other departures from common norms. Refusal to help with group projects or to conform to accepted behavior standards is deplored and typically viewed as either "stinginess" or malice.

At the community level, the long-term interests of the greatest number are paramount. Individuals are expected to give, and give in, as requested. Giving, for example, means providing goods, holding public office, participating in communal building projects, and attending public meetings. Giving in means responding positively to criticism and acceding to leaders' requests. Subordination to group well-being is expected at many levels of society and can result in moral dilemmas because of overlapping levels of obligation. A striking example of such a difficulty occurred during our first stay on Nanumea, when a respected elder named Tepou became pitted against the Island Council, which was acting on behalf of the community as a whole. Tepou, for his part, was trying to carry out his father's deathbed wishes and had already withstood community pressure far longer than most other people would have. The resolution of this dispute illustrates how the community responds to people who put their family's needs (or their own needs) above those of the island as a whole.

Tepou's house was located on his own land between the community's playing field and the government school, precisely in the center of the village, with a clear view of the meeting hall and church. Several generations shared the large household and ate from the breadfruit, coconut, and papaya trees that surrounded it. However, the location of this house had been the subject of lengthy dispute. Before the village was rebuilt in the 1930s, the area that became the village playing field had been owned by several families and was dotted with their cookhouses and food-bearing trees. Like everyone else, Tepou's father had a village house, crowded between rows of identical neighbors. He also had a cookhouse-cum-workroom on the present site. When the community decided to enlarge the playing field adjacent to the meeting house, other landowners relinquished their land and it was cleared. Tepou's father, strong willed and proud of his descent from a lineage of warriors, contended that it was wrong for the island to force a family to give up its land. After pleas and arguments were unable to persuade him to change his mind, the playing field was made smaller than had originally been planned, and Tepou's family cookhouse was left standing at its edge. Eventually the family abandoned its village row house and enlarged the cookhouse, making it the family home. The school came to be built nearby, too, on public land reclaimed from the lagoon by the American forces during World War II.

Forty years later, in the mid-1970s, Tepou's house stood between the school and the playing field, a location that rankled other community members. The need to move Tepou's house became a theme at island meetings again and families who had given up land for the playing field years before were particularly bitter about Tepou's insistence that he must uphold his father's refusal. After a committee of island leaders was not able to persuade Tepou to relocate, the Island Council wrote to the chief magistrate in Funafuti, requesting legal permission to force Tepou to relinquish his land for the community's welfare. While they were still waiting for a reply, the council summoned Tepou to its monthly meeting to try one more time to convince him to cooperate.

At the council meeting, Tepou explained his stance somberly. He said he was an old man without the strength to rebuild a house or to replant food trees elsewhere. His family had already given up land for the school and for the airstrip built during World War II, leaving them nowhere else to move in the village. Tepou said he had sympathy for the island but believed that it was nonetheless wrong for Nanumeans to persecute other community members. The six council members in turn reiterated yet again the reasons why Tepou must accede to the island's request: It was a community decision made to further the welfare of everyone's children and many other people had already cooperated. The councilors who were related to Tepou stressed their sympathy for his plight. Others spoke about how his family had always been a pillar of the community and had always been generous with help. A respectful and gentle tone of persuasion permeated these speeches.

Nonetheless, a hint of drama hung in the air as the arguments were repeated, and then repeated again. Several hours had passed. One of the council members wondered, in an aside, what would be done with Tepou if he refused to agree. Another worried aloud what "might happen" if the will of the island continued to be thwarted. Someone sympathized at the hard decision Tepou was being called on to make and noted how "heavy" his heart must be. Finally, one of the councilors suggested that the island buy Tepou's land if he wasn't willing to give it. Tepou rejected this purposely offensive plan, asserting that his refusal was based on the principle set by his father and the fact that he had nowhere else in the village to go nor strength to replant another plot of land and build another house. He pleaded that he was not trying to profit personally, exasperate the community, or deprive the children of a place to play.

The meeting dragged on as council members made formal replies, begging Tepou's compliance on behalf of the island. They pleaded with him to agree to their akai, "request," reminding Tepou that the council was the island's government and had an obligation to look after community welfare. One councilor who was related to Tepou wondered aloud: What could the island do to help him become established in a new site? Ignoring Tepou's objection that he still refused to move, other councilors took up this lead. Another plot of village land could be found, his house could be rebuilt there, his trees replanted. Suddenly Tepou capitulated. The Island Executive Officer, who had been keeping notes of the decisions reached at the meeting, quickly read out the agreement. Tepou's land would be used for the playing field and his house would be moved to another site in the village. Everything would be arranged by the Island Council. Both Tepou and the council members then gave thanks for each other's patience and everyone promised that the matter was closed and the issue decided.

As far as the council was concerned, the dispute had been settled—but Tepou still had to tell his family of his capitulation. An emotional but private family argument developed, and Tepou fled to the bush. He was gone for several hours and his relatives, fearing that he might be in danger, went in search of him. Tepou later said that when he left his house he felt completely confused, as though "all he had left to him was his own life." His "heart was burdened" and his "soul was startled." He didn't know where he was going as he wandered in the bush. He said he had been surprised to feel a hand on his shoulder and to see a relative standing behind him. As his relatives led Tepou home, they sympathized with him about the difficult decision he had been forced to make, and some cried with him. But no matter how traumatic Tepou's capitulation was for himself and his family, the rest of the community greeted the arrangements as long overdue.

Most people felt that Tepou was in the wrong and that the community would be justified in forcing him to comply, if necessary. One person who heard of Tepou's flight to the bush commented to us that although he pitied him, it was well that Tepou had agreed, since the island otherwise would have had to tear down his house. That drastic possibility had occurred to other people as well and was probably the "something" that "might happen" mentioned by one of the councilors. The council itself was counting on legal enforcement powers if Tepou continued to refuse. However, before destroying the house, the community certainly would have sought mediation by the pastor and agreement from the national government.

House destruction sometimes is also used to punish individuals who refuse to conform to decisions of the wider kin group. During our first period of fieldwork, relatives tore down a woman's house, reportedly to punish her selfish and uncooperative behavior. Such a drastic "solution" to domestic problems is rare but effective. By forcing the recalcitrant individual to join other kin who are still sympathetic enough to be welcoming but are located some distance away, animosities within a family may gradually subside. The British-based court system, as well as contemporary public opinion, looks with disfavor on such a violent solution to intracommunity disputes, though this form of social control does seem to parallel the treatment meted out in traditional times to those considered troublemakers.

Ostracism (*fakatapu*) is another sanction that can be used to punish lack of cooperation. In one case we encountered, ostracism was combined with a threat to inform a potential overseas employer of a man's bad character. Mataio (a pseudonym) was about fifty years old, unmarried, a man of solitary temperament. He lived alone on Lakena Islet, where he was notorious as the only able-bodied man regularly absent from communal work projects. When he did come, he used the excuse of having to do all his household tasks himself to justify arriving when the work was almost over. Even then, angry Lakena residents charged, he would stand and watch rather than pitching in to help. Complaints from other workers finally led the work leader to scold Mataio privately. Mataio responded by leaving Lakena on communal work days, thus absenting himself completely. The Lakena community finally forbade anyone to socialize with Mataio or to help him in even the smallest way. All but one Lakena resident obeyed the ban, but no one was happy about this solution.

At the next Island Council meeting, the Lakena representative requested that Lakena residents not helping with communal work be required to return to live in Nanumea village. Mataio's case, the cause of this request, was discussed and the following decision was reached. Mataio, who had good references from his past employment, was hoping to be rehired overseas. The council decided to draft a letter to Mataio, warning that if he continued to show his character by refusing to help with the communal work, they would feel obliged to disclose it to his prospective employer. They also threatened to "refuse to let him leave the island" lest he hurt the community's reputation, presumably by being as uncooperative overseas as he was at home. The letter had its desired effect and Mataio reformed.

Uncooperative behavior also weakens an individual's social and economic security by reducing the person's circle of sympathetic kin and by blemishing his or her reputation. However, what is good for an individual and immediate family members does not always coincide with the best interests of the whole community. As in Mataio's case, specific sanctions may sometimes be needed to force stubborn individuals to subordinate their desires to the community's needs. Violence, public shame, or ostracism always serve as a last resort, however, used only after other possible avenues of persuasion have failed. Sanctions are viewed as a lever to change antisocial behavior rather than as a punishment.

When Nanumeans assess and judge people's behavior, they focus on what has actually been said and done rather than on what might have been thought or meant. The actual occurrence is given more weight than the person's intent. Maa, "shame," is a vital part of local social control since, as Nanumeans realize, fear of being shamed often motivates people's obedience to social norms. Since Nanumeans expect each other to be humble, people must maintain a delicate balance between modesty and admitting special abilities. Behavior that displays differences in ability or achievement could upset the equality on which Nanumean society is premised.

*Ano game at "Big Days" celebration (1984)*

The community's resolute insistence on equality was demonstrated in 1974 at the island meeting where the schools organizer explained the need for amalgamating the Catholic and government elementary schools. As was mentioned earlier, the organizer faced a hostile audience unanimously opposed to the amalgamation. When discussion turned to the Catholic school's students' recent success in passing the secondary school examination, the schools organizer argued that the exam success resulted from good home environments, not from a particular school's curriculum. Several people in the audience laughed in derision, and the Island Council president was quick to object: "No, we are all equal in our homes here. There are no differences between us!" Another speaker, familiar with the Western assumptions of individual achievement implicit in the organizer's statement (and in the education system as well), added: "It is true. Here we are all the same. Don't try to divide us like that. It would be a shameful thing for us to have some households pointed out as bad for the education of the children in them." It was clear that the schools organizer unwittingly had struck a cultural nerve.

The community's egalitarian ideology is also reflected in the limits imposed by the Island Council on wedding food displays. Traditionally, kin groups put on a splendid feast and urge a large turnout of relatives for the festivities. The goal is to show off the family's wealth, productivity, and cohesion in implicit competition with the other family. In the early 1970s, the Island Council limited participation in wedding festivities to specified close kin and restricted the type and amount of food presented. For example, relatives more distant than second cousins were prohibited from attending the festivities and imported food such as bread was banned from the trays of food each family laid out before the couple. These rules were intended to preserve subsistence resources from conspicuous consumption and to guarantee the equivalency of the two kin groups. Even minimal differences in wedding displays appeared to discomfit the community. The rules were not popular with all, however, and were not fully observed.

Control and regulation are equally important on the personal level. People expect each other to hold anger in check and to maintain a calm demeanor. Though fights occasionally erupt, they are usually broken up quickly by bystanders. Disorderly behavior and physical aggression are explicitly forbidden by law, as are trespassing, malicious gossip, and taunting. Convicted offenders are punished by fines or by sentences of community service. In most of the serious public disputes and disturbances that occur on the island, at least one of the participants is brought to court. Court cases usually result in conviction of the offender.

On the surface, at least, village life is placid. Table 7 lists the court cases during our fieldwork in 1973–74 that involved some aspect of interpersonal antagonism or dispute. This profile is still reasonably representative of the situation today. For a population of nearly a thousand people, twenty-nine incidents involving twenty-three individuals over an eighteen-month period is a very low level of discord. While aggression was involved in about half of these incidents, no deaths or serious injuries resulted.

Tellingly, over 60 percent of these cases stemmed from consumption of alcohol, mainly by young men. Usually several youths begin drinking together in an atmosphere of relaxed camaraderie, but as they become increasingly intoxicated, they argue and often fight. Rarely are bystanders menaced, but a drunken man may try to impose himself on women,

Table 7
Interpersonal Disputes Heard as Court Cases on Nanumea, 1973–1974

| Charge | Number of Cases | Individuals Charged | | |
| --- | --- | --- | --- | --- |
| | | Young Men | Adults | Total |
| Disorderly Conduct (while drunk) | 12 | 9 | 1 | 10 |
| Theft (while drunk) | 2 | 2 | — | 2 |
| Destruction of Property (while drunk) | 2 | 1 | 1 | 2 |
| Assault (Stabbing, Beating) | 2 | 1 | 1 | 2 |
| Bullying a Minor | 1 | 1 | — | 1 |
| Criminal Trespass[a] | 3 | 2 | 1 | 3 |
| Extended Family Squabble (manifested as fighting, slander) | 6 | — | 6 | 6 |
| Disrespectful Words to a Government Official | 1 | 1 | — | 1 |
| **Totals** | 29 | In all, 23 separate individuals were involved: 14 young men, 5 adult women, 4 adult men. Some were repeat offenders. | | |

Source: Data from nine court sittings held while we were resident on Nanumea (between July 1973 and December 1974). The local court also heard many cases contravening the Island Council Bylaw requiring that pigs be penned outside the village. Another common offense was drunkenness, charged as drinking without a license or drinking under legal age. Only interpersonal dispute cases are tabulated here.

[a]Two of these cases involved undesired sexual advances made at night, while the offender was drunk.

destroy property, or take a motorbike for a joy ride. Young, unmarried men (*tamatane*) are most commonly involved in these offenses, perhaps in keeping with their generally marginal role in island life. While young men are expected to help out with household and community activities, they receive little recognition for their efforts and have scant role in public decision making. Unlike young women who are carefully chaperoned by their families, young men are allowed considerable freedom to "play." Their drinking parties and carousing are tolerated as long as they are relatively discrete and nondisruptive, but should any fighting erupt, the combatants are locked up until they are sober. They are then charged in court with disorderly conduct and often receive sentences of community service, which are served locally under supervision of the local government.

The other main cause of incidents brought to court are long-standing family disagreements, whose genesis usually can be traced back a generation or more. Arguments over land division or resource allocation sometimes smolder on even after an ostensible settlement has been reached and eventually may erupt in an angry altercation. Of course, family arguments that reach public attention in this way reflect badly on the individuals and families involved.

## ❧
## Heirs of Tefolaha

The general peace and cooperation of island life are accepted simply as part of daily routine. Against this background, times of turmoil come and go. Perhaps it is these difficult moments, in which a community must summon up its collective unity, that best define it. For Nanumeans, one such moment of cultural definition occurred late one evening in January 1984 at the annual all-night festivities marking the Po o Tefolaha, "Tefolaha's Day." In the early predawn hours, some of the young men began a drunken commotion that verged out of control. The pastor was roused from his sleep to address the aahiga crowd. He spoke eloquently, with fervor matching the seriousness of a disrupted community event. "*Gaa tama a Tefolaha*," (children of Tefolaha), the pastor began, carefully choosing this phrase to evoke the community's unity and all the commitments that follow from shared descent. He urged the assembled crowd to remember the history that they were celebrating and, as he spoke, calm returned. The dance was able to resume.

By invoking Nanumea's legendary founder and former god, the pastor (himself an outsider) spoke to the heart of what it is to be Nanumean. His choice was intended to resonate deeply, yet it had ironic overtones, too. In how many equally fervent speeches had the pastor's predecessors urged these "children" to abandon Tefolaha and other aspects of the island's traditional religious heritage? Though devoutly Christian for a century, Nanumeans derive strength from their steadfast determination to remain the children of Tefolaha. Over the last century, periods of wrenching change have left many aspects of "traditional" culture just cloudy memories. The founder's relics, including his venerated skull and his shrine, have disappeared. Yet it is clear that Tefolaha's unifying presence has endured. Nanumeans today emphatically declare themselves to be the communal heirs of Tefolaha, the rightful inheritors of the island his cleverness won for them. These children of Tefolaha have produced an enduring and resilient community in which social cohesion has been raised to the level of an art.

### ❧

## NOTES AND SUGGESTIONS FOR FURTHER READING

### *Polynesian Chiefly Organization*
The nature of Polynesian chieftainship has been much analyzed by anthropologists and historians. Comparisons within this culture area have related political forms and social organization to resource availability and other economic factors. Two classic works by Marshall Sahlins (1958, 1963) originally sparked debate (see also Goldman, 1970). A review of these comparative generalizations is provided by Alan Howard (1972). Sahlins's more recent work on "divine" kingship in Hawaii and Polynesia (1981, 1985), along with Valeri's (1985), has generated new interest in this topic. Volume 2 of Douglas Oliver's (1989) encyclopedic survey of Oceanic society and culture also summarizes political organization in the region. A thoughtful analysis by George Marcus (1989) explores the tension between hierarchy and egalitarianism in Polynesian chieftainship.

### *Meeting Hall Institution*
The community meeting hall is a core social institution throughout Tuvalu. Ironically, on most Tuvalu islands it is referred to as *maneapa*, a name suggestive of Kiribati (and hence, Micronesian) origins. Michael Goldsmith's (1985) provocative article explores meeting house terminology and origins in Tuvalu, beginning with this anomaly: why, if the meeting hall is "traditional" and a key piece of Tuvalu social organization, was its Tuvaluan name (though not including aahiga in Nanumea) borrowed from a neighboring society? Two books by Harry Maude (1963, 1980) describe the meeting hall institution in Kiribati and provide a useful comparison.

Interestingly, all evidence points to an indigenous origin for the Nanumean term *aahiga*. Its etymology, according to elderly Nanumeans we worked with in 1973–74, derives from the phrase *te aahiga o muna*, which roughly translates as "[the place of] the display of words." The hall is the place where oratory takes place, where the eloquence and persuasiveness of words are compared and admired (cf. "The House of Words" in Keith Chambers 1984).

### *Shame as Social Control Mechanism*
Shame as a mechanism for social control is mentioned in most ethnographic accounts of Polynesia. A useful place to begin exploring issues concerned with motivation, behavior, and social control is Bradd Shore's (1982) analysis of village life in Western Samoa, which focuses on relationships among moral ideas, concepts of personhood, and wider social obligations. Robert Levy (1973) provides a comprehensive account of Tahitian personality and behavioral expectations. Niko Besnier's (1994) analysis of gossip also offers useful insights on social control in Tuvalu.

# Challenges of the Twenty-first Century

"Tell us about the cruise ship that visited Nanumea," we asked our friend Laina. "People could not believe it," he said. "The ship was so huge, so white, just off the reef beyond the boat passage. Its boats brought the *paalagi* [European-descent] tourists in through the channel and let them off. They walked around looking at things. Some of the women in bathing suits were almost naked, and they did not seem to care. A few older people brought them *hulu* wrap arounds to cover up with—they thought it was shameful to see them walk around like that."

"How long did the tour ship stay?" we asked. "It was here the whole afternoon. They were served a meal in the community hall, and then they got into the boats and left. I think the ship's captain paid a few hundred dollars to the island. We haven't seen them again."

Field Journal, Nanumea
July 1996

The *Symphony* looms gigantically out in the lagoon, blinding white, twelve stories high. To some of her passengers, she must look like

Mother Earth did to the first astronauts. For most of the
Funafutians, . . . this has to be the biggest thing they've ever seen.

Tom Huth, writing of visit of
cruise liner *Crystal Symphony*
to Funafuti, January 1996

Massaged by the wind, the Pacific Ocean is in a constant state of upheaval.
Waves roll endlessly in patterned sets, swelling or receding with the tides.
Though there may be days of calm, the ocean is never still. In much the
same way, human culture and the social forms it generates take shape,
mutate, merge and re-form again, and again, and yet again—continually
through time.

The past and present inhabitants of Nanumea are actors in a drama
that has always been unfolding. They play roles that are slowly being
invented anew, with freedom to interpret the commonplace in novel ways
and assign new meanings to convention. For them, as for human beings
everywhere, "tradition" emerges only from a backward glance through
time. The community's shared heritage and traditional ways are shaped
and reshaped to fit the demands of current realities. From Tefolaha's first
words to Pai and Vau, to the contemporary concerns that have threatened
the village side organization, the process of Nanumean society has always
been evolving. Periods of turbulence have counterbalanced eras of relative
calm. Though inevitable, coping with social upheaval has never been easy.

Not just Nanumea, but all of Tuvalu is now engulfed in one of these
periods of massive change. People are contending with new opportunities, reaching out to try new technologies, articulating new aspirations,
and questioning tradition—even as they value tradition more than ever
before. The contemporary situation seems comparable to other times of
great challenge in Nanumea and Tuvalu—the missionary era perhaps, or
the sudden arrival of occupying forces during World War II. At the start of
the twenty-first century there are clearly more difficult questions than
easy answers. When the tides of change run high, as they do now, it is difficult to know which social institutions will endure and which will disap-
pear or be transmuted. Those who are embroiled in the complexities of
the present cannot help but find it both worrisome and daunting to
choose wisely, especially when so many of the choices are set by outside
cultures, market forces, or the political agendas of distant nations.

The local issues that engage Nanumeans (and all Tuvaluans) are
connected with concerns that all of us share. While atolls like Nanumea
are physically isolated, their isolation is increasingly an illusion. Tourist
ships, though they call only infrequently, offer both opportunities and
new problems. Economic imperatives, geopolitics, pervasive popular cul-

*Young Nanumeans of the twenty-first century (1996)*

ture, and global ecological change press closer with each video that is rented from the cooperative store, each labor contract signed by a seaman, each aid application submitted by a government ministry, each storm weathered. The challenges we describe in the following pages have no easy solutions. They will require wisdom, energy, and goodwill to resolve. In today's global society, none of us can dismiss them as only a Nanumean (or even a Tuvaluan) problem.

### 🙙

## RISING SEA LEVELS

On the moonlit evening of January 3, 1993, a series of three waves struck the leeward side of Nanumea between 8 P.M. and midnight. Locally, the waves were named *Te Ofa*, "The Destroyer," perhaps because they swept over the reef and up onto the village peninsula, knocking down houses and sending a low wall of water cascading inland through the main village. Fortunately, no one was injured, but the night was filled with worry about worse destruction that might occur. In retrospect, it seems that the three waves may have been connected to the hurricanes, Nina and Te Kina, that were then threatening southern Tuvalu and other parts of the western Pacific. But waves of this magnitude, without an associated local storm, are unusual in the northern islands. Similar surges are increasingly being reported, however, from other low Pacific Islands: waves that reportedly swell up without any apparent provocation from a nearby storm, often wreaking havoc on the less-protected leeward side of islands. Weather oscillations such as El Niño and La Niña, which have rearranged weather patterns globally, may be implicated in these unusual waves. Recent meteorological research confirms that an abrupt eastward shift occurred in the South Pacific Convergence Zone beginning in 1977. For some island groups, the primary result has been devastating drought. Others have experienced increased rainfall (up to 30 percent higher than normal), temperature changes, and unusual storms. For people living close to the ocean's margins, these changes are worrisome. But a graver threat looms even more ominously in the future. Increases of only a few degrees in global temperatures are likely to bring a marked elevation in ocean levels. Should sea levels rise as some predict, Tuvalu and other low lying nations worldwide will be engulfed. As proverbial "canaries in a coal mine," their fate may presage environmental change with severe global impacts.

The fragile atolls and reef islands that Tuvaluans inhabit stand no more than twelve to eighteen feet above sea level, often less. When tropical storms lash the shore, the reef often gives way before them. The worst hurricanes bring huge waves that can wash completely across an island, as did Hurricane Bebe on Funafuti in October 1972, killing six people. The most serious storm to hit Tuvalu in this century, Bebe destroyed most buildings and devastated vegetation. The island's palms were flattened to the ground, nearly every one of them, and most islets were inundated with salt water. A huge rampart of coral rubble along the windward side of the atoll was dredged up from the surrounding reef shelf by the large wave that swept the atoll. Lesser storms result in shorelines scoured by erosion and the precious sand accretions of centuries can be washed seaward in hours. While Tuvalu has apparently suffered only three or four hurricanes as severe as Bebe in the last hundred years, hurricane-force storms may be becoming more common. Hurricanes caused extensive damage at Vaitupu in 1990 and struck both Niulakita (twice in so many days) and Nukulaelae again in 1997. Any rise in ocean levels severely exacerbates the threat that all storms pose to low lying islands.

Tuvalu is one of forty-two members of the Alliance of Small Island States, a coalition advocating mandatory reductions in greenhouse gas emissions, which are believed to be the cause of global warming. The members of this group see themselves as probable first victims of a global catastrophe disrupting the planet's entire ecosystem. Island nations, whose tiny populations and subsistence-oriented economies contribute relatively little in the way of emissions, are disheartened to realize that they themselves can do little to combat global warming. Their survival depends on changing public opinion and behavior in much larger nations where resource consumption is infinitely higher, as are greenhouse gas emissions, but where there is little interest in the problem. Frustration with this situation led one delegate to a 1992 climate change convention to observe bitterly: "If Pacific Islanders were whales, people would make more effort to conserve them." Indeed.

ॐ

## LOCAL IDENTITY, NATIONAL IDENTITY, AND PRESSURES FOR WESTERNIZATION

Over the last century, Nanumeans have had no choice but to contend with the changes imposed and offered by outsiders. Theirs has been a complex encounter with the West, involving both continuity and disruption, decision making and cultural imposition. One product of the encounter, we believe, has been Nanumeans' development of a shared identity as "Children of Tefolaha," an identity that interweaves traditional ways and local versions of island history with the demands of Western institutions. Through this identity, Nanumeans distinguish themselves from neighboring Tuvaluans—and the rest of the world—and assert a reference point for their own cultural autonomy.

When we lived in Nanumea in 1973–74, its sharing-based economy was still intact and personal goals were routinely achieved through collective endeavors. Even overseas work contracts were short-term, so that community identity continued to be important away from the home island. Workers in the central Pacific phosphate mining islands of Nauru and Banaba created home-island enclaves under the leadership of elders who organized regular remittances of money home. Funafuti was then a small district center of the colony rather than a national capital, its amenities and lifestyle not much different from the outer islands. Tuvaluan was spoken almost exclusively, clothing bore no relationship to current world fashion trends, and direct media influences were limited to an occasional film shown on a 16mm projector set up for the occasion, or the BBC or Australian world news rebroadcast over a small radio station in Funafuti twice a day in English and Tuvaluan. Only a few magazines, cassette tapes, or books circulated. Two-way radio connections linked outer islands with the capital, but the equipment was prone to break down in the salty, humid air. A radio station might be off the air for months at a time before repairs could be made. Satellite connections, television, and even telephone service between islands were all unknown and unimagined.

Some twenty-five years later, Tuvalu is awash in Western culture. Plane arrivals and departures link the capital's international airport with

Fiji, the South Pacific's transportation hub. Air links north to Kiribati and to the Marshall Islands have sometimes been available, too. The govern-ment-owned hotel in Funafuti is usually filled to capacity with expatriate advisors, representatives of aid organizations, and government visitors. Small guest houses, charging rates tailored to the high per-diem levels of officials, dot the capital. There are few tourists as yet but (ever hopeful) development plans target their increase. Urban streets bear increasing loads of vehicular traffic. Minivans provide public transport along the main roads, while pickup trucks, cars, and vans from government minis-tries, churches, the hospital, some outer island communities and a grow-ing number of private individuals meander through town and north out along the road to the cooperative store warehouse and deep-water wharf and beyond. Motor scooters and bicycles weave slowly along the sandy streets, swerving around pedestrians and potholes. This traffic and the urban style of it all adds a sense of busyness to capital life that is in sharp contrast to the slower pace of the outer islands.

The capital has a wide range of consumer items offered for sale. The main cooperative store and its secondary outlet near the airport stock fro-zen meats and fresh vegetables (seldom seen on the outer islands), mayon-naise and cheese, even, as well as the familiar canned goods, staple starches, and household items. Small family-operated storefronts along the main streets, as well as general stores operated by outer island communi-ties and a shop specializing in clothing, offer Funafuti residents a range of shopping venues. A large general store owned by Fijian expatriates (with local partners) has opened recently, offering attractively displayed mer-chandise at prices lower than those of the cooperative store. Another expa-triate shop now sells frozen pizzas! Several modest restaurants compete with the government-run hotel for lunch or dinner patrons. Household meals of imported foods, such as rice topped with stew made from frozen mutton or chicken, have become daily fare for many. In the urban crush of the capital, local produce is scarce and costly. People eagerly buy any fish that is offered for sale, and coconuts shipped in from the outer islands and locally made bread both find a ready market. Money is in chronically short supply for most people but has become vital for subsistence. With employ-ment opportunities limited, everything seems expensive.

Life in the capital hones the economic aspirations of Tuvaluans. Not only do people there come into daily contact with a vast array of imported goods, but some Tuvaluans also have considerable money to spend, at least for a short period of time. Though most people must use their scarce incomes to purchase household necessities and fulfill social obligations first, the consumer culture that has transformed Western society seems to wait in the offing for Tuvaluans, too. Higher wages for seamen who work on overseas ships, as well as rising educational aspirations, which send many students to study at high schools in Fiji, support the expectation that wage labor, rather than subsistence production, will feed families in the future. But many local jobs pay little more than a dollar per hour minimum wage, making all but the most basic imported goods unaffordable.

Westernized media exert a powerful influence on capital life, too. Rental videotapes are widely available, ranging in content from *The Sound of Music* to C-minus epics of sleaze and violence. The latter are watched routinely in many households because children and older people appreciate the fast pace and lack of dialogue in action films. As products of Western society, most videos portray the individualistic, materialistic, and conflict-oriented themes that resonate with Western audiences. Their powerful but creeping influence on Tuvaluan viewers' expectations has been called "visual imperialism" by some critics. Such media exert a subliminal direction on local worldview. Their influence is not a matter of control by a political elite but a generic laissez faire cultural explosion.

Television now engages the attention of capital residents as well. A down-link antenna from the Indonesian *Palapa* satellite made television available in Funafuti for the first time in July 1996, a spin-off from the contract leasing Tuvalu's telephone country code. The only channel available at first was Australian MTV, but shortly thereafter CNN, an American sports channel (ESPN), and an American entertainment channel could be viewed as well. In the years since then, the channels available have varied, sometimes being limited to only a single station from Australia. The outer islands were not included, for cost reasons, in the establishment of broadcast television, but plans call for satellite connections for the outer islands when funding permits.

Long before the local influence of MTV, popular songs made their way to Tuvalu while still on the hit list overseas. In 1996, a teasing tune with words we could never quite make out played so often on the national radio station and in nearby houses that we assumed it was a new local composition. Imagine our surprise when we returned home and learned that the song, the "Makarena," was a worldwide hit, not Tuvaluan at all. Another popular song that year was "Alice," with a refrain of profanity that was masked when it was played on Radio Tuvalu but not at local dance nights. Such affinity for Western popular culture notwithstanding, new ballads, pop songs with local themes and rhythms, and hymns continue to be composed and performed by local band musicians and church choirs alike. Local musical compositions get considerable radio time and engage keen local interest when they are performed at festivities, competitions, and dances. Nonetheless, especially among young people, attraction to overseas popular culture is strong. Storytelling sessions, which

*Recording a new composition, Nanumea (1996)*

used to occupy leisurely family evenings, are increasingly giving way to television or videos, focusing people's attention away from cultural messages of their own invention to those created by global media. While cultural borrowing has always been an intrinsic part of human history, seldom has the pattern been so one-sided or so sweeping as at present.

The amenities and employment opportunities located in the capital, and its pivotal role in national politics, have made Funafuti the focus of Tuvaluan social life. The Funafuti people, as the capital's indigenous inhabitants, retain land rights to their atoll, but many Nanumeans and other outer Islanders have created secure niches for themselves as long-time civil servants, elected officials, or entrepreneurs, accessing land through marriage, kinship, or friendship connections with Funafuti folk. Though the somewhat Westernized atmosphere of the capital allows pursuit of personal ambition outside communal goals, even the lives of long-term capital residents are never fully autonomous. Lotofenua, loyalty to home-island communities, is a structure of urban life too. Tuvalu uses the eight home-island communities as primary units of national government. Capital residents rely on fellow community members for support and join forces with them to achieve common goals. As a result, public life in the capital focuses around each community's meeting hall, just as at home. Both social events and fund-raising endeavors draw forth commitments of considerable time, energy, and money. For Nanumeans living in the capital, involvement with the Nanumean community provides their primary social connection.

Increasingly, the distinctive customs and traditional histories of outer island communities provide emblems of identity for capital residents. One example of this revived interest in traditional custom by urban Tuvaluans is the *Fakavae* ("cultural foundation") project initiated in the early 1990s by Tagisia Kilei and other Nanumean elders residing in the capital. (This group calls itself Nanufuti.) The Fakavae project aims to codify key aspects of Nanumean sociopolitical organization, using a fifteen-page list of typed questions, topics, and statements about Nanumea's traditional history, chiefly political system, social customs, and vocabulary. Tagisia told us that he originally hoped that the resulting compilation of cultural information would serve as a "guidebook" for the Nanumean community. For future generations of Nanumeans, he believed, it would provide a "mirror." As he explained to us in a note, "in case someone wants to see his real identity, just pick up the mirror and see his reflection, check up the balance, if it is more or less Nanumean." Once the survey began to take shape and had the backing of the Nanufuti community, Tagisia began to envision how the collected information could be reviewed and evaluated. Anything determined to be "obsolescent traditions" could be "obliterated" while customs "which need alterations" could be adjusted. Tagisia drafted a list of questions and the Nanufuti community in the capital sent the list to Nanumea for response. On Nanumea, a group of elder men met to work their way slowly through the items, topic by topic, a process that generated lengthy discussion and some disagreement. We were told during our visit in 1996 that the group's response was just about ready to be typed and returned to the leaders of the community in Funafuti. But we also heard that parts of the requested information were disputed, other parts were highly sensitive because they related to the community's ongoing dispute, and that the participating elders could not provide some of the requested information. A definitive document seems unlikely to result soon.

But regardless of the immediate outcome of the "constitution" project, its existence emphasizes the importance of "tradition" as a marker of community and personal identity. Nanumeans are the only people in Tuvalu (or in the world!) who can authoritatively answer a question like "Who was Tefolaha? Was he a real person or not?" By knowing Tefolaha's local significance, what a maatua ofo or a kopiti is, or how the complicated chiefly organization should work, people prove that they truly are Nanumeans, that they have rights to a place in that community and a platform from which to participate in wider Tuvaluan society. They show that they have a unique identity in the world. As Westernization infiltrates capital life more and more, perhaps it is not surprising that Nanufuti elders feel the need of a cultural outline to set themselves apart from other Tuvaluans and from Westerners. More than outer island Nanumeans, but just like other outer Islanders living in Funafuti, they are most acutely aware of the gulf between modern life and the expectations of their home-island childhoods. The cultural constitution toward which the Fakavae project aims could one day be used to decide ceremonial protocol or settle a dispute. Its Nanufuti instigators intend it to protect the cultural knowledge that their own parents took for granted, but about which their own children show little interest and they themselves sometimes feel uncertain. This knowledge, always undergoing some change but never before changing as rapidly as it is in the capital now, has given meaning and structure to island life for generations.

### ❧

## INROADS OF CAPITALISM

The dominant exchange mode of a society not only channels the distribution of resources but also creates the tenor of social relationships and prescribes the strategies used to obtain goods and services. Economic practices everywhere are intricately interwoven together, too. Nanumea developed an economic system that emphasized the survival of the community as a whole. Extensive sharing obligations and a range of related institutions, such as the vaelua division to cope with drought, ensured that everyone's needs would be met equally, to the level allowed by resources available at any given time. Though market-based capitalism was proffered as the natural and superior replacement by explorers, missionaries, traders, and colonial officials alike, sharing-based exchange practices have survived a century of contact.

In the 1970s at least, virtually all Nanumeans still championed sharing obligations. Even though some individuals toyed with ideas for future small businesses, the customers that would bring life to such visions were seldom imagined. People still compartmentalized their exchange relationships, saying that with people one cared about (relatives, neighbors, even the entire Nanumean community in some situations), resources should be shared as needed. Only in socially attenuated relationships were buying and selling acceptable. Even people with quite distant relationships were linked by gift-giving obligations. Customs such as maatua ofo and hai taina (honorary siblings) made virtually all community members potentially connected. Within this milieu, individuals could bestow gifts in ways that strengthened their economic security and social support, but withholding participation was not really an option.

Both sharing-based and market exchange economies are kept in motion by discrepancies between some people's resources and others' perceived needs or wants, though the ostensible goal of each system is quite different. In market exchange, buyers and sellers each strive separately to maximize their material rewards; the relationships between them are impersonal (to large degree) and subordinated to that goal. In a sharing system, maintaining supportive social relationships is so intrinsic to the exchange process that short-term tallies of material benefit are meaningless. As a result, sharing equalizes access to resources across a community and serves as a socioeconomic leveling mechanism. Market exchange systems, on the other hand, tolerate (even encourage) differences in wealth. Both systems are supported by cultural incentives, sanctions, status considerations, behavioral expectations, needs, and so on. Supports for Nanumean sharing include a stigma on "stinginess," prestige accorded on the basis of community service and generosity, expectations about when resources should be shared and when recipient-initiated requests should be honored, and discouragement of individual autonomy.

Exchange activities are heavy with ethical implications, and transactions that contradict key values must be rationalized or condemned. Thus, in the 1970s Nanumeans enjoyed auctions that raised money for public projects and shopped readily at the cooperative store, but looked askance at sales between individuals unless these could be justified, as was done with motorboat-caught tuna. Similarly, Westerners share readily with family members and friends but shift "naturally" into a competitive, consumer mode that takes note of even minor price differences when shopping for everything from groceries to new cars. In both societies, people learn when they should follow dominant expectations and when circumstances allow alternative rules to apply.

Market exchange is becoming increasingly accepted in Tuvalu, especially in Funafuti. This shift has been encouraged by several decades of aid projects, ranging from efforts at small business development to support for outer island fish markets. More intensive work experiences, residence overseas for work and education, increased dependence on imported foods and goods, as well as media influences, all support the weakening of sharing obligations. Many people expect to purchase (or at least to offer to purchase) what they need from everyone but closest relatives. In the capital, but also often in the outer islands, sharing expectations are sometimes ridiculed now as a foolish waste of entrepreneurial opportunity. Such a change in attitude can only mandate a revolution in social relationships. Will Tuvaluans increasingly come to define themselves through personal accomplishment (rather than through group membership), as is typical in Western society? Will individuality, self-assertion, and personal autonomy become accepted ways to access social and economic rewards? If so, relationships among relatives, neighbors, community members, and fellow citizens will be fundamentally and irrevocably changed.

Early in the contact period, Nanumeans required all visitors to wait on the beach below the high-tide line while the community conducted a lengthy ritual. These ceremonies were believed to protect the community against a vaguely defined contamination. Nanumeans also resisted the introduction of a Christian teacher to the island, fearing (as contemporary Nanumeans explain) that their island would *fuli* ("turn over") with the new teachings. Yet, of all the Western influences intruded on Nanumeans over the last century, none has been a more powerful acculturative agent than market exchange. The social impacts of capitalism are far-reaching and subtle. They may indeed have the potential to "turn over" Nanumean society, requiring that community members hold different expectations of each other and forge a new model of community life.

### ❧

## EQUALITY UNDER THREAT

This shift toward market-based values and relationships also impacts traditional political organization. Nanumeans used to say that "here, we are all the same" with some pride, stating both local ideology and a fairly obvious social fact. Differences in family wealth certainly existed, but they were ephemeral. Extended families with exceptional land resources could expect more relatives to affiliate and, in future generations, family land holdings would be dispersed among a wider pool of heirs. People returning from overseas work would try to bring home nest eggs of cash, piles of gifts, and durable household goods. Much of this would be given to or borrowed by relatives, and then further dispersed through the local reciprocal exchange network. The returnees themselves would benefit, too, from the accumulated savings of other returning workers. A constant round of community projects required donations of resources and labor, keeping attention focused on group well-being rather than on personal ambition. A tradition of decision making by consensus and specifications about when an incumbent should step down from public office undermined power differences. Expectations of the old sharing-based economy were that having more meant being able to give more until the abundance was dissipated. Matakea's generous disposal of his coconuts to feed the community was a perfect example of a sharing-based economy in action.

Now that people "live from money," they are increasingly expected to husband their own resources to provide for present and future needs.

Resulting socioeconomic disparities have the potential to threaten the "unique culture based on co-operation and on common welfare," which the national government recognizes as an asset. In the 1995 National Development Strategy, an "equitable distribution of resources" was articulated as a cornerstone of current development policy. Indeed, up to the middle of this century in Tuvalu resources were equally distributed. However, for people who have worked overseas or in the capital for years, or have substantial income from a business or political office, using their resources to build positions of power seems attractive, too. This possibility may even be encouraged by government commitments of support for "enduring small enterprises," the profits from which are expected to raise income levels and improve living conditions.

An "Education for Life" program now mandates that all children be educated through the tenth grade, using a curriculum aimed at developing life skills appropriate to modern Tuvalu and creating an educated workforce better able to implement the country's development plans. Children attend their home-island primary school through the eighth grade and then go on for at least two more years of secondary schooling on Vaitupu. After that, test scores and student aspirations determine whether a child continues with high school or pursues other vocational training. Technical or commercial training options allow for further education, as does academic education beyond tenth grade. Previously, only six years of primary schooling were available on the outer islands, and, according to the Tuvalu government, the national secondary school on Vaitupu admitted only about one quarter of all students. But these new hopes of secondary education for all do not entirely erase differences in children's educational options. Some families can barely scrape together the required secondary school fees, while others can afford to send a child to school overseas, where English immersion may result in higher exam scores, a university scholarship, and a future white-collar job. Government employees who have contact with other elites at regional and international conferences tend to hold high academic expectations for their children and assume that they will obtain professional employment. Parents whose world is more insular are often satisfied when their children are able to send home remittances.

Socioeconomic stratification, and the development of a local elite, has usually followed Westernization throughout the Pacific. In Nanumea (and Tuvalu), social class–like distinctions would contradict the egalitarian premise of local society. Expecting people to look out for their own well-being, to amass resources to buy a secure future, and to vote to consolidate political interests can build only an individualistic (and potentially divided) society. If the economic benefits of Western capitalist-style development were dispassionately weighed against their likely social costs, might strengthening the traditional sharing economy make better social and economic sense than displacing it? Can market-based initiatives really interface successfully with traditional social obligations and customary leveling mechanisms? How can community solidarity and individual economic security best be integrated? A national discussion about "development" should address these questions.

Community cohesion, evocatively dubbed "unity of heart" by Nanumeans, is often regarded as fundamental to entrepreneurial development. There seems little recognition, however, that communal values are at odds with the individualistic orientation of capitalistic-based development. In societies where competitive achievement by individuals or small family groups is basic to social life, modern development goals can extend traditional opportunities and increase access to material items without threatening existing social institutions. Nanumea's (and Tuvalu's) egalitarian and communal value system, supported by its sharing-based economy, is basically at odds with Western capitalism and cannot be pressed into its service intact.

"Development," some analysts maintain, simply perpetuates colonialism in a new form. Ton Otto, for example, views development as "little more than the adaptation of local institutions and economies to better suit Western interests." From this perspective, a skeptical approach to Western development projects and philosophy might serve Tuvaluan interests. Could island-specific development profiles be developed by each community through a process of national discussion? Might some traditional socioeconomic arenas be demarcated for protection?

## LEADERSHIP ISSUES

Precontact Nanumeans relied on older men in each family to grapple with political issues and to make decisions that would secure the extended family's well-being. These men served as spokesmen for their relatives in internal kopiti decision making, in debates in the island meeting hall, and in communion with ancestral spirits. Opinions of women and young men were voiced in family discussions but, in public forums, male elders were the ones who had the deliberative roles. As family representatives, elders were bound to maximize their extended family's welfare over the long term. This commitment was widely accepted in reference to personal decisions and ambitions, too, though not everyone invariably set aside personal desires in every situation. While the activities and responsibilities allocated to men and women differed, they were complementary, each seen as necessary to family welfare. The woman's domain was primarily domestic while men were expected to provide food and link the family with community activities. Young men contributed their energies to family endeavors and learned leadership skills gradually by observing the deliberations of older men. In a social life shaped by the meeting house and extended family corporations, equal representation of individual interests was simply not the issue. Instead, family well-being assured individual well-being.

This is no longer the case, however. Tuvalu is committed to creating a democratic society in which women and men, old and young alike, can enjoy equal rights to sociopolitical involvement and have an equal say in decisions. This commitment calls into question the traditional exclusion of younger citizens and women from public leadership roles. The national development strategy articulated in 1995 committed the government to policies that "ensure that women are able to fully participate in the development process, and all walks of life in Tuvalu, and to enjoy the benefits of that participation." Women's political participation is to be specifically encouraged and any "bias against women" is to be identified and eliminated. The government also aims to increase "youth participation in island community affairs," "encourage respect for the rights of youth," and "ensure the youth voice is heard at all decision-making levels."

The government has supported international conventions guaranteeing youth and women's rights and is currently seeking ways to better represent their interests in government and community affairs. In response to current world concern about gender equity, the collection of specific data about women's socioeconomic situation is mandated, with the results to be used to monitor the effects of government policies. Increased sports activities and facilities are planned in order to involve youth more actively in local life. Though these efforts respond, at one level, to the concerns of international organizations, they also reflect the government's genuine desire that all Tuvaluans be able to pursue a "full, free and happy life," a goal that is warmly embraced by Tuvaluans themselves.

It is difficult to see how some of these aspirations for women and young people can be met without recasting traditional institutions. While universal adult suffrage is accepted as the basis for governmental decision making at both the national and island levels, many Nanumeans would like to see their indigenous political institutions (such as the meeting house and chieftainship) remain dominated by elderly men. The idea of women serving as family representatives in the "house of men" or acting as ruling chiefs seems a grievous break with tradition to many people. Lacking evidence that elders have ever systematically discounted the needs of women, many people argue that traditional political institutions are based on an inclusive approach to decision making that implicitly takes the well-being of everyone (women and youths included) into comprehensive account. In this view, Tuvalu's "unique culture based on cooperation and on a common welfare," as the National Development Strategy document phrases it, provides a fundamental structure of equality. Some advocates see the dismantling of traditional institutions as too high a price to pay to address inequities that may be more pressing in Western societies than in their own. On the other hand, a single minded commitment to gender equity is obvious in the Tuvalu National Women's Policy Statement (July 1998), which explicitly advocates "abolishing traditional and cultural practices that hinder the advancement and full participation of women in social activities. . . ." Resolving this complex issue in a way that is both equitable and protective of the social fabric will clearly require patience and wisdom.

In Nanumea, changes are evident in community leadership patterns. Forced by recent disputes to look beyond the village side organization, the community has sometimes used age groupings to structure festivities and feasts. This structure crosscuts extended families, creating an organization that is radically different from time-honored social divisions. The groups formed are usually equivalent in size and embrace everyone in attendance, but they also place the community's younger men, who have been pushing for greater recognition in community affairs, in symbolic opposition to the elders. Though men aged forty to fifty-five may head families with grown children, be skilled at subsistence tasks, and often have had decades of experience in wage employment, traditionally they are expected to listen, as are women of all ages, while elder men publicly debate issues. Recent events on Nanumea have pushed some middle-aged men to expressions of passion that others stigmatize as lacking in self-control and respect. Given Tuvalu's commitment to democracy, customary political institutions excluding younger men and women are increasingly difficult to maintain, especially when these same people vote to determine other political decisions and contribute valuable intelligence and energy to island activities.

ॐ

## Balancing Urban and Outer Island Opportunities

Movement from outer islands to the capital has resulted in levels of urban crowding that are widely recognized as a national problem. The last census in 1991 found 43 percent of the country's population (of 9,043) enumerated in Funafuti, a population increase for the capital of 441 percent since the 1973 census, nearly two decades before. The National Development Strategy of 1995 (*Kakeega*) estimates Funafuti's population growth at 5 percent a year, versus a 1.7 percent annual growth rate for Tuvalu as a whole. Capital residents must cope with scarce housing, scarcer jobs, sanitation and water supply problems, and increases in minor crime. These create difficult urban living conditions.

However, by world standards, even life in the capital is far from squalid. As the Kakeega notes,

> In some respects, Tuvaluans have quite a high quality of life compared to some countries. There is very little hunger, most people have adequate shelter, the climate usually provides plenty of fresh water, and Tuvalu has remained free of many serious diseases that affect other nations. Few people can be said to experience abject poverty. Tuvaluans benefit from political stability and strong cultural and community ties. Serious criminal activity is quite rare.

Life expectancy at birth averaged sixty-seven years in 1991, and school attendance for children aged six to fourteen was over 97 percent. Though some economic indicators, including gross domestic product per person and the numbers of people in cash employment, were quite low, these reflect the country's subsistence orientation more than they do impoverishment and privation. Nonetheless, concentrating nearly half the nation's population in urban Funafuti's 1.08 square miles (2.79 square kilometers) with little access to traditional subsistence resources, exacerbates social tensions and economic disparities alike. Movement to a cash economy, through which goods and services can be purchased, thus becomes essential to life in the capital.

The government has not yet had much success in finding ways to discourage in-migration from the outer islands, though this has been perceived as a problem for over two decades. Decentralizing government operations by moving some government departments to the outer islands has been attempted but did not prove feasible. For several years in the 1990s the Agriculture and the Education Departments were moved to Vaitupu Island, which has been the site of the government secondary school since the 1930s. Establishment of fax and phone service offered hope that these moves might be workable, though Vaitupu was a half-day's boat journey away from Funafuti and ship visits were infrequent. Both department headquarters have recently been returned to Funafuti, however. Decentralization of business enterprises and of development projects is also being encouraged—a recent example being the Australian-funded project to establish outer island fish markets and processing facilities on Nanumea and Nukufetau, which served as prototypes for centers built in 1999 on Nanumaga, Niutao, Nui, and Nukulaelae through government funding. The extent of infrastructure already established in Funafuti (which includes all external air and shipping links, the national parliament, and most governmental and nongovernmental aid activities) adds significant time costs to most outer island enterprises. For the foreseeable future, people certainly will continue to be attracted to Funafuti for a host of pragmatic reasons: health care, education, employment, private business opportunities, travel, not to mention its "bright lights" and bustle. Since the government recognizes "freedom to migrate" as a basic right, restricting movement to the capital is not a viable solution to urban drift.

Despite Funafuti's attractions, most Tuvaluans view the outer islands as the real place they come from, owe loyalty to, and draw on for support. Only when they are overseas do people identify themselves as simply "Tuvaluan." Home-island origins are often apparent in speech patterns, so people implicitly communicate their origins when they talk. More importantly, social connections based on land ownership, rights to share in land produce, and to participate in social life all make home islands personal reference points. Land cannot be sold to foreigners in Tuvalu and, until recently, sale was forbidden by most island land codes. Land sales are still rare, if not nonexistent, in the outer islands.

Outer island identity may be on the wane for some urban residents, however. The situation of Pita (not his real name), a thirty-year-old Nanumean man now living in Funafuti, is increasingly common. Born and raised in the phosphate islands (Banaba and Nauru), he lived overseas while attending university and now works in the capital in an influential government position. He views himself as a Nanumean, is universally identified as such by others, and takes part in Nanumean community events in the capital. Yet, he has spent no more than several weeks ashore in his outer island community. Speaking somewhat ruefully, in a characteristically southern (not Nanumean) dialect of Tuvaluan, he told us that he had found his first and only visit to Nanumea a few years earlier somewhat awkward. Pita, and others like him, will probably not be drawn back to live on Nanumea in the future. Fortunately, his income and established connections in the capital make it feasible for him to remain there. For others like him, from all of Tuvalu's outer islands, Funafuti is beginning to seem like home.

In the capital, a well-educated, affluent, sophisticated, and influential urban elite increasingly stands out from the outer island majority. Some members of this elite view outer island life as problematic because it lacks conveniences that they now see as necessities: electricity, power appliances, running water, motorized transport, and "bright lights" entertainment. Many find themselves reluctant to move home permanently, despite wanting to live close to relatives and be settled on family land.

In response to these concerns, Nanumeans have been pressuring the national government for several years to electrify the village. While all of the outer islands have had small electricity generators for occasional use since the 1960s, most systems supply only the church or meeting house with power and then only on specific occasions. Since 1984, small solar-powered systems, made up of one to three solar panels connected to a storage battery, have been available to households in the outer islands. Initiated by the Save the Children Foundation, this project is now administered as a cooperative society through the central government. For a share costing $50 and a monthly payment (in 1996) of $7.60 per month, outer island households can run two to three low wattage florescent lights for several hours each night. A radio can be powered for an additional $.60. This photovoltaic system is too small to run larger appliances or higher wattage lights for any length of time and has been difficult to maintain in Tuvalu's humid and salty climate, especially given the remote and scattered nature of the installed systems. Many outer Islanders now perceive solar power as a costly technology with only limited value, insufficient to improve standards of living or allow future economic development. It is unlikely to reduce population drift to the capital or to encourage Nanumeans living there to come home.

In 1993, in response to these concerns, the Nanufuti community commissioned a feasibility study for a village electrical system for Nanumea. The resulting report estimated that a simple low-voltage system providing electricity to homes and public buildings in the main village area would cost A$355,000 (approx. U.S.$250,000). Diesel generation was projected as the only practical option, and the consultant suggested that

*Nanufuti leaders, Tagisia Kilei and Fili Homasi (1998)*

Nanumea establish a customer-owned cooperative. (A solar generated system, perhaps the most reliable and environmentally friendly alternative, could cost A$2,000,000.) Encouraged by this report, Nanumeans at home and in the capital are enthusiastic about making village electrification a reality, and many view it as imminent, whether funded by the central government or by themselves. Some believe that the Nanumean project provides a model that could be used on other outer islands, too.

However, government experts dispute both the projected costs and the feasibility of the village electrification study. Setting up the system in Nanumea alone would cost between A$750,000 and A$1,000,000, they say. Even if this could be funded successfully, recurrent operational costs are viewed as well beyond local community resources. Further, technical expertise to operate and maintain the system may be lacking, while transportation of such large amounts of diesel fuel is thought to be beyond what the nation's single ship can accommodate. Whether electrification actually would provide the social benefits its proponents hope for is also questioned.

Nanufuti officers estimated in 1996 that about five hundred Nanumeans lived in the capital. Like their relatives still on Nanumea, capital residents are represented politically by two members of the national parliament who are elected at large by all island electors, whether living at home or on other islands. These representatives are responsible for furthering the community's interests as a whole. At present, Tuvaluan outer Islanders living in the capital are not represented as a specific interest group, though whether this would be advisable is being debated. Do urban Tuvaluans from the outer islands share enough interests to justify their representation as a single group? Some people worry that common interests will not be strong enough to cancel out home-island loyalties and that urban voters simply would continue to vote by outer island block. Others believe that urban conditions have become unique enough that combining urban residents and the outer Islander portion of each community together into a single constituency makes it impossible to represent the interests of either. The indigenous Funafuti community tends to favor separate representation for outer Islanders residing in the capital, an option that would require a costly duplication of administrative support.

Up until now, Tuvalu effectively has been a collection of autonomous, cohesive outer island communities. Outside advisors and consultants, focused on policies and projects that are nationally oriented, sometimes complain that Tuvalu seems to be more a handful of separate communities than a single nation. This may make nationwide politics complex and factional, but could a nation barely two decades old split into eight communities with distinctive histories, cultures, and linguistic features, separated from each over centuries, be otherwise? Clearly, home-island loyalties, and the effort that community goals can bring forth, are still important social resources. Forging a supracommunity identity is one of the challenges facing Tuvalu as a democratic nation.

ॐ

## LOOKING TO THE FUTURE

Tuvaluans are now contending with cultural upheavals and socioeconomic transformations that rival the historic changes of the last century and question the integrity of local society. Most of these changes are acculturative. They stem from a newly imposed way of life, one that insists that traditional responses be set aside so that a new lifestyle can come into being.

Tagisia Kilei, a Nanumean elder whose adult life largely has been spent in urban centers overseas and in Tuvalu, has long grappled with the dilemmas posed by this onslaught of change. He uses the metaphor of a tidal wave to describe the current situation. With water sweeping completely over the island, he asserts, "You have no way to dodge the breaking wave. All you can do is stand firm and face it yieldingly." In his view, running away can only be foolish and dangerous—you might be washed completely away or pushed down to drown fathoms below the surface. Survival, he claims, can best come by facing the wave and coming to terms with the transformation it brings. If money is now the key to life, he insists, Tuvaluans must find new ways to earn it. This involves taking advantage of every small business opportunity and searching for more ways to benefit from global market opportunities.

But how can a society "stand firm" in its cultural traditions? Can a cultural system withstand change forces whose potential for cultural devastation parallels the force of a tidal wave on a low-lying atoll? How can the essential core of Nanumean culture—its sharing-based economy, service-oriented leadership, social groupings with cross-cutting membership, egalitarian values—survive under the onslaught of Westernization? Can Tuvaluans choose to protect these (or any other) cultural features that are especially valued? Should they try to? In an increasingly differentiated society, who should decide the answers to these questions?

ॐ

## NOTES AND SUGGESTIONS FOR FURTHER READING

### Storm Damage and Environmental Change
Environmental change on atolls through storm-produced rubble has received considerable attention, particularly following Hurricane Bebe in 1972. See Maragos (1973), McLean (1975), or Baines and McLean (1976a,

1976b). McLean and Hosking (1991) provide an overview of hurricane history in Tuvalu. For a firsthand description of the terrifying power a major hurricane can unleash on a tropical environment, read Paul Cox's (1997) gripping *Nafanua*. Research findings regarding major changes in Pacific climate come from press releases of the South Pacific Regional Environment Programme (SPREP) in Apia, Samoa.

### Tourism
Tourism currently appears to offer limited development potential for Tuvalu. A small number of "adventure travelers" visit annually. Sporadic visits by tour ships create encounters such as that depicted at the start of this chapter. Our friend Laina referred in his description to the visit of a Lindblad liner, which called at Nanumea in the 1980s. Tom Huth's condescending travel story (1997) about the opulent liner *Crystal Symphony*'s stop at Funafuti in 1996 highlights the dissonance this type of tourism may create. James Conway, an American advisor to government, resident in Funafuti at the time, described the ship's visit to us: "Even anchored in the [huge] Funafuti lagoon, its enormous size and whiteness was unparalleled, totally incongruous, dropped from outer space." Phillip Ells' (2000) recent account of contemporary life in Funafuti draws on two years' volunteer service as "people's lawyer." While vivid and engaging, the ironic humor typical of this travel writing genre can be biting.

### Class Divisions and Concerns Related to Westernization
Hooper et al. (1987) provide a good starting place for understanding class issues in Oceania. The collection edited by Ton Otto (Otto 1993b) as well as Otto's own essay (1993a) effectively present concerns about the impact of development on class creation and economic disparities in the Pacific region. "Visual imperialism" is discussed in Crawford and Turton (1992:166). Of related interest is Conrad Kottak's (1999) analysis of the effects of television on a remote Brazilian village.

The metaphor of a tidal wave has also been used by other Pacific Islanders to describe the irresistible and sometimes devastating effects of Westernization. For example, Papua New Guinea political leader Bernard Narokobi (quoted in Otto 1997:62) wrote in 1980:

> Melanesia has been invaded by a huge tidal wave from the West in the form of colonization and Christianization. Like any tidal wave, the West came mercilessly, with all the force and power, toppling over our earth, destroying our treasures, depositing some rich soil, but also leaving behind much rubbish. This Western tidal wave has also set in motion chain reactions within ourselves and a thirst for a better future. . . .

## Tuvalu Government Policy and Planning

Tuvalu's most recent National Development Strategy, *Kakeega* (Tuvalu Government 1995), provides extensive information on government policy and social context. Among topics considered are: participation by women and youth, urban growth, quality of life, wealth distribution, and access to education. Population data and land areas are drawn from the 1991 census (Tuvalu Government 1991b:1–5). Information on Tuvalu's Trust Fund is found in Bell (n.d.). Changes in educational policy are described in Tuvalu Government (1993). The recent National Women's Policy is Tuvalu Government (1998). Nanumea's disputed electricity feasibility study was prepared by Maurice French (1994). A good overview of social, economic, and health-related issues throughout the Pacific region is *Pacific Human Development Report, 1999* published by the United Nations Development Programme, UNDP.

## Pacific Island Focused Web Resources

**Pacific Climate and Related Issues (global warming, greenhouse emissions, ozone layer, etc.)**
- SPREP's web site is http://www.sprep.org.ws
- Australian government Pacific climate site is http://www.dar.csiro.au/

**NGO and Regional Sites**
- Secretariat of the Pacific Community (SPC): http://www.spc.org.nc/
- The South Pacific Forum (SPF): http://www.forumsec.org.fj/
- The Small Island Developing States Network (SIDSnet): http://www.sidsnet.org/
- The Alliance of Small Island States (AOSIS): http://www.sosis.org/

**Pacific Island News Sites**
*Pacific Islands Monthly*, published for many decades from Fiji, provides ongoing coverage of regional news and issues, such as Aiavao's (1996) report on the meeting of the Alliance of Small Island States and his quotation about the fate of whales generating more concern than those of Pacific Island peoples. A newer Fiji-based periodical, *Islands Business*, is considered by many to be today's leading news magazine for the Island Pacific. Web-based resources are of increasing importance:
- A good place to start is the comprehensive *Pacific Islands Report* from the Pacific Islands Development Program of the East-West Center and the Center for Pacific Islands Studies, University of Hawaii at Manoa: http://pidp.ewc.hawaii.edu/
- South Pacific Information Network (SPIN): http://sunsite.anu.edu.au/spin/
- *Pacific Islands Monthly* can be accessed at http://www.pim.com.fj

- Pacific Journalism Online, maintained by the Journalism Department at the University of the South Pacific, Suva, provides a daily news update and a broad range of related links at http://www.usp.ac.fj/journ/

**Tuvalu Focused Web Sites**

- http://members.xoom.com/tuvaluonline/ Known as Tuvalu Online, this privately run site is a good starting place. It serves as a worldwide "chat place" and communications link for Tuvaluans and interested others.
- http://members.xoom.com/janeresture/tu8/aboutus.htm/ Maintained by Jane Resture-Grey, a descendant of nineteenth century trader at Nukufetau Alfred Restieaux, mentioned in chapter 4.

# ❧ 10

# Unity of Heart

It is May 1984, and the community is gathered in Nanumea's aahiga. A murmur of voices, accompanied by the hiss of kerosene pressure lanterns and the rustle of dance skirts, fills the hall. The council president sits cross-legged at his accustomed pillar. To his left and right are members of the Haumaefa and Lolua sides, seated on the floor in two roughly concentric circles around wooden box drums. People wear leaf and flower garlands on their heads and bodies over colorful print wrap-arounds and dresses. Coconut oil is glistening on bare skin. The men closest to the drum box are ready. Slowly, the lead singer's solo falsetto intones the beginning of the first lines of the faatele song, and then in deeper cadence, a hundred voices pick up the melody. On the drum box, four or five men maintain a sturdy beat that pounds through the hall and reverberates out into the darkness. Slowly, the song accelerates through its first stanza, rising in pitch, stopping abruptly with the final drum beat. A momentary pause and then the singing begins again, the rhythm slightly faster. A few women stand up and take their places behind the singers seated on the floor. They tie on fragrant dance skirts and ready themselves for the next yet faster verse. Faatele are narratives, expressing poetic images and evocatively describing memorable events.

Tonight's dance is no different than dozens we have attended before in Nanumea, but the words of this faatele song converge so powerfully with the values of island life that the moment is imprinted forever on our memories:

| *A Galiga o Fenua* | *True Beauty in a Land* |
|---|---|
| *A galiga o fenua* | True beauty in a land |
| *Ko te loto gaatasi* | Lies in the unity of hearts |
| *Ke maopoopo tou malosi* | To put our efforts together |
| *I mea katoa tau o taa ola* | For the things we need in life |
| *Ke lagona, kau lagona* | You feel this, I feel this |

Nanumean faatele attributed to<br>Taumaia Faga, Christmas 1943

To one side is Haumaefa, representing half the village. Its men drum to outdo their Lolua rivals, and its women dance to uphold the honor of their village side. To the other side is Lolua, sitting silently watching Haumaefa's performance, ready with their own repertoire. Their turn is next. The rivalry of the village sides is so intense that we have always sat first with one group and then the other, emphasizing our affiliation with the

*Faatele in the aabiga, Nanumea (1974)*

community as a whole. The faatele explodes through the meeting house, celebrating in both word and performance Nanumea's unity. Within this cohesion, the village sides can emphasize their differences. This faatele, we realize, could serve as the Nanumean anthem.

It is June 1996, twelve years later. Nanumeans are welcoming us back to Tuvalu with a feast in *Seimeana*, their meeting hall in Funafuti. Electric lights illuminate the meeting hall's interior and seep out into the darkness around the building. The steady wind off the ocean and the pounding of waves on the nearby reef muffle the meeting house sounds. Tonight, a festive meal and speech making are followed by a much-anticipated faatele. Soon the lead singers gather around the drum box, and the first, slow stanzas of the first song begin. We smile in recognition. We know this song carries special meaning for the "heirs of Tefolaha." It is *A Galiga o Fenua*, our favorite faatele, the first song sung at every faatele celebration, both here and in Nanumea during our visit this year.

Over many years we have been convinced by Nanumeans that "true beauty in a land lies in its unity of heart." Choosing an opening song that celebrates this value so explicitly shows how much cooperation and collective well-being are still valued. But the increasing popularity of this faatele, and the tendency to use it as a community emblem, may have other overtones as well. This faatele reminds all those who sing it that their community's strength is its cohesion and that "unity of heart" has so far endured the test of time. Nonetheless, many must now wonder (as do we ourselves) whether Nanumea's collective solidarity can remain intact in the face of increasing Western pressure in so many areas of Tuvaluan life.

In most Western industrialized societies, individualism is the basic value that defines personal goals, social organization, and moral relationships, creating a fundamental structure into which other institutions (social, political, and economic) must fit. In the United States, Robert Bellah and his colleagues have likened individualism to a dominant "first language," one to which other values relate as supplemental extensions, playing support roles equivalent to "second languages." Economic "rationality" and the tenor of social commitments, in particular, must conform closely to the dominant cultural paradigm—in the American case, to individualism.

Perhaps not surprisingly, few Westerners are willing to privilege community well-being over the welfare of themselves and their immediate families. Nor are most people willing to yoke their personal goals to the ones most important in (and achievable by) society as a whole. In the United States, and many other Western societies as well, socioeconomic inequality and community disintegration are creating urgent social problems. Increasingly, we realize that the individualism we revere erodes our otherwise-enviable quality of life.

Nanumea's enduring "unity of heart" (paralleled in the values and social organization of other Tuvaluan communities, too) is a cultural treasure. While Western readers will be reassured to read of a modern society that remains premised on cooperation and solidarity, Tuvaluans and other Pacific Islanders may wonder about the fit between their traditions and economic "modernization." Important questions about cultural survival may be raised, too.

Can societies like Tuvalu retain their valued cultural core of community solidarity and still engage in a global economy dominated by market forces? What will happen to local society when market rationality replaces the values of a sharing-based economy? Can relatives, neighbors, and community members give priority to short-term economic gain but still bring collective goals into being? Does economic development offer Tuvalu progress and modernity—or only certain destruction of traditional values and culture?

The present inexorably becomes the future and, in this process, the worlds we know become strange new ones. What ways of life will the children of Nanumea and Tuvalu inherit?

*Celebration after successful community fund-raising campaign, Nanumea's aahiga in Funafuti (1998)*

## 🐚
## NOTES AND SUGGESTIONS FOR FURTHER READING

### Faatele Dance Traditions

Faatele is a remarkable traditional song and dance form common to all Tuvalu communities. Participants sit in an inward facing circle around a group of lead singers in a performance characterized by a heart-pounding accelerating tempo accompanied by rhythmic clapping and drumming on a mat or specially constructed box. The term *faatele* (possibly of Samoan derivation) means "to multiply," probably referring to the rhythm's increasing speed as the song progresses. Christensen and Koch's study of traditional Tuvaluan music (1964) includes a 45-rpm recording with one archaic style of faatele included. A more recent CD is *Tuvalu, a Polynesian Atoll Society*, recorded in 1990 with liner notes by Ad Linkels (Linkels 1994). Thomas (1996) provides an ethnomusical analysis of faatele from the neighboring (and culturally related) Tokelau Islands. Mervyn McLean's encyclopedic *Weavers of Song* (2000) includes a chapter on Tuvalu music and a sampler CD; his earlier annotated bibliography of oceanic music and dance is useful for comparative purposes (1995). The Tuvalu government allocated funds in its 2000 budget for the digitizing and preservation in CD format of Koch's music recordings made in 1960 and 1961.

Those who stand to dance in the faatele, male or female, tie around their waist a short brown dance skirt which in Nanumea is called *titi fakamanumanu*. These skirts are laboriously made of four or five different types of prepared leaves and perfumed with fragrant smoke before each dance. The skirts and the racks used to perfume them are pictured in Koch (1961).

### Community and "Civil Society"

Issues of community-mindedness (vs. extreme individualism) in Western society have been of concern to philosophers and social critics for some time. Especially notable is *Habits of the Heart* by Robert Bellah and colleagues (1996). Amitai Etzioni (1993) offers suggestions for increasing the communitarian focus in contemporary life. The contrast between Tuvalu's communal values and Western individualism was also noted several decades ago in an official history of Britain's Pacific empire—see Coates 1970:75.

# Glossary of
# Tuvaluan Words

## PRONUNCIATION KEY

Tuvaluan, along with other Polynesian languages, pronounces its vowels very much as does Italian. Thus, /a/ is pronounced as in English "ah," /e/ as in "*echo,*" /i/ as the double *ee* in "feel," /o/ as the first *o* in "Orion," and /u/ as the *oo* in "goo." When two dissimilar vowels occur together, as in *aitu*, (ghost, spirit), each is pronounced separately, with less tendency to form a diphthong than in English. Thus, it is pronounced "ah-ee-too." Consonants are generally unvoiced, but otherwise similar to English; the exception is /g/, which is pronounced as is the *ng* in "singer." There is no /r/ in Tuvaluan. When this letter occurs in loan words, it is frequently pronounced as /l/.

Both consonants and vowels can be lengthened, or "doubled," a grammatical feature that normally signals pluralization or verb forms where repetitive action is taking place—we have indicated this by simply doubling the letter. For double consonants, the effect is to make that consonant more emphatic and explosive. An example is *mmalu*, "honor, respect," which is pronounced by holding the lips closed longer than one would for an English *m*. The Tuvalu Language Board, currently working to standardize spelling and produce the first Tuvalu language dictionary, may prefer the use of macrons (as in ā instead of aa) to indicate length.

ॐ

## Tuvaluan Words Used in the Text

| | |
|---|---|
| *aahiga* | community meeting hall. Known as *maneapa* in most other islands of Tuvalu |
| *aava* | respect, honor |
| *afaga* | canoe landing place, especially of the precontact gods |
| *aitu* | ghost, spirit |
| *akai* | to request, as a gift, something from someone; to beg |
| *aliki* | traditional chief; also "Lord," in biblical usage. Often referred to today as *Tokofitu*, a polite euphemism referring to the seven traditional chiefly families. The reigning chief is *Pulefenua*, leader of the island. |
| *alofa* | love, compassion, empathy, pity |
| *ano* | traditional ball game played by two teams on ceremonial occasions |
| *atu* | skipjack tuna, bonito (*Euthynnus pelamis*), one of the staple ocean-going fish caught by trolling |
| *epa* | finely plaited sleeping mat, a form of traditional wealth |
| *faatele* | traditional song/dance form characterized by accelerating rhythm and tempo and drumming on a mat, low box structure, and *kapa* tin |
| *fakaalofa* | landless person (a non-Nanumean), "pitiable" |
| *fakaatea* | different |
| *fakatapu* | ban, forbid; ostracize |
| *fakatupuna* | classificatory relative in grandparent generation |
| *fakaua* | household-based work and food production groups that are required to provide foods and contributions for island-wide feasts in the *aahiga* |
| *fakavae* | foundation; constitution; one's share in local cooperative society |
| *fakkai* | village, community |
| *fale* | house, household |
| *Falekaupule* | Elected local island government (instituted 1997); the traditional leadership, elders and chiefs, who meet in the meeting hall on each island |
| *fehuiaki* | to trade, exchange |

| | |
|---|---|
| *feitu* | side; either of two named village "sides" or halves, Lolua and Haumaefa, to which most Nanumeans belong |
| *felo* | small fig species (*Ficus tinctoria*) |
| *fenua* | island; community; country; land (when used in opposition to sea) |
| *fetau* | *Calophyllum inophyllum*, large hardwood tree, favored for making canoe hulls |
| *fia kano* | to desire to remain related (one reason given by families that may not wish to approve a marriage between their young people) |
| *folau* | to sail, to voyage; set oneself adrift at sea |
| *fugao* | spouse of one's child |
| *gafa* | length of a man's double arm span; a fathom; descent line |
| *galo* | gone, missing |
| *hahave* | flying fish (*Exocoetidae*) |
| *hai taina* | fictive sibling, honorary sibling (lit.: "tie same sex sibling [or cousin]") |
| *hakulaa* | marlin, swordfish |
| *huihui* | to trade, exchange |
| *kaaiga* | extended family, family |
| *kai fakatahi* | to eat together, to eat in a group; share |
| *kaitahi* | group land tenure, a group of related individuals who share rights to and use of one or more land parcels; lit., "eat as one" |
| *kaleve* | coconut sap, collected from specially prepared spathes when the tree is just flowering out. If fresh, *kaleve fou*, if fermented and alcoholic, *kaleve vii*, if boiled to molasses-like consistency, *kaleve kula* |
| *kanava* | *Cordia subcordata*, medium-sized shoreline tree whose rot-resistant wood is used for house posts |
| *kano* | a relative; related |
| *kapa* | tin can (from English "copper"); large empty biscuit tins are used as drums in faatele dances |
| *kapau* | coarse mat of coconut fronds, used on ground beneath finer mats (such as *papa* and *epa*) |
| *Kau Aliki* | council of chiefs |
| *Kaumaile* | the spear said to have been brought to Nanumea by its founder, Tefolaha, and later used by his descendant, Lapi; emblem of Nanumea |
| *Kaupule* | elected local government ("Council of Leaders"), replacing Island Council in 1997 |

| | |
|---|---|
| *kopiti* | extended patrilateral and patrilocal family residential group, now archaic |
| *llama* | to fish for flying fish in canoe or small boat using pressure lamp or, formerly, torches (*lama*) braided of dried coconut fronds |
| *lotofenua* | "community heartedness," loyalty to one's home island community, the virtue of caring about one's community; patriotism |
| *maa* | shame; to be shy or ashamed; brother-in-law |
| *maalosi* | strong, hardworking; strength |
| *maatua* | parents or relative in parents' generation; mother or one of her female relatives in same generation |
| *maatua ofo* | "volunteer mother," a ceremonial kinship role undertaken by distant female cousins of a newborn child's father |
| *maga o aliki* | "branch of chiefs," one of the seven chiefly branches or lineages said to spring from Nanumea's founder, Tefolaha |
| *magoo* | shark |
| *mako* | traditional song commemorating an individual or event |
| *malae* | open area, field, airfield; traditionally adjacent to community meeting hall |
| *maneapa* | meeting hall (*aahiga* in Nanumea, *maneaba* in Kiribati) |
| *matakaaiga* | household |
| *meaalofa* | gift |
| *mmalu* | honor, respect |
| *ofaga* | a nest; sometimes appears as variant of *afaga* |
| *oge* | stingy |
| *paa* | mother-of-pearl shell tuna fishing lure (an important piece of fishing equipment as well as a traditional valuable and mark of status) |
| *paalagi* | foreigner; usually (but not always) in reference to individuals of European descent |
| *Pai* | one of two women (the other is Vau) said to have originally been in possession of Nanumea; name of one of two sports or competitive teams at Nanumea's Kaumaile primary school |
| *paiee* | lazy |
| *pakupaku* | the portion (about 10%) of fishing catch provided by canoe captain to the individual who supplied the tree from which its hull was hewn, sometimes given to another person designated by captain |
| *palu* | deep-sea fish (*Ruvettus* sp.) caught deep on baited longline hooks, sometimes called "castor oil fish" because of its oily flesh |

| | |
|---|---|
| *papa* | plaited all-purpose sitting mat, made of ca. 3/4″ to 1″-wide strips of pandanus leaf. Papa are about 1 yard by 2 yards in size. |
| *pologa* | special responsibilities associated with particular lineages; servant |
| *pou* | pillar, post (of a building); by metaphorical extension, the family heads who sit in the *aahiga* |
| *pouliuli* | word characterizing Nanumea and Tuvalu society before Christianization; lit. "black black night," i.e., "dark ages" |
| *pulaka* | "atoll taro" (*Cyrtosperma chamissonis*), similar to but larger and more salt tolerant than taro |
| *Pulefenua* | reigning chief, formerly *te aliki* (or *ulu aliki*) |
| *taina* | same sex sibling, or cousin of same generation as ego |
| *tafolaa* | dolphin, porpoise; whale |
| *takuo* | yellowfin tuna (probably *Thunnus albacares*), one of the staple ocean-going fish caught by trolling |
| *takutakua* | renowned, famous, "talked about" in a positive sense |
| *talo* | taro (*Colocasia esculenta*); an excavated pit for growing taro or pulaka |
| *tama* | child |
| *tama ofo* | child who is taken on and given food and other gifts by a *matua ofo* |
| *tamana* | father or male relative of his in father's generation |
| *tamatane* | young, unmarried man |
| *taui* | to trade items of exactly equal value; to repay; to exact vengeance |
| *tausi* | to care for; a person who cares for someone |
| *tautai* | master fisherman; captain of a canoe |
| *tavatava* | juvenile stage of yellowfin tuna (*takuo*) |
| *telemo* | telegraphic money order |
| *titi* | traditional skirt, now used in dancing but some types formerly used as everyday garb. Styles include, among others, *titi vao, titi fakamanumanu, titi galegale*. Made of variously prepared leaves and fibers, but none made of "grass" |
| *toa* | warrior; also, a type of hardwood (possible *Pemphis* sp.) used for coconut husking staffs (*koho*), said to grow on neighboring Tuvalu islands but not in Nanumea |
| *toeaina* | elder male leader; male head of a family |
| *togi* | buy, sell; market exchange |
| *Tokofitu* | lit., "the seven," the Council of Chiefs; chiefly lineage |
| *tonu* | real, true, as in *tuagane tonu* (one's sister or brother, as opposed to cousin) |

| | |
|---|---|
| *tuaatina* | mother's brother or sister's child; a culturally marked, special relationship |
| *tuagane* | opposite sex sibling or cousin |
| *Tukumuna* | chief's spokesperson, member of the *aliki* |
| *tupuna* | grandparent or relative of ego in generation above parents |
| *ulua* | trevally fish, a Jack (possibly *Caranx ignobilis*) |
| *uosili* | attendant to bride or groom at wedding; "best man" or "bridesmaid" |
| *uto* | coconut or coconut palm of sweet-husked variety; husk of green nut can be chewed for its sweet juice |
| *vaelua* | "divide in two"—traditional practice of dividing the island population into two parts, each living in separate portion of the island, in order to supervise resource use in times of drought or other hardship |
| *vaevae* | divided, individual form of land tenure |
| *vaka* | canoe, in Nanumea traditionally with dug-out hull hewn from mahogony-like *fetau* tree (*Calophylum inophyllum*), but sometimes hewn from the softer *pukavai* tree (*Hernandia peltata*) |
| *vaka kaiva* | four-person, ocean-going fishing canoe—the highest state of the canoe builder's art; in some respects sacred, since not used for routine work |
| *vaka malaga* | four-person canoe used for work purposes, not ocean fishing—usually not as strong or as well-fitted out as *vaka kaiva* |
| *vao* | bush, bushland; conceptual opposite of village land (*fakkai*) |
| *Vau* | one of two women (the other is Pai) said to have originally been in possession of Nanumea; name of one of two sports teams at Nanumea's Kaumaile primary school |

# Bibliography

Agar, Michael
    1996    *The Professional Stranger: An Informal Introduction to Anthropology*, 2nd edition. San Diego: Academic Press.

Aiavao, Ulafala
    1996    Global Warming's Missing Link. *Islands Business* 22(7):35.

Bailey, Eric
    1975    *Report on the 1973 Census of Population*. Vol. I: *Basic Information*. Tarawa, Gilbert Islands: Office of the Chief Minister.
    1977    *The Christmas Island Story*. London: Stacey International.

Baines, Graham B. K., and R. F. McLean
    1976a    Re-Surveys of 1972 Hurricane Rampart of Funafuti Atoll, Ellice Islands. *Search* 7(no. 1–2, Jan–Feb):36–37.
    1976b    Sequential Studies of Hurricane Deposit Evolution at Funafuti Atoll. *Marine Geology* 21:M1–M8.

Becke, Louis
    1967    *South Sea Supercargo: Stories by Louis Becke*, comp. and ed. A. Grove Day. Honolulu: University of Hawaii Press.

Becker, Anne
    1995    *Body, Self and Society: The View from Fiji*. Philadelphia: University of Pennsylvania Press.

Bedford, Richard, Barrie Macdonald, and Doug Munro
  1980    Population Estimates in Kiribati and Tuvalu: Review and Speculation. *Journal of the Polynesian Society* 89:119–246.
Belich, James
  1996    *Making Peoples: A History of the New Zealanders.* Auckland: Allen Lane, The Penguin Press.
Bell, Brian
  n.d.    *Tuvalu Trust Fund: 10th Anniversary Profile, 1987–1997.* Funafuti: Tuvalu Trust Fund Advisory Committee.
Bellah, Robert N., Richard Madsen, William M. Sullivan, Ann Swidler, and Steven M. Tipton
  1996    *Habits of the Heart: Individualism and Commitment in American Life* [updated edition]. Berkeley: University of California Press.
Bellwood, Peter
  1987    *The Polynesians: Prehistory of an Island People,* rev. ed. London: Thames and Hudson.
  1989    The Colonization of the Pacific: Some Current Hypotheses. In Adrian V. S. Hill and Susan W. Serjeantson, eds., *The Colonization of the Pacific: A Genetic Trail,* pp. 1–59. Oxford: Clarendon Press.
Bernard, H. Russell
  1995    *Research Methods in Anthropology: Qualitative and Quantitative Approaches.* Walnut Creek, CA: AltaMira Press.
Bertram, Geoff
  1999    The MIRAB Model Twelve Years On. *The Contemporary Pacific* 11(1):105–138.
Bertram, I. G., and R. F. Watters
  1985    The MIRAB Economy in South Pacific Microstates. *Pacific Viewpoint* 26(3):497–519.
Besnier, Niko
  1981a   The History of the Tuvaluan Language. In *Ttou Tauloto te Ggana Tuvalu: a Course in the Tuvaluan Language.* Funafuti: United States Peace Corps., pp. xxi–xxviii.
  1981b   *Tuvaluan Lexicon.* Funafuti: United States Peace Corps.
  1994    The Truth and Other Irrelevant Aspects of Nukulaelae Gossip. *Pacific Studies* 17(3):1–39.
  1995    *Literacy, Emotion and Authority: Reading and Writing on a Polynesian Atoll.* Cambridge: Cambridge University Press.
Borofsky, Robert
  1987    *Making History: Pukapukan and Anthropological Constructions of Knowledge.* Cambridge: Cambridge University Press.
  1997    Cook, Lono, Obeyesekere, and Sahlins. *Current Anthropology* 38(2):255–282.
Borofsky, Robert, and Alan Howard
  1989    The Early Contact Period. In Alan Howard and Robert Borofsky, eds., *Developments in Polynesian Ethnology,* pp. 241–275. Honolulu: University of Hawaii Press.

Bowen, Elenore Smith
1964    *Return to Laughter: An Anthropological Novel.* New York: Doubleday [orig. published 1954].
Brady, Ivan
1972    Kinship Reciprocity in the Ellice Islands: An Evaluation of Sahlins' Model of the Sociology of Primitive Exchange. *Journal of the Polynesian Society* 81:290–316.
1974    Land Tenure in the Ellice Islands: A Changing Profile. In Henry Lundsgaarde, ed., *Land Tenure in Oceania.* Honolulu: University Press of Hawaii, pp. 130–178.
1975    Christians, Pagans and Government Men: Culture Change in the Ellice Islands. In Ivan Brady and Barry Isaac, eds., *A Reader in Culture Change*, vol. 2. New York: John Wiley, pp. 111–146.
Buck, Sir Peter [Te Rangi Hiroa]
1959    *Vikings of the Pacific.* Chicago: University of Chicago Press. [Originally published in 1938 as *Vikings of the Sunrise*, Frederick A. Stokes Co.]
Catala, René L.A.
1957    *Report on the Gilbert Islands: Some Aspects of Human Ecology.* Washington, D.C.: Pacific Science Board, Atoll Research Bulletin no. 59.
Chambers, Anne
1983    Exchange and Social Organization in Nanumea, a Polynesian Atoll Society. PhD dissertation, University of California, Berkeley, Dept. of Anthropology.
1984    *Nanumea.* Canberra: Australian National University Development Studies Center. *Atoll Economy: Social Change in Kiribati and Tuvalu*, no. 6 [reissue, with minor revisions, of *Nanumea Report: A Socio-Economic Survey of Nanumea Atoll, Tuvalu.* Wellington: Victoria University, Rural Socio–Economic Survey of the Gilbert and Ellice Islands, 1975].
1986    *Reproduction in Nanumea (Tuvalu): An Ethnography of Fertility and Birth.* Auckland, University of Auckland Working Papers in Anthropology, Archaeology, Linguistics and Maori Studies, no. 72.
Chambers, Keith S.
1984    Heirs of Tefolaha: Tradition and Social Organization in Nanumea, a Polynesian Atoll Community. PhD dissertation, University of California, Berkeley, Dept. of Anthropology.
Chambers, Keith S., and Anne Chambers
1975    Comment: A Note on the Ellice Referendum. *Pacific Viewpoint* 16:221–222.
Chambers, Keith S., and Doug Munro
1980    The "Mystery" of Gran Cocal: European Discovery and Mis-Discovery in Tuvalu. *Journal of the Polynesian Society* 89:167–198.
Christensen, Dieter, and Gerd Koch
1964    *Die Musik der Ellice-Inseln.* Berlin: Museum für Völkerkunde.
Coates, Austin
1970    *Western Pacific Islands.* London: Her Majesty's Stationery Office.

Connell, John
  1980    Tuvalu: Independence or Dependence? *Current Affairs Bulletin* (University of Sydney, Department of Adult Education) 56(9):27–31.
  1991    Island Microstates: The Mirage of Development. *The Contemporary Pacific* 3(2):251–287.
Counts, David
  2000    Too Many Bananas, Not Enough Pineapples, and No Watermelon at All: Three Object Lessons in Living with Reciprocity. In *Stumbling Toward Truth: Anthropologists at Work*, ed. Philip R. DeVita. Prospect Heights, IL: Waveland Press, pp. 177–183. [Originally published 1990 in *The Humbled Anthropologist: Tales from the Pacific*, Wadsworth.]
Cox, Paul Alan
  1997    *Nafanua: Saving the Samoan Rainforest*. New York: W. W. Freeman.
Crane, Julia G., and Michael V. Angrosino
  1992    *Field Projects in Anthropology: A Student Handbook*, 3rd ed. Prospect Heights, IL: Waveland Press.
Crawford, Peter Ian, and David Turton, eds.
  1992    *Film as Ethnography*. Manchester: Manchester University Press.
Darwin, Charles
  1962    *The Voyage of the Beagle*, ed. and annotated by Leonard Engel. Garden City, NY: Doubleday.
Davenport, William
  1959    Nonunilinear Descent and Descent Groups. *American Anthropologist* 61:557–572.
David, Mrs. Edgeworth
  1899    *Funafuti, or Three Months on a Coral Atoll: An Unscientific Account of a Scientific Expedition*. London: John Murray.
Day, A. Grove
  1966    *Louis Becke*. Melbourne: Hill of Content.
Dening, Greg
  1980    *Islands and Beaches: Discourse on a Silent Land: Marquesas 1774–1880*. Honolulu: University of Hawaii Press.
Denoon, Donald, ed.
  1997    *The Cambridge History of the Pacific Islanders*. Cambridge: Cambridge University Press.
DeVita, Philip R., ed.
  2000    *Stumbling Toward Truth: Anthropologists at Work*. Prospect Heights, IL: Waveland Press.
Dickinson, William R., Jun Takayama, Eleanour A. Snow, and Richard Shutler Jr.
  1990    Sand Temper of Probable Fijian Origin in Prehistoric Potsherds from Tuvalu. *Antiquity* 64:307–312.
Dodd, Edward
  1972    *Polynesian Seafaring*. New York: Dodd, Mead and Co.
Dodge, Ernest S.
  1976    *Islands and Empires: Western Impact on the Pacific and East Asia*. Minneapolis: University of Minnesota Press, and Oxford: Oxford University Press.

Ellen, R. F., ed.
1984    *Ethnographic Research: A Guide to General Conduct.* London: Academic Press.
Ells, Phillip
2000    *The People's Lawyer.* London: Virgin Publishing.
Engel, Leonard
1962    Darwin and the *Beagle.* Introduction to Charles Darwin, *The Voyage of the Beagle.* Garden City, NY: Doubleday, pp. ix–xxiv.
Etzioni, Amitai
1993    *The Spirit of Community: Rights, Responsibilities, and the Communitarian Agenda.* New York: Crown Publishers.
Feinberg, Richard
1988    *Polynesian Seafaring and Navigation: Ocean Travel in Anutan Culture and Society.* Kent, Ohio: Kent State University Press.
1998    *Oral Traditions of Anuta, a Polynesian Outlier in the Solomon Islands.* New York and Oxford: Oxford University Press (Oxford Studies in Anthropological Linguistics 15).
Fernea, Elizabeth Warnock
1965    *Guests of the Sheik: An Ethnography of an Iraqi Village.* New York: Doubleday.
Finney, Ben
1976 (ed.)   *Pacific Navigation and Voyaging.* Wellington, New Zealand: The Polynesian Society.
1994    *Voyage of Rediscovery: a Cultural Odyssey Through Polynesia.* Berkeley: University of California Press.
1999    *The Sin at Awarua.* The Contemporary Pacific 11(1):1–33.
Firth, Raymond
1954    Anuta and Tikopia: Symbiotic Elements in Social Organization. *Journal of the Polynesian Society* 63:87–131.
1957    A Note on Descent Groups in Polynesia. *Man* 57:4–8.
1961    *History and Traditions of Tikopia.* Wellington: The Polynesian Society.
1963    Bilateral Descent Groups: An Operational Viewpoint. In I. Shapera, ed., *Studies in Kinship and Marriage.* Royal Anthropological Institute, Occasional Paper 16:22–37.
1970    Sibling Terms in Polynesia. *Journal of the Polynesian Society* 79:272–287.
Flinn, Juliana, Leslie Marshall, and Jocelyn Armstrong, eds.
1998    *Fieldwork and Families: Constructing New Models for Ethnographic Research.* Honolulu: University of Hawaii Press.
Fosberg, F. R., ed.
1965    *Man's Place in the Island Ecosystem: A Symposium.* Honolulu: B. P. Bishop Museum Press.
Fosberg, F. R., and Marie-Helene Sachet, eds.
1953    *Handbook for Atoll Research*, 2nd preliminary ed. Washington, D.C.: Pacific Science Board, Atoll Research Bulletin No. 17.

French, Maurice V.
1994    Report on an Electricity Supply for Nanumea Island, Tuvalu for the
        Nanumean Community. Australian Executive Service Overseas Project
        No. TV 0006 (photocopy—July 1994).
Geddes, W. H., Anne Chambers, Betsy Sewell, Roger Lawrence, and Ray Watters
1979    *Rural Socio-Economic Change in the Gilbert and Ellice Islands: Team
        Report*. Tarawa: Ministry of Local Government and Rural Develop-
        ment [The Victoria University of Wellington Rural Socio-economic
        Survey of the Gilbert and Ellice Islands; reissued 1982 in different for-
        mat as *Islands on the Line: Team Report*. Canberra, Australian
        National University, Development Studies Centre, no. 1 in its *Atoll
        Economy: Social Change in Kiribati and Tuvalu*.]
Gibson, Herbert W. S.
1892    Report of Proceedings, H.M.S. *Curacoa* at Suva, Fiji, 20 September
        1892. Ms., Western Pacific High Commission Archives, Suva. [Orig-
        inally formed Enclosure no. 3 in Australian Letter No. 464 of 6 Octo-
        ber, 1892, Royal Navy, Australian Station.]
Gill, W. W.
1885    *Jottings from the Pacific*. London: The Religious Tract Society.
Gladwin, Thomas
1970    *East Is a Big Bird: Navigation and Logic on Puluwat Atoll*. Cam-
        bridge: Harvard University Press.
Goldman, Irving
1970    *Ancient Polynesian Society*. Chicago: University of Chicago Press.
Goldsmith, Michael
1985    Transformations of the Meeting-House in Tuvalu. In Antony Hooper
        and Judith Huntsman, eds., *Transformations of Polynesian Culture*.
        Auckland: The Polynesian Society, pp. 151–175.
1989    Church and Society in Tuvalu. Ph.D. dissertation, University of Illinois
        at Urbana-Champaign, Department of Anthropology.
1995    Decentering Pacific Biographies. In *Messy Entanglements: Papers of
        the 10th Pacific History Association Conference, Tarawa, Kiribati*.
        Brisbane: Pacific History Association, pp. 5–14.
Goldsmith, Michael, and Doug Munro
1992a   Conversion and Church Formation in Tuvalu. *Journal of Pacific His-
        tory* 27:44–54.
1992b   Encountering Elekana Encountering Tuvalu. In Donald Rubenstein,
        ed., *Pacific History: Papers from the 8th Pacific History Association
        Conference*. Mangilao, Guam: University of Guam Press and Microne-
        sian Area Research Center, pp. 25–41.
Goodenough, Ward
1955    A Problem in Malayo-Polynesian Social Organization. *American
        Anthropologist* 57:71–83.
1996    (ed.) *Prehistoric Settlement of the Pacific*. Philadelphia: American Philo-
        sophical Society (transactions v. 86, pt. 5).

Grimble, Arthur
 1952  *A Pattern of Islands*. London: John Murray.
 1957  *Return to the Islands: Life and Legends in the Gilberts*. New York: William Morrow.
Haddon, A. C., and James Hornell
 1975  *Canoes of Oceania*. Honolulu: B. P. Bishop Museum Press. [Reprint of its Special Publications 27, 28, 29, originally published 1936–38.]
Halapua, Sitivini
 1993  *Sustainable Development: From Ideal to Reality in the Pacific Islands*. Honolulu: East West Center, Pacific Islands Development Program.
Hayter, Francis
 1871–73  Logbook and Journal, H.M.S. *Basilisk*, January 1871–July 1873. Canberra, Pacific Manuscripts Bureau microfilm PMB 626.
Hedley, Charles
 1896  General Account of the Atoll of Funafuti. Australian Museum Memoir 3 (Pt. 1):1–71.
Heyerdahl, Thor
 1952  *American Indians in the Pacific*. Chicago: Rand McNally.
Hill, Captain A. R.
 1945  Travelling Diaries of District Officer, Ellice Islands. Diary for May 1945 of Captain A. R. Hill. Western Pacific High Commission, Suva, GEIC File 10/30/1.
Hooper, Antony, Steve Britton, Ron Crocombe, Judith Huntsman, and Cluny Macpherson, eds.
 1987  *Class and Culture in the South Pacific*. Auckland: University of Auckland, Centre for Pacific Studies, and Suva: University of the South Pacific, Institute of Pacific Studies.
Hooper, Antony, and Kerry James
 1993  *Sustainability and Pacific Cultures*. Honolulu: East-West Center, Pacific Islands Development Program (paper prepared for the Fourth Pacific Islands Conference of Leaders, Tahiti, French Polynesia, June 24–26, 1993).
Howard, Alan
 1972  Polynesian Social Stratification Revisited: Reflections on Castles Built of Sand (and a Few Bits of Coral). *American Anthropologist* 74:811–823.
Huntsman, Judith, and Antony Hooper
 1996  *Tokelau: A Historical Ethnography*. Auckland: Auckland University Press.
Huth, Tom
 1997  Hi. Nice Little Island You Have Here. Mind if My 775 Passengers Come Ashore? *Conde Nast Traveller 32* (April 1997):136–144.
Igarashi, Yuriko, Kazumichi Katayama, and Jun Takayama
 1987  Human Skeletal Remains from Tuvalu with Special Reference to Artificial Cranial Deformation. *Man and Culture in Oceania* 3:105–124.
Irwin, Geoffrey
 1992  *The Prehistoric Exploration and Colonisation of the Pacific*. Cambridge: Cambridge University Press.

1998        The Colonisation of the Pacific Plate: Chronological, Navigational and
            Social Issues. *Journal of the Polynesian Society* 107(2):111–143.
Isala, Tito
1983a      Secession and Independence. In Hugh Laracy, ed., *Tuvalu: A History*.
            Suva: University of the South Pacific, Institute of Pacific Studies, and
            Funafuti: Ministry of Social Services, pp. 153–177, 198–199.
1983b      Tuvalu: Atoll Nation. In Ron Crocombe and Ahmed Ali, eds., *Politics
            in Polynesia*. Suva: University of the South Pacific, Institute of Pacific
            Studies, pp. 20–54.
Isala, Tito, and Doug Munro
1987        *Te Aso Fiafia: Te Tala o te Kamupane Vaitupu 1877–1887*. Funafuti
            and Suva: Tuvalu Extension Services Centre and the Institute of
            Pacific Studies of the University of the South Pacific.
Jackson, Geoffrey W.
1994        *Te Tikisionale o te 'Gana Tuvalu: A Tuvaluan-English Dictionary*, rev.
            ed. Suva: Oceania Printers. [Originally published 1993.]
Jackson, Geoff, and Genny Jackson
1999        *An Introduction to Tuvaluan*. Suva: Oceania Printers.
Keesing, Roger
1975        *Kin Groups and Social Structure*. New York: Holt, Rinehart and Win-
            ston.
Kennedy, Donald G.
1931        *Field Notes on the Culture of Vaitupu, Ellice Islands*. Wellington: The
            Polynesian Society, Memoir no. 9.
1953        Land Tenure in the Ellice Islands. *Journal of the Polynesian Society*
            62:348–358.
Kirch, Patrick V.
1984        *The Evolution of the Polynesian Chiefdoms*. Cambridge: Cambridge
            University Press.
1989        The Early Contact Period. In Alan Howard and Robert Borofsky, eds.,
            *Developments in Polynesian Ethnology*. Honolulu: University of
            Hawaii Press, pp. 13–46.
Kirch, Patrick V., and Roger C. Green
1987        History, Phylogeny and Evolution in Polynesia. *Current Anthropology*
            28:431–456.
Kirch, Patrick V., and Marshall I. Weisler
1994        Archaeology in the Pacific Islands: An Appraisal of Recent Research.
            *Journal of Archaeological Research* 2(4):285–328.
Kirtley, Bacil F.
1971        *A Motif-Index of Traditional Polynesian Narratives*. Honolulu: Uni-
            versity of Hawaii Press.
Koch, Gerd
1961        *Die Materielle Kultur der Ellice-Inseln*. Berlin: Museum für
            VölkerkundeVeröffentlichungen, neue folge 3, Abteilung Südsee I.
            Translated n.d. [ca.1984] as *The Material Culture of Tuvalu* by Guy
            Slater. Suva, University of the South Pacific, Institute of Pacific Studies.

Kofe, Laumua
   1976   The Tuvalu Church: A Socio-Historical Survey of its Development
          Towards an Indigenous Church. Thesis (Bachelor of Divinity), Pacific
          Theological College, Suva.
Kottak, Conrad
   1999   *Assault on Paradise: Social Change in a Brazilian Village*, 3rd ed.
          Boston: McGraw Hill.
Lake, A. G.
   1947   Annual Report for 1946, Ellice Islands District (Mar. 8, 1947).
          Included in Reports and Returns, Annual Colony Reports, Ellice
          Islands District, GEIC File 3/1/6, vol. II (housed, in 1974, at Western
          Pacific High Commission Archives, Suva).
   1949   Genealogical, historical and traditional data collected by Land's Com-
          missioner A. G. Lake. Gilbert and Ellice Islands Colony archival file,
          29/2, "History and Traditions of Various Ellice Islands," F. 9, No. 9,
          February 20, 1949 (correspondence between Lands Commissioner
          and Chief Lands Commissioner).
   1950   Letter from A. G. Lake, Chief Lands Commissioner, to District Officer
          R.C.D. McKenzie, included in McKenzie's Annual Report for 1949,
          Ellice Islands District [July 10, 1950]. In Reports and Returns, Annual
          Colony Reports, Ellice Islands District, GEIC File 3/1/6, vol. II (housed,
          in 1974, at Western Pacific High Commission Archives, Suva).
Laracy, Hugh, ed.
   1983   *Tuvalu: A History.* Suva: University of the South Pacific, and Funafuti,
          Government of Tuvalu, Ministry of Social Services.
Lewis, David
   1972   *We the Navigators: The Ancient Art of Landfinding in the Pacific.*
          Honolulu: University of Hawaii Press.
Levison, Michael, R. Gerard Ward, and John W. Webb
   1973   *The Settlement of Polynesia: A Computer Simulation.* Minneapolis:
          University of Minnesota Press.
Levy, Robert I.
   1973   *Tahitians: Mind and Experience in the Society Islands.* Chicago and
          London: University of Chicago Press.
Lieber, Michael
   1994   *More Than a Living: Fishing and the Social Order on a Polynesian
          Atoll.* Boulder, CO: Westview Press.
Linkels, Ad, and Lucia Linkels
   1994   *Tuvalu, a Polynesian Atoll Society.* CD2055. Leiden, the Netherlands:
          PAN records (32 selections recorded in 1990 in Tuvalu).
Lockwood, Victoria S., Thomas G. Harding, and Ben J. Wallace, eds.
   1993   *Contemporary Pacific Societies: Studies in Development and Change.*
          Englewood Cliffs, NJ: Prentice Hall.
Macdonald, Barrie
   1970   Constitutional Development in the Gilbert and Ellice Islands Colony.
          *Journal of Pacific History* 5:139–145.

1971a    Local Government in the Gilbert and Ellice Islands 1892–1969, Part I. *Journal of Administration Overseas* 10:280–293.

1971b    Policy and Practice in an Atoll Territory: British Rule in the Gilbert and Ellice Islands, 1892–1970. PhD Thesis, Australian National University, Canberra, Department of History.

1975a    Secession in the Defence of Identity: The Making of Tuvalu. *Pacific Viewpoint* 16:26–44.

1975b    The Separation of the Gilbert and Ellice Islands. *Journal of Pacific History* 10:84–88.

1982     *Cinderellas of the Empire: Towards a History of Kiribati and Tuvalu.* Canberra: Australian National University Press.

Mahaffy, Arthur

1909     *Report . . . on a Visit to the Gilbert and Ellice Islands, 1909. . . . London, Colonial Office.* (Seen at Western Pacific Archives, Suva: Despatches from Secretary of State, Numbered 1909, pp. 509–516.)

Maragos, James E.

1973     Tropical Cyclone Bebe Creates a New Land Formation on Funafuti Atoll. *Science* 181(21 Sept, 1973):1161–1164.

Marck, Jeff

1996     Kin Terms in the Polynesian Protolanguages. *Oceanic Linguistics* 35(2):195–257.

Marcus, George E.

1989     Chieftainship. In Alan Howard and Robert Borofsky, eds., *Developments in Polynesian Ethnology.* Honolulu: University of Hawaii Press, pp. 175–209.

Maude, H. E.

1932     Report on the 1931 Census of the Gilbert, Ellice and Phoenix Islands. Manuscript: Western Pacific High Commission Archives.

1949     *The Cooperative Movement in the Gilbert and Ellice Islands.* Sydney: South Pacific Commission (Technical Paper no. 1).

1963     *The Evolution of the Gilbertese Boti: An Ethnohistorical Interpretation.* Wellington: The Polynesian Society, Memoir No. 35.

1968     *Of Islands and Men: Studies in Pacific History.* Melbourne: Oxford University Press.

1980     *The Gilbertese Maneaba.* Suva: University of the South Pacific, Institute of Pacific Studies, and Tarawa: Kiribati Extension Centre of the University of the South Pacific.

1981     *Slavers in Paradise: The Peruvian Labour Trade in Polynesia, 1862–1864.* Canberra: Australian National University Press.

Maude, H. E., and Ida Leeson

1968     The Coconut Oil Trade of the Gilbert Islands. In H. E. Maude, *Of Islands and Men: Studies in Pacific History.* Melbourne: Oxford University Press, pp. 233–283.

Maurelle, Francisco Antonio

1799     Narrative of an Interesting Voyage in the Frigate *La Princesa*, from Manila to San Blaz, in 1780 and 1781. In J. F. G. de la Perouse, *A Voy-*

*age Round the World in the Years 1785, 1786, 1787, and 1788,* 2nd ed., ed. L. A. Milet-Mureau, 3 vols. London: G. G. and J. Johnson.

Mauss, Marcel
1967 [1934] *The Gift: Forms and Functions of Exchange in Archaic Societies.* New York: W. W. Norton.

McArthur, Norma
1967 *Island Populations of the Pacific.* Canberra: Australian National University Press.

McArthur, Norma, and J. B. McCaig
1964 *A Report on the Results of the Census of the Population, Gilbert and Ellice Islands Colony 1963.* Suva: Government Printer.

McLean, Mervyn
1995 *An Annotated Bibliography of Oceanic Music and Dance,* 2nd revised edition. Warren, MI: Harmonie Park Press. [First edition 1977, Wellington: The Polynesian Society.]
2000 *Weavers of Song: Polynesian Music and Dance.* Honolulu: University of Hawaii Press.

McLean, R. F.
1975 Morphology of Hurricane Banks at Funafuti Atoll, Ellice Islands. In William Brockie, Richard Le heron, and Evelyn Stokes, eds., *Proceedings of the International Geographical Union Regional Conference and Eighth New Zealand Geography Conference,* pp. 269–277. New Zealand Geographical Society, Conference Series no. 8.

McLean, R. F., P. F. Holthus, P. L. Hosking, and C. D. Woodroffe
1986 *Tuvalu Land Resources Survey: Nanumea.* Auckland: University of Auckland, Department of Geography, Tuvalu Land Resources Survey, Island Report no. 1 ("A report prepared for the Food and Agriculture Organisation of the United Nations acting as executing agency for the United Nations Development Programme").

McLean, R. F., and P. L. Hosking
1991 *Tuvalu Land Resources Survey: Country Report.* Auckland, Department of Geography, University of Auckland. ("A report prepared for the Food and Agriculture Organisation of the United Nations acting as executing agency for the United Nations Development Programme.")

McQuarrie, Peter
1994 *Strategic Atolls: Tuvalu and the Second World War.* Christchurch: University of Canterbury Macmillan Brown Centre for Pacific Studies, and Suva: University of the South Pacific Institute of Pacific Studies.

Moresby, John
1876 *Discoveries and Surveys in New Guinea and the D'Entrecasteaux Islands. . . . a Cruise in Polynesia . . . in . . . H.M.S. Basilisk.* London: John Murray.

Morton, Helen
1996 *Becoming Tongan: An Ethnography of Childhood.* Honolulu: University of Hawaii Press.

Munro, Doug
1982    The Lagoon Islands: A History of Tuvalu 1820–1908. Ph.D. thesis, Macquarie University (Australia), School of History, Philosophy and Politics.
1990    Migration and the Shift to Dependence in Tuvalu: A Historical Perspective. In John Connell, ed., *Migration and Development in the South Pacific*. Canberra: Australian National University, Pacific Research Monograph No. 24, pp. 29–41.

Murray, A. W.
1866    London Missionary Society Journals, South Sea Journals 157 (microfilm at Alexander Turnbull Library, Wellington, New Zealand). Records of the London Missionary Society, School of Oriental and African Studies, London.
1876    *Forty Years' Mission Work in Polynesia and New Guinea, from 1835 to 1875*. London: James Nisbet.

Newell, J. E.
1895    Notes, Chiefly Ethnological, of the Tokelau, Ellice, and Gilbert Islanders. *Proceedings of the Australasian Association for the Advancement of Science* 6:603–612.

Newton, W. F.
1967    The Early Population of the Ellice Islands. *Journal of the Polynesian Society* 76(2):197–204.

Noricks, Jay Smith
1981    *A Tuvalu Dictionary*, 2 vols. New Haven: Human Relations Area Files.
1983    Unrestricted Cognatic Descent and Corporateness on Niutao, a Polynesian Island of Tuvalu. *American Ethnologist* 10(3):571–584.

Obeyesekere, Gananath
1992    *The Apotheosis of Captain Cook: European Mythmaking in the Pacific*. Princeton: Princeton University Press.

Oliver, Douglas
1989    *Oceania: The Native Cultures of Australia and the Pacific Islands*, vol. 2. Honolulu: University of Hawaii Press.

Otto, Ton
1993a    Empty Tins for Lost Traditions? The West's Material and Intellectual Involvement in the Pacific, in Otto, ed., 1993, pp. 1–28.
1993b (ed.)    Pacific Islands Trajectories: Five Personal Views. Canberra: Australian National University, Department of Anthropology, Research School of Pacific Studies Occasional Paper.
1997    After the "Tidal Wave": Bernard Narokobi and the Creation of a Melanesian Way. In Ton Otto and Nicholas Thomas, eds., *Narratives of Nation in the South Pacific*. Amsterdam: Harwood Academic Publishers, pp. 33–64.

Pease, Henry II
1854    Account of an Adventure on St. Augustine Island, Lat. 5 35 S., Lon. 176 12 E., Near Ellis' Group. *Vineyard Gazette* (Martha's Vineyard, Massachusetts), May 26, 1854, vol. 9(4):1–2.
1962    Adventure on St. Augustine Island. *The Dukes County Intelligencer* (Edgartown, Massachussetts) 3(4):3–13.

Peterson, Glenn
   1993    Some Pohnpei Strategies for Economic Survival. In Victoria S. Lock-
           wood, Thomas G. Harding, and Ben J. Wallace, eds., *Contemporary
           Pacific Societies: Studies in Development and Change*. Englewood
           Cliffs, NJ: Prentice Hall, pp. 185–196.
Phillips, C.
   1881    London Missionary Society Journal (microfilm at Alexander Turnbull
           Library, Wellington, New Zealand). Records of the London Missionary
           Society, School of Oriental and African Studies, London.
Pollard, Stephen
   1988    *Atoll Economies: Issues and Strategy Options for Development—A
           Review of the Literature*. Islands/Australia Working Paper No. 88/5.
           Canberra: Australian National University, National Centre for Devel-
           opment Studies.
   1989    Pacific Atoll Economies. *Asian-Pacific Economic Literature* 3(1):63–
           81 [March 1989, Guildford, Surrey].
Pollard, Stephen, and Ropate R. Qalo
   1993    *Development Sustained by Enterprise: Toward Policies for Economic
           Stimulation*. Honolulu: East-West Center, Pacific Islands Develop-
           ment Program.
Pusinelli, F. N. M.
   1947    *A Report on the Results of the Census of the Population, Gilbert and
           Ellice Islands Colony, 1947*. Suva: Government Printer.
Radcliffe-Brown, A. R.
   1965    The Mother's Brother in South Africa. In *Structure and Function in
           Primitive Society*. New York: The Free Press, pp 15–31. [Essay originally
           published in 1924 in South African Journal of Science 21:542–555.]
Ranby, Peter
   1973    Nanumean Syntax. Master's Thesis, Department of Anthropology, Uni-
           versity of Auckland.
   1980    *A Nanumea Lexicon*. Pacific Linguistics Series C - No. 65. Canberra:
           Australian National University Press.
Raskin, Andrew
   1998    Buy This Domain. *Wired* 6.09 (September 1998):106–110.
Read, Kenneth E.
   1965    *The High Valley*. New York: Charles Scribner's Sons.
Roberts, R. G.
   1946    Annual Report for 1945, Ellice Islands District (Feb. 4, 1946).
           Included in Reports and Returns, Annual Colony Reports, Ellice
           Islands District, GEIC File 3/1/6, vol. I (housed, in 1974, at Western
           Pacific High Commission Archives, Suva).
   1958    Te Atu Tuvalu: A Short History of the Ellice Islands. *Journal of the
           Polynesian Society* 67:394–423.
Rodgers, K. A.
   1991    A Brief History of Tuvalu's Natural History. *South Pacific Journal of
           Natural Science* 11:1–14.

Rodgers, K. A., and Carol Cantrell
    1991    Incidents from Edgeworth David's 1897 Royal Society Coral Reef Boring Expedition to Funafuti. *South Pacific Journal of Natural Science* 11:15–35.

Rogers, Garth
    1977    "The Father's Sister is Black": A Consideration of Female Rank and Power in Tonga. *Journal of the Polynesian Society* 86:157–182.

Sahlins, Marshall D.
    1958    *Social Stratification in Polynesia.* Seattle: University of Washington Press.
    1963    Poor Man, Rich Man, Big Man, Chief: Political Types in Melanesia and Polynesia. *Comparative Studies in Society and History* 5:285–303.
    1972    *Stone Age Economics.* Chicago: Aldine.
    1981    *Historical Metaphors and Mythical Realities: Structure in the Early History of the Sandwich Islands Kingdom.* Ann Arbor: University of Michigan Press.
    1985    *Islands of History.* Chicago: University of Chicago Press.
    1995    *How "Natives" Think: About Captain Cook, for Example.* Chicago: University of Chicago Press.

Salmond, Anne
    1991    *Two Worlds: First Meetings between Maori and Europeans, 1642–1772.* Honolulu: University of Hawaii Press.
    1997    *Between Worlds: Early Exchanges between Maori and Europeans, 1773–1815.* Honolulu: University of Hawaii Press.

Scarr, Deryck
    1967    *Fragments of Empire: A History of the Western Pacific High Commission, 1877–1914.* Canberra: Australian National University Press.

Shore, Bradd
    1982    *Sala'ilua: A Samoan Mystery.* New York: Columbia University Press.

Shweder, Richard A., and Edmund J. Bourne
    1984    Does the Concept of the Person Vary Cross-Culturally? In Richard A. Shweder and Robert A. LeVine, eds., *Culture Theory: Essays on Mind, Self and Emotion.* Cambridge: Cambridge University Press.

Sinoto, Yoshiko H.
    1966    *Brief Description of Funafuti* [Archaeological] *Survey in 1966.* Honolulu: B.P. Bishop Museum. Typescript, 7pp, ca. 1966.

Small, Cathy A.
    1997    *Voyages: From Tongan Villages to American Suburbs.* Ithaca, NY: Cornell University Press.

Smith, Bernard
    1960    *European Vision and the South Pacific 1768–1850: A Study in the History of Art and Ideas.* New York: Oxford University Press.

Sollas, W. J.
    1899    *Funafuti: The Story of a Coral Atoll.* Annual Report of the Smithsonian Institution for the Year ending June 30, 1898, pp. 389–406. Washington D.C.: Government Printing Office.

Spiro, Melford
    1993    Is the Western Concept of the Self "Peculiar" within the Context of World Cultures? *Ethos* 21:107–153.

Spradley, James P.
1979    *The Ethnographic Interview.* New York: Holt, Rinehart and Winston.
Takayama, Jun
1987    The Western Origin for Early Eastern Polynesian Fishhooks in Light of the
        Excavation of Vaitupu, Tuvalu. *Tezukayama University Review* 57:16–46.
Takayama, Jun, and Akane Saito
1987    The Discovery of the Davidson Type 1a Hooks on Vaitupu Island,
        Tuvalu. *Tezukayama University Review* 55:29–49.
Takayama, Jun, Bwere Eritaia, and Akane Saito
1987    Preliminary Observation of the Origins of the Vaitupuans in View of
        Pottery. In Eikichi Ishikawa, ed., *Cultural Adaptation to Atolls in
        Micronesia and West Polynesia.* Tokyo: Tokyo Metropolitan Univer-
        sity, Committee for Micronesian Research, 1985, pp. 1–13.
Thomas, Allan
1996    *New Song and Dance from the Central Pacific: Creating and Per-
        forming the* Faatele *of Tokelau in the Islands and in New Zealand.*
        Stuyvesant, NY: Pendragon Press (Dance and Music Series, no. 9).
Thomas, Stephen D.
1987    *The Last Navigator.* New York: Henry Holt.
Thomson, David S.
1997    The Sapir-Whorf Hypothesis: Worlds Shaped by Words. In James Spra-
        dley and David W. McCurdy, eds., *Conformity and Conflict*, 9th ed.
        New York: Longman, pp. 80–92. [Originally published 1975, in
        *Human Behavior: Language*, New York: Time-Life Books.]
Turbott, I. G.
1950    Fishing for Flying Fish in the Gilbert and Ellice Islands. *Journal of the
        Polynesian Society* 59:349–367.
Turner, George
1876    London Missionary Society Journals, SSJ 168, consulted on microfilm
        at Alexander Turnbull Library, Wellington.
1884    *Samoa a Hundred Years Ago and Long Before.* London: Macmillan.
Tuvalu Government
1979    *Laws of Tuvalu: Revised Edition, 1978.* Funafuti: Office of the Attor-
        ney General.
1984    Third Development Plan for Tuvalu, 1984–1987 (draft, as presented
        to the Tuvalu Parliament in 1984). Funafuti: Government of Tuvalu.
1986    *Cadastral Map of Tuvalu.* Nanumea (13 sheets, plus index sheet). Funafuti:
        Ministry of Natural Resources (work carried out under the auspices of the
        United Nations Development Programme and United Nations CHS).
1991a   *Tuvalu: 1991 Population and Housing Census.* Vol. 1: *Basic Informa-
        tion.* Funafuti: Central Statistics Division, Ministry of Finance, Eco-
        nomic Planning, Commerce and Industry.
1991b   *Tuvalu: 1991 Population and Housing Census.* Vol. 2: *Analytical
        Report*, prepared by Habtemariam Tesfaghiorghis. Funafuti: Central
        Statistics Division, Ministry of Finance, Economic Planning, Com-
        merce and Industry.

1993     Education for Life Programme: Round Table Meeting on Development Assistance Requirements. (Prepared under the auspices of the UNDP/ Unesco Preparatory Assistance Project TUV 90/001, Unesco Office for the Pacific States, Apia, Western Samoa, October 1993.)

1995     *Kakeega o Tuvalu: National Development Strategy, 1995 to 1998.* Funafuti: Ministry of Finance, Economic Planning, Commerce and Industry.

1996     Printout summary of meteorological data for 1947–1993, provided by Tuvalu Meteorological Service, Funafuti.

1998     Tuvalu National Women's Policy (draft). Funafuti: Department of Health, Women and Community Affairs.

1999     *Tuvalu National Accounts, 1996–1998, Report* (September 1999). Funafuti: Ministry of Finance and Economic Planning.

Tuvalu National Archives

1893     *Agreement Between the High Commissioner for the Western Pacific and the Chief and Councillors of Nanomea* [sic] *1893.* Funafuti: Tuvalu National Archives, TUV 1/I/2.

UNDP

1999     *Pacific Human Development Report 1999: Creating Opportunities.* Suva: United Nations Development Programme.

Valeri, Valerio

1985     *Kingship and Sacrifice: Ritual and Society in Ancient Hawaii.* Chicago: University of Chicago Press.

Vansina, Jan

1985     *Oral Tradition as History.* Madison: University of Wisconsin Press.

Waqa, Vasiti, and Robert Keith-Reid

1996     Now Tuvalu's got "Live Sex" On Line. *Islands Business,* July 1996, 22(7):40–41 (Suva).

Ward, Martha C.

1989     *Nest in the Wind: Adventures in Anthropology on a Tropical Island.* Prospect Heights, IL: Waveland Press.

Ward, R. Gerard

1993     South Pacific Futures: Paradise, Prosperity, or Pauperism? *The Contemporary Pacific* 5(1):1–21.

Weisler, Marshall I.

1999a     *Atolls as Settlement Landscapes: Ujae, Marshall Islands.* Washington D.C.: National Museum of Natural History, Smithsonian Institution, Atoll Research Bulletin No. 460.

1999b     The Antiquity of Aroid Pit Agriculture and Significance of Buried A Horizons on Pacific Atolls. *Geoarchaeology: An International Journal* 14(7):621–654.

Western Pacific High Commission

1947–48     Western Pacific High Commission (Suva), GEIC File 48/41, "People of Nanumea, GEIC—Desirous of Purchasing an Island in the Fiji group."

White, Geoffrey M., and Lamont Lindstrom

1989     *The Pacific Theater: Island Representations of World War II.* Honolulu: University of Hawaii Press.

Wiens, Herold J.
  1962    *Atoll Environment and Ecology.* New Haven and London: Yale University Press.
Wilk, Richard R.
  1996    *Economics and Cultures: Foundations of Economic Anthropology.* Boulder, CO: Westview Press.
Zwart, F. H., and Ko Groenewegen
  1970    *A Report on the Results of the Census of the Population, Gilbert and Ellice Islands Colony 1968.* Suva: Government Printer.

# Study Guide

prepared by
*Holly Ambler-Jones*

## *Introduction*

- Where is Nanumea? Of which culture area is it a part? What was Tuvalu's name under British Colonial rule? What does the atoll look like?

- The authors mention taking a "relativistic" stance. What does this involve? What are the advantages of cultural relativism? Are there potential pitfalls? What might they be?

- Consider the concept of culture. Can you offer a definition? What characteristics do you think all cultures have in common?

- Where can one "do" anthropology? Must it be confined to "exotic" locales? How would you apply the anthropological perspective to understand your own culture? What aspects of your own comfortable, familiar world would be interesting to see as "culture"?

- Why have the authors chosen to write in a personal style? What, do you think, is the "experience" of cultural anthropology?

## *Chapter One   Encountering Nanumea*

- Think about the anecdote that introduces this chapter. How do you think the people "studied" by anthropologists may feel about that process? What sorts of dialectic might develop between observer and observed? What metaphors capture the essence of fieldwork relationships? How is a sense of humor useful in fieldwork?

- Why was learning the language so critical to Anne and Keith's work? How would you go about learning a language "in the field"?

- Why did Anne and Keith choose to conduct a census as their first systematic survey? What varied benefits did the census provide?

- What specific areas of interest did Anne and Keith each have on their first trip? On their second? At present?

- What fieldwork methods did they employ? Give some examples of each method.

- Anne and Keith were initially exhausted by participant observation. Why? What do you think the phrase "become a real person" means?

- How can a fieldworker assess whether he/she knows enough to prepare an ethnography? What signs signaled this readiness to Anne and Keith?

- What changes had the Nanumean community undergone in the twelve years separating the 1984 visit and the return in 1996? What are the benefits of long-term fieldwork in the same community? Are there some drawbacks? What understandings emerged as Keith and Anne reflected on the last quarter century of their involvement with Nanumea?

### *Chapter Two  Of the Island*

- Imagine that you are an anthropologist, embarking on your first fieldwork. How would you feel? How did Anne and Keith feel as they arrived on Nanumea, equipped with a refrigerator and bicycles but unable to carry on a casual conversation?

- What is "serendipity"? What role does this play in ethnographic research? Why?

- Were Anne and Keith welcome visitors in the community? Recall that only Ioane met them on the beach. What might the absence of the Island Council have implied? What assumptions were reflected in the location and style of the housing prepared by the community?

- What was the authors' "first ethnographic encounter"? What cultural background do you need to begin to understand the meaning of local events? Can you think of an example from your own life that might be difficult or impossible for a cultural outsider to interpret correctly?

- Who is Sunema? Who are Venu and Seselo? Samuelu? How did the socially constructed roles of each of these people involve them with Anne and Keith's research? Describe the political organization of the community. What role, if any, did the "old men" play in island life?

- What might being classified as "of the government" rather than as "of the island" have meant for Anne and Keith's research? What significance do Nanumeans attach to these categories? How did being "of the island' affect Anne and Keith's relationship to the community (and their research) in the long term?

- "Local categories" offer important ethnographic clues. What do categories contribute to culture exactly? Why do you think it is important to understand a culture's systems of classification and conceptual organization?

### Chapter Three   Tefolaha in the Cookhouse

- What is a *kopiti*? How were they important in traditional life? How was membership determined? What resonance do kopiti still have today?
- How did kopiti groups interface with overall community organization? What were the main village landmarks and how have these changed through time?
- What benefits does the flexibility of cognatic descent provide Nanumeans?
- What are Lolua and Haumaefa? How did they come about? Think about the other changes imposed by missionaries and the colonial government. Do you think Nanumeans benefited from these? Why or why not? How did these changes affect island life and institutions?
- Adze heads, cowrie lures, and other pieces of material culture litter the ground in Nanumea, tangible reminders of the past. Imagine that you are an archaeologist in the far future, studying the tumble of objects that once comprised a dump or landfill. What do you think you might find? Could you guess at the objects' uses? Their meanings? What might you infer about the culture that produced these objects?
- What is the significance of Nanumean cookhouses? How are they linked to kopiti? Consider why the authors referred to them as the "backstage" of Nanumean life. What aspects of your own life are expected to take place "backstage"? Do any institutions in Western culture play analogous roles to the cookhouse?
- What motivated Takitua's visit? (Recall that descent groups and land rights are directly linked on Nanumea.) What did he hope Anne and Keith could clarify? Could they accept his "text" as historically definitive? Why or why not?
- Takitua relates Nanumea's "creation" myth. Think of other creation stories you know. Does Tefolaha's tale share any elements with these other stories? Do you think Nanumea once had other myths about the actual formation of the world? Why might Takitua not have shared them with Anne and Keith? What can we learn about people through their narrative traditions?
- Who are Pai and Vau? What critique did some Nanumeans offer of Takitua's tale? Why were there different versions of the same story?
- Tefolaha's story functions on several levels. It affirms Nanumean rights to their atoll, acts as a keystone in their shared identity, and has a sacred element, too. How does it accomplish all this? What does it mean to be an "heir of Tefolaha"?

### Chapter Four   Emerging from the "Days of Darkness"

- Compare the two nineteenth-century accounts that introduce this chapter. What could account for their wildly different perspectives?

278 UNITY OF HEART

- What estimates could Anne and Keith offer for how long ago Tefolaha might have settled the atoll? How does genealogical dating differ from dating via historic documents? From archaeological dating? What are the benefits of each dating method? Which method do you think might be more reliable? Why?

- What do archaeologists say about the settlement of Oceania generally, and Nanumea specifically? From where are the settlers believed to have originated? What have studies conducted by other researchers shown about these early Polynesian travelers?

- Provide a brief description of precontact political and social life in Nanumea. What "core principles" governed precontact society? Why was an egalitarian ethos sensible (even necessary, perhaps) for Nanumeans in traditional times?

- What is an *aliki*? What incongruities arise when aliki is viewed as a simple equivalent to "chief" or "king"?

- What might have prompted the Taua i Talo (taro pit war)? How did early Nanumeans exert social control? What behaviors were likely to incite the community's wrath?

- The authors write, ". . . the threat of social disruption runs as a common thread through all these stories of long ago." Why are "troublemakers" so problematic for Nanumeans? Do you think it is a matter of values, of atoll logistics, or a combination of the two? Why might a community come to stigmatize "showoffs"? Think about the behaviors your own community sanctions and censors. How do these contrast with behaviors that are especially valued?

- What does Nanumean oral tradition have to say about earliest contact with European explorers? What meaning can you draw from this?

- Who was Captain Henry Pease? Why was his 1853 visit to Nanumea so remarkable?

- The Congregationalist London Missionary Society (LMS) wasn't particularly successful at first in converting Nanumea. What made the island such a hard sell? Why did the Nanumeans finally capitulate? How did the acceptance of Christianity connect with the adoption of other Western values? How was village life affected by conversion to Christianity?

- Who was George Holomoana, and what did he do for Nanumeans?

- Describe the time frame and the stages in Tuvalu's political assimilation by Great Britain. What effects did colonial status have for outer Islanders during the next fifty years? How do contemporary Nanumeans describe this period?

- Why did the colonial government undertake the creation of a land code? What were the goals of the Kennedy Land Commission? Why did the commission's decisions result in 25 percent of Nanumean land parcels changing ownership?

- Nanumea was occupied during World War II by U.S. forces. How did the Islanders react to this? What restrictions were imposed on the people? On the soldiers? What were the main local effects of the wartime occupation?

- Tuvalu became independent in October 1978. How has the country fared since independence? What have been its main sources of income? What new opportunities are appearing on Tuvalu's economic horizon?

## Chapter Five   Coral and Sand

- Why are atolls "marginal human habitats"? How are they formed? Of what are they made? What determines their shape? What resources do they provide for settlers?

- How big is Nanumea? How does its size and resources relate to land tenure customs? According to Venu, what is the staff of life for Nanumeans?

- What types of tenure does the land code recognize? What social contract does the local system of *kaitahi* land tenure support? Can you trace the line of descent in Figure 4?

- How does cognatic descent "allow people to maximize resources for themselves and their children"? In what sense are land use decisions "actually decisions about relationships"? Is this true in your society too? Give an example.

- Patrilocal residence refers to a cultural preference for married couples to settle near or with the man's family. How does the Nanumean preference for this arrangement impact descent groups?

- What did Anne and Keith learn from their survey of household land ownership and usage? Were family parcels bunched all together? Were they uniform? Why did they collect that information? What economic patterns were revealed? Why might a "simple count of land holdings" have been misleading?

- Why did Venu call out "Come and eat some coconut, come and drink some water"? In your society, what might be the equivalent of this phrase?

- What is evapotranspiration? How does this process affect plants on Nanumea? With drought a recurrent problem, how do people collect and store water? What have been the effects of changes in these practices? What subsistence practices in your own society have negative consequences? Who tends to be most affected by them?

- How did Nanumeans traditionally cope with drought? What principles underlie this practice? If faced with the same emergency, how do you think your community would respond?

- What root crops are grown on Lakena islet? What must one do to render pulaka and taro edible? What other flora grows on the atoll?

- What are Nanumea's "convenience foods"? How are local taste patterns changing? Do you think McDonald's, that ubiquitous agent of Westernization, will ever make inroads in Tuvalu?

- It seems that in Nanumea, the proverbial "better mousetrap" has arrived in the form of the motorboat. Or has it? How have fishing practices changed? How have social expectations changed? What problems does motorboat maintenance present? In your opinion, is the switch from canoes to motorboats a positive thing? Why or why not?

- Do you come away from this chapter with the impression that making a living for oneself and one's family is easy in Nanumea? What social and cultural adaptations make life on the atoll possible?

### Chapter Six   Something for All

- What is meant by the term "sharing economy"? What type of reciprocity do Nanumeans advocate? What assumptions underlie this form of reciprocity? How does the Nanumean form of reciprocity distribute resources?

- What is *alofa*? What do expectations regarding alofa accomplish? What parallel principle structures life in your own society?

- The authors say that "economics and values are tightly interdependent" and that economic practices are "rich with connotations and ethical imperatives, many of which are tacit parts of local worldview and cultural expectations." What cultural expectations are demonstrated by the Nanumean principle of "eating as one"?

- Nanumeans break exchange into several categories. What are the distinctions between *togi, taui, meaalofa,* and *akai*? Why is taui stigmatized as "stingy"? Why is being labeled *oge* (stingy) such a serious insult? How do people in your society conceptualize and talk about exchange?

- What customary rules regulate fish exchange? Do you find it surprising that households with an active fisherman actually ate fish less often than households without a fisherman? What strategies do people sometimes use to keep more of their catch (or other resources) for their own use? Do you ever catch yourself or people you know avoiding full engagement with a social expectation? Which cultural strategies tend to be used?

- How dependent are Nanumeans on imported consumer goods? How do they obtain them? What role does subsistence production still play in the Nanumean economy?

- Who is most likely to launch a small business on Nanumea? How are group selling efforts regarded? Why?

- What percentage of their monetary income do Nanumeans donate to public causes? How does this compare to your own society? Discuss the relevance of social pressure to these kinds of decisions.

- Why do Nanumeans need money? What four methods can they use to obtain it? What are the advantages and limitations of each income source? Do households in your own society usually rely on multiple subsistence sources? Explain and give some examples.

- What cultural changes has the presence of money brought? How do you think the Nanumean economic paradigm is shifting? Provide some examples to support your analysis.

### Chapter Seven   Family Matters

- What divisions do Nanumeans recognize in their social world? What is the Nanumean understanding of the category of *kaaiga*? Why is it desirable to have many relatives? What basic rule governs Nanumean family life?

- How do Nanumeans classify their relatives? Within their "classificatory" kinship system, what distinctions do Nanumeans draw? What does the classifier *tonu* indicate? How does a classificatory system of kinship terminology differ from that used by English speakers? What relationships are highlighted as important in each?

- What is one possible reason for the institutionalized mother's brother (*tuaa-tina*) bond? The *maatua ofo* bond? How do tuaatina and maatua ofo complement each other?

- What are *taina*? What are *tuagane*? How do Nanumean sibling categories differ from English ones? In what ways are "tuagane more venerated than siblings of the same sex"? Why would Nanumeans consider a relationship between fourth or fifth cousins incestuous? Under what circumstances can an affine be like a taina? What, according to Raymond Firth, makes such a relationship permissible?

- Marriage, the authors write, realigns social relationships. How does it pare down kinship obligations in Nanumea?

- Imagine being a new Nanumean bride. How would your life change? How would your household be organized? Do you think this arrangement would ease the transition to married life, or do you think it might be stressful? Why? What role does romantic love play?

- What leads unmarried women to decide to have a child? Is this socially acceptable? Why is there "a scarcity of marriageable men"? Do women have any alternatives to marriage? Why could choosing to remain unmarried be an attractive option for some women?

- Why do Nanumeans think it is optimal to have two children of each sex? Why is having an opposite sex sibling particularly important for women?

- Now did Tuvaluans limit and equalize family size in traditional times? Why did they feel these limits were necessary?

- Relatives living together are the basic socio-economic unit in Nanumea. How have residence patterns changed? Is the community's egalitarian ideal strained by these changes?

## *Chapter Eight   Community*

- How is Nanumea organized as a community? What roles do the village "sides" play? How did their friendly rivalry galvanize community action? To what extent does solidarity wax and wane?

- What was at issue in the recent factional dispute? Summarize and discuss some of the current threats to Nanumean solidarity. Do you think the community will remain intact in spite of these threats? Why? What issues threaten your own community's cohesion? How similar are they to those faced by Nanumea?

- How are *fakaua* both economic and social groups? How do they reflect Nanumea's traditional emphasis on organized competition? How is structured competition important to Nanumeans? Why might this be?

- What two institutions bind Nanumeans together? What is meant by *lotofenua* (community heartedness)? Why might rejection of the dominant religion be construed as rejection of the community itself? Do you think religious freedom is workable in Nanumea? What might be considered more precious to the average Nanumean, religious freedom or community solidarity? What is more precious to you, personally? Why?

- What is the *aahiga?* Describe the hall's three zones. How do these zones manifest hierarchy? Who traditionally speaks for families in the aahiga? In what sense is it "the house of men"?

- What qualities do Nanumeans value in their leaders? Which people are eligible to be leaders in "affairs of the island"? Which have the best chance to play a part in public life in "affairs of the government"? How do the two institutions—chiefly lineage and representative government—divide power? Do they peaceably coexist?

- Contrast Nanumeans' understanding of the word *fakaatea* ("different") with the understanding most prevalent in our society. How would you fare socially in Nanumea? How would a Nanumean fare here?

- Do you think the council's treatment of Tepou was fair? Why was it necessary through the lens of Nanumean logic? How might have Tepou's situation paralleled that of earlier "troublemakers"?

- Shame and ostracism are "the big guns" of social control in Polynesia. Give an example of Nanumeans' use of these tactics. Have you noticed these tactics used in your own society? Are they as effective in your own society as they seem to be in Nanumea? Why?

- Who is responsible for most acts of violence on Nanumea? What role does alcohol play? Why can the invocation of Tefolaha help to restore peace and cooperation on Nanumea?

- Like all societies, Nanumea is dynamic and changing; it is neither simply an academic curiosity nor an idealized paradise. Did you find yourself tending to idealize Nanumean life as you read this book? Why or why not? What challenges face ethnographers in their attempts to portray social and cultural complexity?

## *Chapter Nine   Challenges of the Twenty-first Century*

- What globalizing forces are acting on Tuvalu? Do any of these affect your life too?

- How is global climate change threatening Tuvalu? What is the Alliance of Small Island States urging the global community to do? What is frustrating their efforts?

- Is Funafuti in danger of being afflicted by urban blight?

- What do you think of "visual imperialism"? Do you find it worrisome? Is it inevitable?

- How is identity reckoned in the capital?

- What has been the most powerful acculturative agent in Tuvalu? What would a "turning over" mean for Nanumean society?

- Judging from recent trends, do you think stratification is making inroads in Tuvalu? Should some traditional socioeconomic arenas be demarcated for protection? Why or why not?

- In accord with Western democratic standards, all adults, not just old men, should participate in Tuvalu's civic life. Why have women and youths tradition- ally been left out of public decision making? How might the community deal with the conflicts between traditional and democratic ideals?

- In what sense do Tuvaluans enjoy a high quality of life? Which of the conven- tional socioeconomic indicators can be problematic in a traditional, subsistence society? What "development" does the community itself most want for Nanumea?

- What metaphor was used by Tagisia to describe the changes brought by mis- sionization, colonization, and Westernization over the last century? Does this seem an appropriate metaphor to you? Could you suggest another?

### *Chapter 10   Unity of Heart*

- How is the Nanumean ethos different from that of your own society? Would you like to live with the degree of community-mindedness that is traditional on Nanu- mea? What benefits might this lifestyle bring? What costs could you envision?

- What insights has reading this ethnography given you about human differences and similarities? Does Nanumea offer any lessons to the rest of the world? If so, what might they be? In your view, what qualities would a "truly civil society" have?